THE ARCHITECTVRE
OF
EDWARD & W.S. MAXWELL

The Montreal Museum of Fine Arts

*A travelling exhibition funded by the Museum Assistance
Program of Communications Canada and
organized by the Travelling Exhibitions Service of
The Montreal Museum of Fine Arts*

To
John Bland
and
Mary Maxwell Rabbani

This catalogue was published on the occasion of the exhibition *The Architecture of Edward & W.S. Maxwell*, presented at the Montreal Museum of Fine Arts from December 13, 1991 to March 22, 1992, and organized by the Travelling Exhibitions Service, under the direction of Marc Pitre, with the assistance of Jasmine Landry, in co-operation with the members of The Maxwell Project.

Exhibition design: Glenn Bydwell with James Fox (Associate Designer)
Exhibition production: Pierre Dion, Karen Forsley, Jean-François Castonguay,
Nathalie Bourcier and Chantal Doolub
Conservation of works: Karen Colby, Estelle Richard with Alain Laferrière
Photographs of works: Brian Merrett and Brigitte Ostiguy
All Notman photographs were made by Thomas Humphry, the photographic technician for the Notman Photographic Archives.
Conception of models: Michel Bergeron (Château Frontenac), Gerald Laforest and François Leblanc of GLAF Maquettes (Saskatchewan Legislative Building), La Boîte du Pinceau d'Arlequin, under the direction of Jean-François Pinsonneault (Main doorway, Royal Bank of Canada, Westmount Branch), Duncain Swain with Gerald Laforest of GLAF Maquettes (The Square Mile), John Tusa Design Inc. (Shrine of the Báb)

The exhibition will circulate from June 15, 1992 to June 30, 1993, and will be presented at the Winnipeg Art Gallery, the New Brunswick Museum in Saint John and the Musée du Québec in Quebec City.

Communications Department
of The Montreal Museum of Fine Arts
Danielle Sauvage, Director

A production of the Publications Service

Co-ordination: Denise L. Bissonnette
Revision: Donald Pistolesi
Graphic Design: Ikram Schelhot
and Caroline Landry, Concept I.S.
Photocomposition: Compo Em Inc.
Photo-engraving and Printing: Litho Acme Inc.

© The Montreal Museum of Fine Arts, 1991
Legal deposit – 4th trimester 1991
Bibliothèque nationale du Québec
National Library of Canada
ISBN: 2-89192-150-X

PRINTED IN CANADA

THE MONTREAL MUSEUM OF FINE ARTS
P.O. Box 3000, Station "H"
Montreal, Quebec H3G 2T9

Cover:
Charles Meredith House, front door
1130 Pine Avenue West, Montreal

CONTENTS

CONTENTS

THE MAXWELL PROJECT

The exhibition *The Architecture of Edward & W.S. Maxwell* has been conceived and planned by The Maxwell Project in co-operation with The Montreal Museum of Fine Arts. The Maxwell Project, a federally registered non-profit organization, has undertaken research into the architectural practice of the brothers Edward and William Sutherland Maxwell in order to make their work known to a wide audience. All directors of The Maxwell Project have contributed to the exhibition and catalogue.

BOARD OF DIRECTORS

John Bland, Chairman
Emeritus Professor of Architecture and Honorary Curator, Canadian Architecture Collection, McGill University

France Gagnon Pratte, Vice-chairman
Architectural historian and Président du Conseil des monuments et sites du Québec

Henry B. Yates, Treasurer
Executive, The Standard Life Assurance Company, and grandson of Edward Maxwell

Hugh Locke, Executive Director and Secretary
Director, Only One Earth, Ltd.

Peter Jacobs
Professor, School of Landscape Architecture, Faculté de l'aménagement, Université de Montréal

Ellen James
Associate Professor of Art and Architectural History, Concordia University

Robert Lemire
Architectural historian

Irena Murray
Head, Blackader-Lauterman Library of Architecture and Art, McGill University

Rosalind M. Pepall
Curator of Canadian Decorative Arts, The Montreal Museum of Fine Arts

Susan Wagg
Architectural historian and independent curator

Jeanne M. Wolfe
Director and Professor, School of Urban Planning, McGill University

Curators responsible for research, conception, planning and selection of works:
France Gagnon Pratte, Ellen James, Rosalind M. Pepall, Susan Wagg

Curators responsible for development and realization of the exhibition:
Ellen James, Susan Wagg, Sandra Coley Byron (Assistant Guest Curator)

General editors of the catalogue:
Harold Kalman, Susan Wagg

The Montrealers Edward and William Sutherland Maxwell were among the most important architects in Canada at the turn of the century. However, today they are little known as the creators of architectural works, even though these works still hold a place of prominence in the country's major cities. Maxwell buildings, both public and private, are scattered from New Brunswick to British Columbia and include such splendid structures as a substantial portion of the Château Frontenac in Quebec City, the Montreal Museum of Fine Arts' 1912 building and the Birks store in Montreal, the Saskatchewan parliament in Regina, and the Palliser Hotel in Calgary.

We hope that the exhibition *The Architecture of Edward & W.S. Maxwell* will at long last help the Maxwell brothers to become better known as the creators of these and other marvellous works.

We warmly congratulate the members of The Maxwell Project, who have spent several years putting this exhibition together for us. Thanks to their enthusiasm and devotion, the work of the Maxwell brothers will now be adequately documented. We would like to extend special thanks to the Blackader-Lauterman Library of McGill University, which made available its wealth of information regarding the Maxwells, as well as to the lenders, whose generosity has made the exhibition possible.

On our own staff, we are also grateful to Marc Pitre, Head of the Travelling Exhibitions Service, and his assistant Jasmine Landry for having assumed responsibility for co-ordinating the organization of the exhibition, its presentation at our Museum and its circulation to other Canadian museums, which in turn we thank for having agreed to host the exhibition in their galleries. We should also like to mention in particular Rosalind M. Pepall, Curator of Canadian Decorative Arts, for serving as a vital link between the Museum and The Maxwell Project.

This exhibition is among the events planned in conjunction with the opening of the Montreal Museum of Fine Arts' Jean-Noël Desmarais Pavilion, designed by the outstanding architect Moshe Safdie. This seemed an entirely appropriate way to celebrate the eightieth anniversary of the 1912 building, to which Moshe Safdie has paid a handsome tribute through his creation.

We must also thank the Quebec Ministère des Affaires culturelles, the Conseil des arts of the Communauté urbaine de Montréal, and Communications Canada's Museum Assistance Program, as well as the National Spiritual Assembly of the Bahá'ís of Canada, the Royal Bank of Canada, and Canadian Pacific Ltd, all of which lent their financial support to the preparation of the exhibition.

Pierre Théberge
Director of The Montreal Museum of Fine Arts

LENDERS TO THE EXHIBITION

HAIFA
Mary Maxwell Rabbani

MONTREAL
Henry Birks & Sons, Ltd

Canadian Architecture Collection, Blackader-Lauterman Library of Architecture and Art, McGill University

Canadian Pacific Archives

Church of the Messiah

McCord Museum of Canadian History

McGill University

Brian Merrett collection

Montreal Museum of Decorative Arts, Château Dufresne

Notman Photographic Archives, McCord Museum of Canadian History

Henry B. Yates

OTTAWA
National Gallery of Canada

QUEBEC CITY
France Gagnon Pratte

REGINA
Saskatchewan Archives Board

SAINT-CONSTANT, Que.
Canadian Railroad Historical Association

THORNHILL, Ont.
National Spiritual Assembly of the Bahá'ís of Canada

John B. Dempsey II
Helen P. Mackey
Dr. and Mrs. John A. Findlay
and those lenders who prefer to remain anonymous

ACKNOWLEDGEMENTS

The exhibition *The Architecture of Edward & W.S. Maxwell* has been a co-operative effort calling on the talents of many individuals. Most of the research material on the Maxwells and the majority of the exhibited works have come from the Maxwell Archive in the Canadian Architecture Collection, Blackader-Lauterman Library of Architecture and Art at McGill University. Special thanks are due to John Bland, Emeritus Professor of Architecture and Honorary Curator of the Canadian Architecture Collection, who serves as Chairman of The Maxwell Project, and Irena Murray, Head, Blackader-Lauterman Library of Architecture and Art, and her staff, Cindy Campbell, Françoise Roux, Marilyn Berger and Jewel Lowenstein. An exhibition on the Maxwell firm could not have been realized without their expertise and generous support.

Our sincere thanks go to Madame Mary Maxwell Rabbani for her invaluable help in documenting her father William Maxwell's career and in recalling aspects of his work, and for her hospitality in Haifa. In addition we are very grateful for her generosity in donating many of her father's records and papers to McGill University and in lending works from her collection to the exhibition. Madame Rabbani's staff has been most helpful with our many inquiries and requests, in particular, Violette Nakhjavani, Nell Golden and Ken Gretton.

During the preparation of the exhibition, other Maxwell family members have been most encouraging and willing to help with research. Henry Yates, grandson of Edward Maxwell, has supported the project with great enthusiasm.

We are indebted to the current owners of many of the Maxwell buildings, who very kindly allowed us to visit their properties. A special thanks goes to Mrs. Aileen Smith of St. Andrews Civic Trust, who guided our curators around Saint Andrews, New Brunswick.

We also thank descendants of the Maxwells' clients, who offered archival material or their reminiscences of a building's history, especially John B. Dempsey II, Mrs. Raymonde Chevalier Bowen, the late Louis Johnson and Mrs. Jerzy Fialkowski.

Other individuals and institutions who have helped in various ways with advice and support include the Bahá'í International Community, Husayn Banani, David Bourke, Jennifer Bydwell, Nicole Cloutier, the Reverend Charles Eddis, the late Mrs. Margaret Vaughan Eller, Alan C. Hammaker, Jonathan Hanna, David Harris, Charles Hill, Robert G. Hill, Margaret M. Hutchison, David James, David Jones, Yves Lacasse, Omer Lavallée, Richard Macklem, Douglas Martin, Sarah McCutcheon, Duncan McDowall, Manuel Menendez, Bahia Mitchell, Linda Rossomme, Abigail Smith, Timothy Wagg, the Faculty of Fine Arts, Concordia University, and the Canadian Pacific Archives.

Many of the early photographs of Maxwell buildings were taken by William Notman & Son. We would like to thank the staff of the Notman Photographic Archives, McCord Museum of Canadian History, for their assistance: Stanley Triggs, Curator; Nora Hague, Assistant to the Curator; Tom Humphry; and Heather McNabb. We are also grateful to Brian Merrett, who, in addition to photographing many of the existing Maxwell buildings, has enthusiastically supported the project from the beginning.

AAM	Art Association of Montreal
ANQM	Archives nationales du Québec à Montréal
CAB	*The Canadian Architect and Builder*
CAC	Canadian Architecture Collection, McGill University, Montreal
JRAIC	*Journal, Royal Architectural Institute of Canada*
MA	Maxwell Archive, Canadian Architecture Collection, Blackader-Lauterman Library of Architecture and Art, McGill University, Montreal
MMFA Archives	The Montreal Museum of Fine Arts Archives
MUA	McGill University Archives, Montreal
NPA	Notman Photographic Archives, McCord Museum of Canadian History, Montreal
PQAA	Province of Quebec Association of Architects
R.C.A.	Royal Canadian Academy of Arts
RAIC	Royal Architectural Institute of Canada
RIBA	Royal Institute of British Architects

INTRODUCTION

This landmark catalogue, published on the occasion of the exhibition *The Architecture of Edward & W.S. Maxwell*, is a welcome addition to the small but growing collection of documents that record and interpret the substantial contribution made by Canadian architects during the nineteenth and twentieth centuries. Any exhibition that attempts to encompass the breadth and originality of the Maxwells' oeuvre is a massive undertaking. The comprehensiveness of this exhibition and the value of its accompanying catalogue are largely due to the perceptive and critical skill of several scholars and historians who have collaborated on the project. They must be congratulated for their originality of conception as well as for their selection of significant and appropriate material, drawn mainly from the valuable Maxwell Archive now held in the Canadian Architecture Collection of the Blackader-Lauterman Library of Architecture and Art at McGill University in Montreal.

From Newfoundland to British Columbia, in major cities and small towns, the talented Montreal team of Edward and William Maxwell received commissions for hundreds of distinctive designs that have added to, and have been an influence upon, the architectural landscape of Canada. Iconographic symbols such as the Château-style railway station and Canadian railway hotel, the Shingle Style country house, and the Beaux-Arts branch bank were all developed or refined in the busy Maxwell office in Montreal. Their partnership also generated schemes for churches, schools, club houses, office buildings, retail stores, farm buildings, industrial warehouses and even hospitals – an extraordinary range of building types that no other Canadian practice of this era could match in number, let alone quality.

It is hoped that this exhibition will not only serve to celebrate the unique and memorable elements of Canadian architectural design as envisaged by two of its most talented proponents, but also to bring recognition to the whole genre of architectural drawing in Canada, which, despite being represented in collections in every major city, has frequently been overlooked or ignored by researchers. These collections, and exhibitions such as this one, hold the key to understanding what buildings mean to those who design them, and to cultivating a greater appreciation of the rich and varied Canadian architectural tradition.

Robert G. Hill, Architect, OAA, MRAIC
Editor, *Biographical Dictionary of Architects in Canada, 1800-1950* (forthcoming)

THE IMPORTANCE OF
THE MAXWELLS IN CANADIAN
ARCHITECTURE

John Bland

The architectural practice of Edward & W. S. Maxwell was one of the most significant in Canadian history. The period between 1892, when Edward Maxwell (1867-1923) went into private practice, and 1939, when William Sutherland Maxwell (1874-1952) retired from his work,[1] was a time of great change in architecture, spanning the late Victorian, Edwardian and early Modern eras. Approaches to design and professional practice were transformed, and the Maxwells were at the forefront of this change. The most vital period was from 1902 to 1923, when the two brothers joined forces and worked together.

The brothers had different personalities, interests and skills. They complemented each other perfectly; the whole was truly greater than the sum of the parts. Edward was gregarious, self-confident and easily held the confidence of those who knew him. Diligent and a good organizer, he had a genius for supervision. All of this was conspicuously demonstrated in his management of the Montreal Board of Trade Building (1891-1893).[2] His wife enjoyed society, and the couple had a flair for entertaining. Their first house is remembered for its oval salon and impressive dining room. Edward had two country houses: one in Saint Andrews, New Brunswick, where he could enjoy Atlantic sailing, and the other in Baie-d'Urfé, on Montreal Island, where he could indulge in raising thoroughbred cattle. William, on the other hand, was introspective, an artist and a bibliophile. An extremely talented draftsman, he had a sure sense of composition and a remarkable feeling for decoration. He especially enjoyed the companionship of the artists and craftsmen with whom he collaborated. He spent long hours in his drafting room, scarcely ever taking a holiday. His wife was philosophical and deeply concerned with human welfare. Their home contained a great many handsome and carefully selected books, covering a broad range of arts. Its top floor was an ideal painter's studio. For many of their friends their house was a spiritual place, and today it remains a shrine for the Bahá'í Faith, which William, his wife and daughter sponsored in Canada.[3]

Edward's family background in construction and the lumber business, and his apprenticeship with the architect A. F. Dunlop (1842-1923), acquainted him with the nature and problems of building in Montreal. His later employment with Shepley, Rutan & Coolidge in Boston, in the shadow of the great American architect H. H. Richardson (1838-1886), with devoted assistants all co-operatively involved in widespread commissions, introduced him to the idea of an extensive practice dependent on expert collaborators.[4] His early work in Montreal stemmed directly from his Boston experience and set new standards in design that were soon to be adopted by Montreal's old leading architects with their new American-trained juniors or partners, such as A. F. Dunlop with J.C.A. Heriot, Andrew Taylor with Huntley Ward Davis, and J. Omer Marchand with Stevens Haskell.[5]

William's apprenticeship with Edward in Montreal and later work in Boston with architects who had had schooling at M.I.T. and in Paris, was supplemented by studies at the Boston Architectural Club. There the principles of Beaux-Arts design were taught by the famous M.I.T. professor Constant Désiré Despradelle (1862-1912),[6] under whom William learned that analysis, composition and presentation were the steps in the production of architectural schemes – principles that were well accepted in the leading schools but only beginning to be practised in professional competitions. While still a draftsman in Boston, William helped Edward win a competition for adding four floors to the Merchants Bank of Canada in Montreal. It posed a major problem in the treatment of elaborate façades and structures; yet on the back of a photograph of the finished work, Edward characteristically wrote a note indicating that "not a single crack has developed in any wall or partition".[7]

Following his return from Boston, William spent time in Paris as a special student in the Atelier Pascal, which was affiliated with the École des Beaux-Arts. There he had the opportunity to confirm and build upon what he had learned from Despradelle. When he joined his brother's firm in 1902, William was an accomplished designer in the Beaux-Arts manner, and with essential links to the practice of H. H. Richardson, the M.I.T. school and the École des Beaux-Arts, the partnership had a stature unique in Canada.

Both brothers had exceptional talent. Edward's was a spontaneous ability to assess requirements and outline solutions, whereas William's was more contemplative and imaginative. From the start Edward succeeded in attracting powerful clients and significant commissions. With William's help, the firm began to win competitions in which their work was selected by well-qualified judges on the basis of design excellence. Their victories over a field of noted architects focussed attention on their special skills and increased their professional opportunities.

Few Canadian practices could have begun more auspiciously than Edward's. Even before the supervision of the Board of Trade Building was completed, commissions began pouring in. First came those of friends of his family. Then there was a splendid house for Vincent Meredith and work for James Bryce Allan (Mrs. Meredith's cousin), for Duncan McIntyre (the merchant railroader and one of the founders of the CPR), and R.B. Angus (the banker and railway's principal financier). There were important houses for James Crathern, Joseph Learmont and Edward Clouston, and a jewellery store for Henry Birks that included a studio for the celebrated photographers William Notman & Son. All of these came to him before 1894, when he was only twenty-six years old. To carry on his private work he resigned from Shepley, Rutan & Coolidge on January 12, 1892.[8] However, when no replacement was found for him, his superintendence of the Board building was continued, provided that he take no further work until it was completed.

Before 1900 many of the leading figures in commercial, financial and professional spheres could be counted among Edward's clients. He had the wit to please them well and to conduct an efficient office, staffed by talented young architects capable of undertaking work from coast to coast. Edward had clearly built upon his experience working with the partnership of Richardson's dedicated assistants, who created an organization for the practice of architecture on a national scale well beyond the scope of the individual architect.

Edward was so busy in 1899 that he brought a former colleague from Boston, George C. Shattuck (1864-1923), to help him conduct his affairs. Shattuck remained his partner until 1902, when William took his place. In the decade 1892-1902, Edward appears to have been the first Canadian to develop the kind of practice that Toronto architect A. H. Chapman (1879-1949) subsequently described:

The tendency in this country, where there is great building activity, is for large offices to accumulate an enormous quantity of work and instead of its being the creation of one man it is the creation of an organization of assistants who became certain office specialists.[9]

Many of Edward's assistants developed rapidly in his office and went on to successful independent practice in the burgeoning Canadian economy.[10]

In the two decades after 1902, the Maxwell office came to be more in the hands of William, and its design philosophy increasingly reflected the view of one individual. More consistent and directed, the office continued to be a training place. Although with fewer opportunities for individual development, it had a stronger artistic discipline, in which the enrichment of a design was frequently the work of collaborating artists and craftsmen, and where landscape architects were often consulted in setting buildings so as to secure the greatest potential of their sites. The firm, which employed as many as fifty-six assistants at one time, was the largest in Canada. Yet, under William's control it became less an organization for the production of building designs and more the "atelier" of an admired master, like the office of Richardson after his Paris experience and that of McKim, Mead & White in New York at its peak. For a time William actually conducted the "Atelier Maxwell", which was related to the Beaux Arts Institute of Design in New York, where young Canadian architects working with him could measure their skills against a wide American field.[11]

When in 1907 the Maxwells won the widely publicized competition for the Legislative Building of Saskatchewan, chosen by a celebrated international jury from among carefully selected submissions from Canada, the United States and Britain, no one could deny that they had reached the top of their profession. Three years later their position was confirmed by winning the competiton for the Art Association of Montreal. The reputation of all Canadian architects benefited from their success.

The completion of the Maxwells' additions to the Château Frontenac – the brothers' last project together – in 1924, by which time Gordon Pitts (1886-1954) had joined the firm, involved all their separate and combined skills. The two great axes of its plan gave a classical order to the scattered romantic parts. The Saint-Louis Wing, courtyards and central tower proved to be precisely the right elements to complete the extraordinary building that William Van Horne and Bruce Price (1845-1903) had set upon Dufferin Terrace in Quebec City. Its varied yet centrally unified form and depth of interest gave Canada a truly memorable building, unique in world architectural terms.

Both individually and together, the Maxwell brothers can be seen to have had an exemplary influence upon architecture in Canada from the standpoint of the inspiration and opportunities they gave to those who worked with them, the quality of the buildings they designed, and the pleasures and satisfactions these buildings have provided.

---

[1] *Canadian Bahá'í News Memorial Issue* (Montreal), March 1952.

[2] "Daily Journal, 1892", unpaginated, MA, Series D.

[3] B. K. Filson, "Maxwell House: Montreal Architect's Home Is Now a Bahá'í Shrine", *Canadian Collector*, vol. 18 (May-June 1983), pp. 18-19.

[4] J. D. Forbes, "Shepley, Bulfinch, Richardson & Abbott, Architects: An Introduction", *Journal of the Society of Architectural Historians*, vol. 17 (Fall 1958), p. 19.

[5] Heriot (1862-1921), a native Montrealer, received his training at Cornell University; Dunlop had worked in Detroit from 1871 to 1874. Davis (1875-1952), also a Montrealer, graduated from M.I.T. in 1898 before returning to Montreal to work for Taylor. The American-born Haskell (1871-1913) worked in the office of Cass Gilbert in New York before coming to Montreal in 1903. I am indebted to Robert Hill for this information.

[6] Despradelle was Professor of Design at M.I.T. from 1893-1912 and patron of the Boston Architectural Club from 1895-1898, when William was in Boston. See Henry F. Withey and Elsie Rathburn Withey, *Biographical Dictionary of American Architects (Deceased)* (Los Angeles: New Age, 1956), p. 171, and W. S. Maxwell, "Architectural Education", *Construction*, vol. 1 (February 1908), pp. 49-52.

[7] Project 211.0, MA.

[8] "Daily Journal, 1892", unpaginated, entry for January 12, MA, Series D.

[9] A. H. Chapman, "Architectural Development in Canada", *The Year Book of Canadian Art 1913* (Toronto: Dent, 1913), p. 267.

[10] Among them were John S. Archibald (1872-1934), D. H. MacFarlane (1875-1950), Kenneth G. Rea (1878-1942) and Charles Saxe (1870-1943).

[11] John Roxborough Smith, "Obituary William Sutherland Maxwell", *JRAIC*, vol. 29 (October 1952), p. 311.

THE LIVES OF
EDWARD AND WILLIAM S. MAXWELL

Henry B. Yates

The family of my grandfather Edward and my great uncle William Maxwell has Scottish origins. "The ancient and honourable house of Maxwell, so conspicuously connected with the history of Scotland, and considered one of the most distinguished ... is generally believed to have been founded by Maccus, son of Undwyn, in the twelfth century."[1] In 1824, a Presbyterian marriage took place in Jedburgh, Scotland, between Edward Maxwell (1805-1876) and Agnes Reid. Edward, a joiner and carpenter, emigrated to Montreal with his wife in 1829.[2] They lived on Saint-Gabriel Street near the waterfront. Several children were born to the couple, and one of them, Edward John, became a builder. In 1862 this son founded E.J. Maxwell & Co., lumber dealers specializing in hardwood and black walnut. "The yard was located on Craig Street (today's St. Antoine St.), a little to the east of Victoria Square and Beaver Hall Hill".[3] This business prospered for three generations, remaining in the family until it was sold in the early 1970s.

After his marriage to Johan MacBean, Edward John lived in a large house with a garden on Côte-Saint-Antoine Road, which at that time was in the country. Two daughters were born and then two sons, Edward (1867-1923) and William (1874-1952) (cat. 2c). The sons were exposed to the basics of building and fine lumber; their father even made violins. Clearly this home environment influenced the decision of both young men to become architects.

Edward and William studied at the High School of Montreal, played sports and enjoyed a happy home. Their parents emphasized the importance of family life, diligent work and integrity. After returning from his employment in Boston in 1891, Edward lived with his parents on Côte-Saint-Antoine Road until his marriage five years later. According to family lore, when he was recovering from an illness, he spied an attractive young lady through a crack in his bedroom door. She was his third cousin Elizabeth Ellen Aitchison, of Scottish origin, from Madrid, New York. In 1896 they were married. Edward then built a small house attached to that of his parents; several years later a house he designed on Peel Street became their home. Edward and Elizabeth had four children between 1900 and 1908: Blythe, Jean, Stirling and Elizabeth (cat. 2e).

Just before William was to write his final-year exams at the High School of Montreal, he became ill and decided not to write them. Following this, William chose to join an architectural firm in Boston. There his talent for drawing was recognized, and he was assigned detailed architectural drawings, especially cornices. His daughter, Mary Maxwell Rabbani, has remarked: "I am sure that he must have bettered the design because he had such a marvellous sense of proportion."[4] At the turn of the century William studied along with American and British students at the Atelier Pascal in Paris. Mary Rabbani recalled two humorous episodes that occurred there. New students were subjected to hazing, which sometimes resulted in being stripped and entirely covered with watercolour paint. William was not spared. The second was a prank involving William and a few other students who lived in a house where the Parisian landlady owned a baby tortoise. Every week or so the students would acquire a larger tortoise and replace the incumbent. The landlady was amazed at the rapid growth and enthusiastically reported it to all her friends.

While in Paris William met Randolph Bolles, an American architectural student also studying at the Atelier Pascal. William and Randolph became devoted friends, and in 1902 William married Randolph's sister May in London.[5] That same year William became a partner in the architectural firm of Edward & W. S. Maxwell in Montreal. The brothers' varied talents combined to make an excellent team. Edward was not only a fine architect but also had a keen business sense. He developed contacts with and entertained the many influential people he knew in business and government. William, on the other hand, had a remarkable ability for fine drawing and design. According to his daughter Mary, he was "fundamentally ... a scholar and a creator and very much of a recluse. He wasn't interested in

Cat. 2c. *Edward John Maxwell family: Edward, William, Johan MacBean Maxwell* (mother), *Amelia, Jessie Gertrude and Edward John* (father)

Cat. 2e. *Edward Maxwell's children: Stirling, Jean, Elizabeth and Blythe*

Fig. 1. Photographer unknown, *Edward Maxwell House ("Tillietudlem")*, Saint Andrews, N.B. (Edward Maxwell, architect), about 1908. Private collection.

social life, but he had a passion for everything to do with art and architecture. He had a knowledge that was literally encyclopedic."

In 1899 Edward was summoned to Saint Andrews, New Brunswick, by Sir William Van Horne, president of the Canadian Pacific Railway, to help with the building of his summer house on Minister's Island. At Sir William's suggestion, Edward purchased a choice piece of land nearby, on the sea, and built a modest summer house, "Tillietudlem" (fig. 1), the name perhaps inspired by Tillietudlem Castle in the Walter Scott novel *Old Mortality*.

In 1908 Edward bought one hundred and sixty acres (65 ha) of farmland in Baie-d'Urfé on Montreal Island. Here he built "Maxwelton", a large fieldstone house (fig. 2), and developed a choice herd of Jersey cattle.

Edward and William knew many leading artists in Montreal, and studio space above their office on Beaver Hall Hill was occupied by artists such as the three Des Clayes sisters, Laura Muntz and G. Horne Russell.[6] An important employee in the office for many decades was Amelia M. Parent, who performed many duties as administrative assistant. Although she was a frail lady, her great ability and sense of loyalty "kept the firm together".[7] William's daughter recalls that the Maxwell firm was the largest and most prominent in Canada before World War I, and she believes that at its height it employed as many as fifty-six draftsmen. However after the war, with the death of Edward in 1923, the firm never regained its former prominence.

Both Edward and William were elected to the Royal Canadian Academy of Arts. William also served as president of the Arts Club in Montreal and belonged to the Pen and Pencil Club of Montreal.[8] Every Friday he would go to the Arts Club with his friends, mostly architects and artists, and spend "the whole evening in a big cloud of blue smoke. There he talked of the subjects that interested him, played poker and billiards."[9] Many leading figures in the art and academic world frequented these clubs, including artists William Brymner, Maurice Cullen, Clarence A. Gagnon, Robert Harris and Robert W. Pilot, and humourist Stephen Leacock.[10]

Over the years William avidly collected books on art and architecture as well as antiques. On one occasion, soon after his marriage, he was taking a streetcar home from work and spotted an auction of carpets. He leapt off the trolley, spent the $100 and more he and his wife had for the next month's living expenses, and happily arrived home with a roll of carpets under each arm.[11]

Edward developed cancer and died in 1923, whereupon William formed a partnership with Gordon Pitts of Montreal. In 1940 William's wife died, and the next year he moved to Haifa, Israel, to live with his daughter Mary, who had married Shoghi Effendi Rabbani, head of the World Bahá'í Faith. It was here that William designed his most unique building, the Shrine of the Báb, located in extensive gardens on the slopes of Mount Carmel. In poor health, William returned to Canada in 1952 and soon died in the city of his birth.

Fig. 2. William Notman & Son, *Edward Maxwell House* (*"Maxwelton"*), Baie-d'Urfé, Que. (Edward Maxwell, architect), about 1921. Private collection.

[1] Florence Wilson Houston, Laura Cowan Blaine and Ella Dunn Mellette, *Maxwell History and Genealogy* (Indianapolis: C.E. Pauley, 1916), p. 1.

[2] Maxwell family papers, private collection, Montreal.

[3] "Montreal Then and Now", *The Gazette* (Montreal), October 24, 1987, p. K-11.

[4] Mary Maxwell Rabbani, interview by France Gagnon Pratte and Rosalind M. Pepall, Haifa, April 1, 1989.

[5] Randolph Bolles worked for Edward & W.S. Maxwell from 1912 to 1926 and then retired to Washington, Connecticut, a small town near New Haven (Jan Bolles Chute [daughter of Randolph], interview by the author, Haifa, March 28, 1989).

[6] Mary Maxwell Rabbani files, Haifa.

[7] Rabbani interview, April 1, 1989.

[8] Canadian Newspaper Service, *National Reference Book on Canadian Men and Women*, 5th edition (Montreal: H. Harrison, 1936), pp. 510-511.

[9] Rabbani interview, April 1, 1989.

[10] Leo Cox, "Fifty Years of Brush and Pen: A Historical Sketch of the Pen and Pencil Club of Montreal" (unpublished manuscript, 1939), pp. 8-10.

[11] Rabbani interview, April 1, 1989.

The Education and Training of Edward Maxwell

Ellen James

*I know the disadvantages that we labour under in Montreal.
In Europe and in the United States students have a great
advantage over Canadians. Canadian architects are in a lower
position than their brethren in the neighbouring country, not
because they have less talent, but because they have not such good
opportunities for studying.*[1] A. F. Dunlop, 1890

Edward Maxwell (cat. 1a) was determined to get the
education that was unavailable to so many Canadian
students. He first learned about construction from his
father E. J., who ran a successful lumber company. In his
father's library, too, Edward had access to a number
of architectural books, including the *Elementary Principles
of Carpentry* by Thomas Tredgold and *Treatise on the
Decorative Part of Civil Architecture* by Sir William
Chambers.[2]

Edward began his formal architectural training in
Montreal as an apprentice in the office of Alexander
Dunlop (1842-1923). This is confirmed in a letter written by Dunlop referring to "my old apprentices,
Maxwell and [David Robertson] Brown".[3] The precise
dates of Edward's pupillage with Dunlop are not clear,
although his student sketchbook confirms that he was
still in Montreal in December 1886, at the age of almost
nineteen.[4]

Dunlop, well established as an architect in
Montreal by the 1880s, had completed his professional
training in Detroit.[5] About 1874 he returned to
Montreal, where he was recognized as an "expert in
designing the best class of heavy structures and the
larger class of residential work".[6] During Edward's time
in Dunlop's office he likely saw the designs for a large
neo-Gothic commission, Saint James Methodist
Church (1887-1888) on Sainte-Catherine Street West.

With Dunlop, Edward would have learned the
fundamentals of drawing, materials, surveying and
construction. Before the 1880s this kind of preparation
would have been sufficient to become a practising
architect in Canada, as the profession was still rooted in
the traditions of the building trades. But by the time
Edward undertook his studies, architecture was at a

Cat. 1a. *Edward Maxwell*

Cat. 7b. *Ames Gate Lodge (North Easton, Massachusetts, by Henry Hobson Richardson)*

crossroads, and apprenticeship was no longer adequate. The profession was about to change profoundly, emphasizing academic training inspired by the École des Beaux-Arts in Paris.[7] Young Canadians were routinely advised "to go to the United States and obtain an education there".[8] A. C. Hutchison, a prominent Montreal architect, observed in 1890:

> It is true that young men may enter an office of an architect and spend a few years there, and pick up a knowledge of architecture ... but as to any systematic teaching it has been completely ignored – in fact there are no means of providing it.[9]

The opportunity for such study did not occur in Canada until 1896, when a chair in architecture was established at McGill.

Edward – surely on Dunlop's advice – went to Boston to pursue his training. By 1888 he was working in the office of Shepley, Rutan & Coolidge, heirs to the prestigious practice of H. H. Richardson (1838-1886). He remained there through 1891.[10] David Robertson Brown (1869-1946) also worked for an unspecified period in the Shepley office. In 1890 both Edward and Brown were living at 138 Boylston Street in Boston.[11]

When Edward arrived in Boston, the Shepley office was completing a number of commissions undertaken prior to Richardson's death in April 1886. These included the Allegheny County Court House and Jail in Pittsburgh, the Marshall Field Wholesale Store in Chicago, and the Cincinnati Chamber of Commerce Building, all landmarks in Richardson's unique synthesis of historicism and modernism.[12] Edward keenly admired these buildings. A print of the Allegheny County buildings would later hang in his house in Montreal, and a cornice detail of the Marshall Field store and a gable detail of the Cincinnati Chamber of Commerce were pasted in his scrapbook. In the Shepley office he also had the opportunity to work on an enlargement of the gardener's cottage on the Frederick L. Ames estate in North Easton, Massachusetts, designed by Richardson in 1884-1885.[13] Edward's initials appear on the Shepley drawing lists beside sections for "staircase windows, cornices, dormer over porch, bay on west front, stone details of front porch and small slate dormers in roof with copper finials".[14] Edward also made plans, elevations and sections for the Ames boathouse.[15] Additionally, in March 1891, he made a watercolour sketch of the Ames Gate Lodge designed by Richardson in 1880 (cat. 7b).[16]

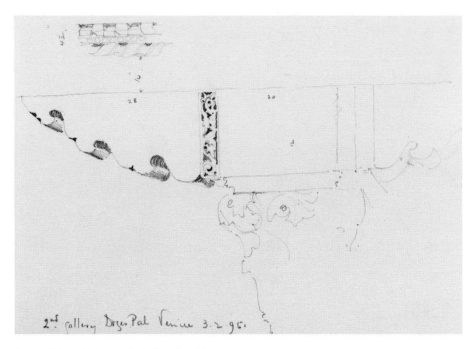

2ⁿᵈ gallery Doges Pal Venice 3.2.95.

Fig. 3. Edward Maxwell, *Gallery detail from the Doge's Palace, Venice*, 1895. Montreal, McGill University, Canadian Architecture Collection.

Since Richardson died two years before Edward's name first appears in *The Boston City Directory*, it is improbable that the two ever met; nevertheless, Richardson's influence on Edward was profound – as it was on countless young architects of the time. Edward's debt to the American architect is apparent in the planning, massing, materials and decoration of his early city and country houses. In his scrapbook he preserved Richardson's signature, his wax seal and several autograph floor plans of the proposed Oliver Ames house, which he probably found in the Shepley office.[17]

From his experience in the ateliers at the École des Beaux-Arts in Paris, Richardson understood the value of artistic collaboration – working, for example, with the sculptor Augustus Saint-Gaudens, the painter-glazier John Lafarge, and the landscape designer Frederick Law Olmsted, who was his neighbour and close friend. When Edward established his own practice, he continued this tradition, employing the Canadian sculptors Henry Beaumont and George W. Hill, and working with the American firm of landscape architects begun by Olmsted and continued by his sons.

Beyond the pervasive legacy of Richardson and the immediate experience of the busy Shepley office, Edward also absorbed ideas from the Massachusetts Institute of Technology, whose Beaux-Arts programme permeated the Boston architectural milieu. In 1890, while Edward was in Boston, Henry Van Brunt, whose former partner William R. Ware founded the department of architecture at M.I.T., wrote a two-part article entitled "The Education of the Architect", which appeared serially in a periodical published by M.I.T. These two issues remain in Edward's extensive library.[18]

In his article, Van Brunt outlined an ideal course of study that included a strong background in the history of architecture and in the theory and practice of design. He also offered advice on how to assemble and use a library and suggested a model bibliography, including books by E. E. Viollet-le-Duc, Léon Château, John Ruskin, James Fergusson, G. E. Street and Joseph Gwilt.[19] Edward owned these volumes and many more, making it clear that although he was not enrolled in the architecture department at M.I.T., he was certainly aware of its teachings.

For Edward, and for many other young North American architecture students, information about European buildings was acquired primarily from literary sources and only secondarily from travel abroad; hence, an extensive library was of the utmost importance to both the student and the practising architect.

17·4·91

Cat. 8b. *Detail of page from Edward Maxwell's scrapbook, vol. 2, with self-portrait*

After opening his office Edward did find opportunities to travel. In 1893 he visited the World's Columbian Exposition in Chicago. His father, writing to his mother, said: "Eddy was at Chicago last week ... He liked the exhibition ... especially the buildings ..."[20] At the fair he would have seen the Beaux-Arts work of McKim, Mead & White, the American firm whose traditional classicism was beginning to dominate the architectural scene and would soon overshadow the innovative work of the pioneer modernists, William LeBaron Jenney and Louis Sullivan. In 1895, Edward went to Venice and Ravenna and in 1896 to Milan. His travel sketchbooks are full of cornices, columns and capitals (fig. 3).[21]

In addition to his library, Edward's scrapbooks provide a glimpse into his learning process. The scrapbooks are just that — two unsequenced volumes of oddments: sketches, drawings, clippings and simplified plans of his early commissions in Montreal. The collection includes such diverse material as the first-floor plan of the A.W. Nickerson house in Dedham, Massachusetts, at one time attributed to Richardson but in fact designed in the Shepley office soon after 1886;[22] the Williams Institute, New London, Connecticut, also by Shepley; floor plans of a museum, a theatre and a courthouse copied from the *Croquis d'architecture;* an elevation of the Hôtel de Cluny, and a self-portrait sketch dated April 17, 1891 (cat. 8b).[23]

Edward's library and scrapbooks sum up much of what he learned in Boston – a creative eclecticism adapting elements from Richardson and the American Beaux-Arts. With this newly gained knowledge, he formed a personal style shaped by his own artistic inclinations toward the Picturesque, the wishes of the client and the particular demands of the commission.

By summer 1891 Shepley, Rutan & Coolidge had enough confidence in Edward to send him to Montreal to supervise one of their commissions, the Board of Trade Building.[24] Early in 1892 the twenty-four-year-old architect, having received a number of commissions from prominent Montrealers while still acting as Shepley superintendent, seized the day and opened his own office with the reluctant blessing of his Boston employer.[25]

After his death in 1923, Edward was praised as an architect who "to a remarkable degree ... combined thorough professional knowledge, fine artistic taste and exceptional business and executive ability, and it was only natural that he was considered one of the leading architects of Canada".[26] His education and training laid the groundwork for this success.

1 CAB, vol. 3 (October 1890), p. 116.

2 According to Henry Yates, Edward's grandson, these books from E. J. Maxwell's library passed into the library of young Edward.

3 Letter from A. F. Dunlop to J. B. Abbott, Montreal, March 24, 1910, MMFA Archives, cited in Rosalind M. Pepall, Construction d'un musée Beaux-Arts/Building a Beaux-Arts Museum, exhib. cat. (Montreal: Montreal Museum of Fine Arts, 1986), p. 36 and note 35.

4 [Sketchbook 1, 1886], unpaginated, MA, Series I.

5 Clark's Directory of Detroit, 1870-1871, p. 199, and Directory of Detroit, 1873-1874. I am grateful to Robert Hill for this information.

6 The Herald (Montreal), quoted in H. Morgan, The Canadian Men and Women of the Time (Toronto: Briggs, 1898), p. 294.

7 J. Draper, "The École des Beaux-Arts and the Architectural Profession in the United States: The Case of John Galen Howard"; Bernard M. Boyle, "Architectural Practice in America, 1865-1965: Ideal and Reality", both in Spiro Kostof, ed., The Architect: Chapters in the History of the Profession (New York: Oxford University Press, 1977), pp. 209ff and 309ff respectively; and K. Crossman, Architecture in Transition: From Art to Practice, 1885-1906 (Montreal: McGill-Queen's University Press, 1987), pp. 51ff.

8 CAB, vol. 4 (September 1891), p. 90.

9 CAB, vol. 3 (October 1890), p. 114.

10 J. D. Forbes, "Shepley, Bulfinch, Richardson & Abbott, Architects: An Introduction", Journal of the Society of Architectural Historians, vol. 17 (Fall 1958), pp. 19ff; Russell Sturgis, Great American Architects Series No. 3, The Architectural Record Co. (New York: Da Capo, 1977), "Boston Architects, Part I: Shepley, Rutan & Coolidge", pp. 1ff; and Pepall, 1986, p. 42. The Boston City Directory, 1888, lists Maxwell as a draftsman and gives his address as 13 Exchange, the Shepley office.

11 The Boston City Directory, 1890, lists Edward Maxwell, draftsman, boarding at 138 Boylston Street. I am indebted to Abigail G. Smith of the Fogg Library, Harvard University, for this information. For David Brown, see Ordre des architectes du Québec, Montreal, D. R. Brown file (as cited in Pepall, 1986, p. 39), and application form for admission as fellow of the Royal Institute of British Architects, RIBA Archive, London, File 2572. I am indebted to Robert Hill for this reference.

12 For an extensive discussion of these commissions, on which Maxwell may have worked, see Forbes, 1958.

13 Henry-Russell Hitchcock, The Architecture of H. H. Richardson and His Times (Cambridge, Massachusetts: M.I.T. Press, 1966), pp. 283-284; J. K. Ochsner, H. H. Richardson, Complete Architectural Works (Cambridge, Massachusetts: M.I.T. Press, 1982), p. 350, item 120; and Larry Homolka, "Richardson's North Easton", Architectural Forum, vol. 124 (May 1966), pp. 72ff.

14 Shepley enlarged the cottage by adding a full second floor (Shepley, Rutan & Coolidge Drawing Lists, 1890-1893, vol. 3, p. 38, Archives of Shepley, Bulfinch, Richardson & Abbott, Architects, Boston, Massachusetts [as cited in Pepall, 1986, p. 137, note 48]).

15 The Ames boathouse drawings are initialed by Edward (Shepley, Rutan & Coolidge Drawing Lists, 1890-1893, vol. 3, p. 54). They are not dated, but Shepley's librarian Katherine Green Meyer suggests 1890 as the most plausible year.

16 Project no. 501.0, "Perspective of the Ames Gate Lodge", MA.

17 [Scrapbook 2, 1889-1894], unpaginated, MA, Series F.

18 Henry Van Brunt, "The Education of the Architect", Technology Architectural Review, vol. 3, no. 6 (October 31, 1890), pp. 31ff, and vol. 3, no. 7 (November 29, 1890), pp. 37ff. The copies in the MA bear the signature of Edward Maxwell.

19 Ibid., vol. 3, no. 7 (November 29, 1890), pp. 38-39.

20 Letter from E. J. Maxwell to Johan Maxwell, August 12, 1893 (private collection, Montreal).

21 [Sketchbook 3, 1895-1909], unpaginated, MA, Series I.

22 Hitchcock, 1966, p. 285.

23 [Scrapbook 2, 1889-1894], unpaginated, MA, Series F.

24 CAB, vol. 4 (February 1891), p. 13; CAB, vol. 6 (June 1891), p. 64. For events surrounding Maxwell's supervision of the Board of Trade Building see also "Daily Journal, 1892", unpaginated, MA, Series D. While the exact date of Maxwell's return to Montreal is not known, his admission to the PQAA was a fait accompli by July 1891, and The Boston City Directory of 1891 has him "removed to Montreal, Canada".

25 "Daily Journal, 1892", unpaginated, entries for January 11 and 12, and February 3; John Bland, "Edward Maxwell: Biography", in Edward & W.S. Maxwell: Guide to the Archive/Guide du fonds (Montreal: Canadian Architecture Collection, McGill University, 1986), p. 5.

26 William Wood, ed., The Storied Province of Quebec, 5 vols. (Toronto: Dominion Publishing, 1931), vol. 3, p. 183.

THE EDUCATION AND
TRAINING OF WILLIAM S. MAXWELL

Rosalind M. Pepall

As the younger brother of a practising architect, William Maxwell (cat. 1b) had an ideal introduction to the profession. From early in Edward's practice, "Willie" was very much a presence behind the scenes. His hours of work for the firm are noted from October 1894 to September 1895 and again from May 1898 to October 1901 in Edward's records of his draftsmen.[1] These records indicate the buildings in which he was involved, and many drawings are initialled *WSM*. By the end of the 1890s his hand is evident in the fine decorative work rendered in detail on the architectural plans and drawings for the buildings of his brother's firm.

It was undoubtedly with Edward's encouragement that William went to Boston to further his training in a large architectural office. Between September 1895 and May 1898 he was in Boston working for Winslow & Wetherell,[2] a long-established practice run by Walter T. Winslow (1843-1909) and George H. Wetherell (1854-1930).[3] In a letter to his brother, written on Winslow & Wetherell letterhead, William gave a glimpse of his work: "I have been working a good deal with Henry Forbes Bigelow lately and am now carrying out a large country house for him, he seems very satisfied with my work ... he is a very clever young fellow (29 or 30) and knows more about planning, designing etc. than anyone else in the office."[4]

Henry F. Bigelow (1867-1929) would become a partner in the firm in 1898. A biographical note on Bigelow states that "In the opinion of one of his contemporaries, Mr. Bigelow probably contributed more to the creation of charming and distinguished house interiors than any one person of his time."[5] William Maxwell's own interest and talent in domestic interior design may well have been awakened by Bigelow.[6]

Winslow & Wetherell was also well known for its large hotels and commercial buildings.[7] One hotel, the Touraine, completed in 1897, was a major commission for the firm during William's years in Boston and was a project in which Bigelow participated. William saved

Cat. 1b. *William Sutherland Maxwell*

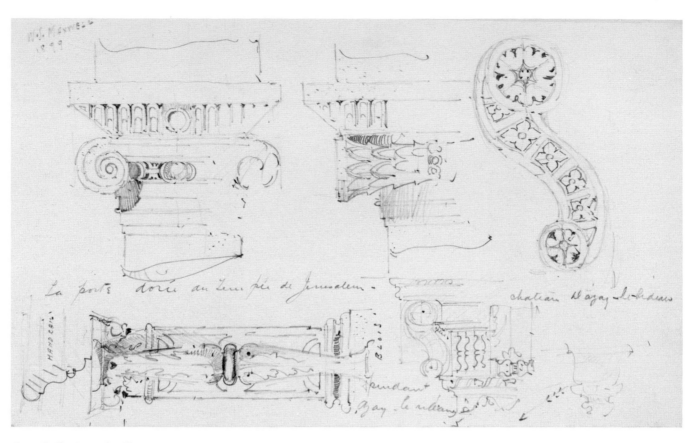

Cat. 6f. *Sketches made in France*

among his personal papers a newspaper clipping on the hotel, suggesting that he too may have been involved in its design.[8]

William made notes and drawings in his sketchbooks of Boston buildings and of his trips to nearby towns such as Marblehead, Massachusetts, and Portsmouth, New Hampshire.[9] He made notes on the Boston Public Library, which opened in 1895, the year he arrived in the city. The library, designed by McKim, Mead & White, is a key monument in American architecture. In the aftermath of the World's Columbian Exposition in Chicago, the building stimulated an interest in Beaux-Arts classicism, and some of the best American sculptors and artists decorated the building in the spirit of the so-called American Renaissance.[10]

The evenings that William spent in drawing classes and in social gatherings at the Boston Architectural Club also provided him with an opportunity to learn about the latest ideas and developments in American architecture.[11] At the turn of the century the École des Beaux-Arts in Paris was having a major impact on American architecture: many of the leading architects in the United States had studied there, and Winslow &

Wetherell was run by graduates of the French school. William's enthusiasm for French architecture was already evident in 1896 when he wrote to Edward about his purchase of the *Concours Publics*, a magazine that illustrated winning competition plans for French government commissions.[12] Upon his return to Montreal in May 1898, clearly excited by French Beaux-Arts models, William delighted in rendering the cartouches, trophies and swags on the façade of Edward Maxwell's London & Lancashire Life Assurance building.[13]

By this time William had set his sights on Paris. He left for Europe in late summer 1899 and by September was in Paris, where he filled his sketchbooks with scenes of the city and of his travels farther afield (cat. 6f).[14] He lived at 83 Boulevard Montparnasse, the same address as the Canadian painter Maurice Cullen.[15] William wrote to the secretary of the Province of Quebec Association of Architects in February 1900: "Paris is delightful and I wish I could prolong my stay for years."[16]

Although William was not registered as a student at the École des Beaux-Arts, he was admitted into the atelier of Jean-Louis Pascal (1837-1920), a leading

Beaux-Arts architect closely associated with the École.[17] It was in the atelier, under the eye of the *patron*, that the student learned planning and design and carried out projects.[18] As architectural historian Richard Chafee explains: "These large ateliers were not architectural offices; they were private schools of architecture."[19] Young French students, "les aspirants", who wished to try the École's rigorous entrance exams would spend as long as two years preparing for them in an atelier.[20] Some American architects with previous education were also admitted to the ateliers to round off their training before taking up practice at home.[21] When William set out for Paris at the age of twenty-four, he probably never intended to embark on the lengthy period of study required to graduate from the École des Beaux-Arts.

In Jean-Louis Pascal's atelier, William would have learned a logical and systematic approach to planning. One of Pascal's students recalled that the master "urged logic, not intuition. He taught simplification: rational plans and decorous elevations. His ideal was architec-

ture that was and looked distinguished."[22] This training served William well in later years when the Maxwell firm entered design competitions for some of Canada's most important and complex public buildings.

William's talent as a painter and his love of drawing made him an ideal student of the Beaux-Arts method. The École des Beaux-Arts considered the architect as an artist, and William would have flourished with the emphasis placed on skilled draftsmanship and beautifully executed drawings and plans. The exquisite study of a nude woman that William executed either in Paris or in Boston shows his facility in drawing (cat. 6a). William would have been inspired by the impressive renderings the architecture students prepared for the monthly and annual competitions. As he said himself, "The exhibitions, in a large hall at the École, exert a powerful influence; they get a man out of a rut, stimulate his imagination and broaden his point of view. The effect of many solutions of a problem all intelligently worked out cannot be other than broadly educative."[23]

Cat. 6a. *Figure study*

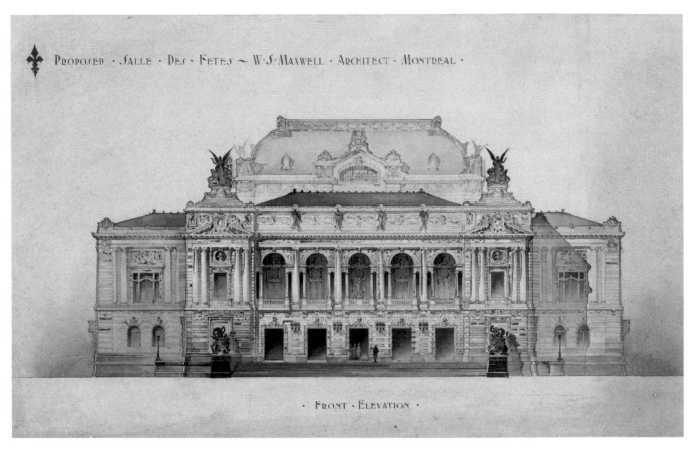

Cat. 6b. *Front elevation for a proposed "salle des fêtes"*

Two of William's own watercolour studies from this period are typical of the drawings prepared by the students. His renderings of the front and side elevations of a proposed "salle des fêtes" (cat. 6b) are modelled on the quintessential Beaux-Arts building: the Paris Opera, completed in 1875 by Charles Garnier.[24] The emphasis on symmetry, classical precedent and the creation of a grand public monument replete with symbolic sculpture was in keeping with the ideals of Beaux-Arts design. William's ability to create such elaborately detailed and lavishly colourful drawings made him well suited to prepare renderings for the Maxwell firm.

Another watercolour, depicting an opulent "state barge" bedecked with flags, exemplifies the type of design the École students were asked to create for prizes in decoration (cat. 6d). William may have painted this watercolour as a practice exercise, following the rules for the competition of the Prix Rougevin, awarded for rendering of ornament in an architectural context. In

1900 this prize was given for "La Décoration arrière d'un navire."[25]

William had the good fortune to be in Paris during the Exposition Universelle of 1900. He was able to visit the two splendid Beaux-Arts buildings constructed especially for the exhibition, the Petit Palais and the Grand Palais.[26] He would also have seen Art nouveau design at its most advanced state in the decorative art exhibits.

In July 1900, William was travelling in the north of France, through Normandy and Brittany, and at the end of the summer he went to Italy to study Renaissance architecture – an essential part of any Beaux-Arts education. In August and September, William sketched in Venice, Padua and Milan, and then went south to Florence and Rome.[27]

In late 1900, when William returned to Montreal, Edward Maxwell's office was busy with a number of important commissions. Once again "Willie" was at work in the drafting room. Many of the drawings of interior elevations and carved exterior ornament for the sumptuous house of Charles R. Hosmer are in William's distinctive hand. With free, loose pen strokes he sketched the decorative details of mouldings and panels (fig. 4). Because of William's outstanding draftsmanship and his interest in ornament, Edward relied on his brother to carry out designs for furniture, plaster, carved woodwork and other fittings.

William's period of study at the Atelier Pascal, though short, came at a critical time in his career. Paris put the finishing touch to his maturity as an architect who had already had years of experience in Montreal and Boston. His Beaux-Arts training in Boston and Paris brought valuable additional skills and prestige to the Maxwell firm.

Cat. 6d. *A State Barge*

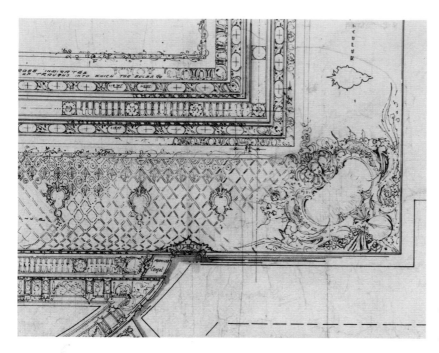

Fig. 4. W. S. Maxwell, *Drawing room ceiling detail for Hosmer House,* undated. Montreal, McGill University, Canadian Architecture Collection.

1 [Draftsmen's Hours per Client Book K, 1894-1901], MA, Series C.

2 One of William's rare extant letters from Boston, written to his cousin Bess, is dated September 11, 1896 (private collection, Montreal). He is first listed in *The Boston City Directory* of 1896 as a "draughtsman" at 3 Hamilton Place, which was the office of Winslow & Wetherell.

3 Winslow & Wetherell were successors to the practice of the prominent architect Nathaniel Bradlee, with whom they became partners. The records of the Winslow & Wetherell firm do not appear to have been preserved (information from the Boston Athenaeum, Boston).

4 The date on this letter (private collection, Montreal) appears to be March 16, 1895; however, judging from the number of hours William worked for Edward in March 1895, it would have been virtually impossible for him to have been in Boston then. Therefore the year in all likelihood is 1896.

5 Henry F. Withey and Elsie Rathburn Withey, *Biographical Dictionary of American Architects (Deceased)* (Los Angeles: New Age, 1956), p. 57.

6 Bigelow exhibited some drawings in the PQAA exhibition in Montreal in 1896, most probably on the recommendation of W. S. Maxwell (*The Gazette* [Montreal], October 9, 1896, in MMFA Library Scrapbook, vol. 4, p. 72).

7 The Steinert Hall office, showroom and concert hall complex with a Beaux-Arts façade on Boylston Street (1896), and the Procter Building on Bedford Street (1897) are two existing works by the firm.

8 *Boston Herald,* April 13, 1896.

9 Seventeen of William's sketchbooks still exist in the collection of his daughter, Mary Maxwell Rabbani. The earliest date from 1893-1894 in Montreal, and they continue throughout his career until 1937. Two remain from his Boston years.

10 See Richard Guy Wilson, *McKim, Mead & White, Architects* (New York: Rizzoli, 1983), pp. 134-145.

11 William Maxwell's participation in the Boston Architectural Club has been discussed in Rosalind M. Pepall, *Construction d'un musée Beaux-Arts/Building a Beaux-Arts Museum,* exhib. cat. (Montreal: Montreal Museum of Fine Arts, 1986), pp. 44-45.

12 Letter of March 16, 1895 (but see note 4 regarding date).

13 Project no. 171.0, "Detail of St. John Street Dormer", signed and dated 26-9-98; "Detail of St. James Street Pavilion", signed and dated 20-9-98.

14 A sketch in one of his notebooks is dated August 23, 1899, Edinburgh. From the period of September 1899 to April 1900, William's sketchbooks are filled with drawings of buildings in, among other places, Paris, Versailles, Fontainebleau, Reims and Tours.

15 Sketchbook, 1899-1900, "W. S. Maxwell/London 1899/Paris 203 Boulevard Raspail" changed to "83 Boulevard Montparnasse", and Sylvia Antoniou, *Maurice Cullen* (Kingston, Ont.: Agnes Etherington Art Centre, 1982), p. 15.

16 Letter from W. S. Maxwell to G. A. Monette, Paris, February 9, 1900, PQAA correspondence, 06-P-124-1, chemise 2, ANQM.

17 William S. Maxwell's name is not found among the lists of architecture students at the École des Beaux-Arts preserved at the Archives Nationales in Paris: AJ52-240, "Registres matricules des élèves de la section d'architecture 1800-1925"; AJ52-248, "Registre d'inscription des élèves dans les ateliers de peinture, sculpture, architecture, ateliers extérieurs 1874-1945"; and AJ52-470, "Élèves étrangers 1878-1928". William Maxwell's training in Paris has been discussed in Pepall, 1986, pp. 45-49.

18 For a thorough discussion of École des Beaux-Arts teaching methods, see Richard Chafee, "The Teaching of Architecture at the École des Beaux-Arts", in Arthur Drexler, *The Architecture of the École des Beaux-Arts* (New York: Museum of Modern Art, 1977), pp. 61-109.

19 *Ibid.,* p. 89.

20 *Ibid,* p. 82, and Edmond Delaire, *Les architectes élèves de l'École des Beaux-Arts 1793-1907* (Paris: Librairie de la construction moderne, 1907), p. 212.

21 The American Society of Beaux-Arts Architects, formed by graduates of the École, was also open to those who had been in a Paris atelier for at least one year (Delaire, 1907, p. 447).

22 Francis Swales, a former student of Pascal, quoted in Chafee, 1977, p. 96.

23 W. S. Maxwell, "Architectural Education", *CAB,* vol. 16 (January 1903), p. 22.

24 This watercolour was exhibited at the AAM Spring Exhibition in March 1901 (*CAB,* vol. 14 [March 1901], p. 65, and vol. 14 [June 1901], suppl., p. 124).

25 The winning design is illustrated in Annie Jacques, *La carrière de l'architecte au XIXᵉ siècle,* Les Dossiers du Musée d'Orsay, vol. 3 (Paris: Éditions de la Réunion des musées nationaux, 1986), p. 34.

26 These two buildings must have impressed William Maxwell, because later in his career he gave a lecture to the PQAA Sketching Club on the Petit Palais and the Grand Palais (*CAB,* vol. 22 [March 1908], p. 15). He also had in his library *Les Palais des Beaux-Arts : M. Girault architecte en chef* (Paris: n.d.).

27 Two sketchbooks remain from this trip (Mary Maxwell Rabbani collection, Haifa). Both are signed and bear the two addresses 83 Boulevard Montparnasse and 188 Côte-Saint-Antoine Road.

V

BUILDING FOR POWER
THE MAXWELL PRACTICE AND
THE MONTREAL BUSINESS COMMUNITY

Robert Sweeny

One of the most remarkable aspects of the Maxwell practice had little to do with architecture – the stability of the Maxwells' clientele, whether individuals or companies, over a thirty-year period was nothing short of extraordinary. Families and firms who first employed Edward Maxwell in the early 1890s were still the backbone of the partnership in 1923 when Edward died.[1] This achievement cannot be explained simply in terms of a prevailing architectural fashion, for the styles in vogue evolved significantly over this period. In large measure the explanation of this client loyalty and, indeed, of the Maxwell firm's success in general lies in the broader social history of the Montreal business community.

In 1891 Edward Maxwell returned to Montreal from Boston to oversee the building of the imposing new offices of what had been the pre-eminent business institution of nineteenth-century English Montreal, the Board of Trade. Undoubtedly this was a great opportunity for the twenty-three-year-old architect. The Board of Trade had been, since its inception in 1825, the principal pressure group for the city's English-speaking merchants. It was, however, an organization whose days of glory were already a thing of the past, for Montreal no longer owed its prominence in the economic life of the Dominion to its historic role as a mercantile centre. The site of Canada's Industrial Revolution at mid-century, Montreal was, by the last quarter of the nineteenth century, the financial, industrial and transportation metropolis of Canada. The city would maintain this leading role in the country's economy until the Great Depression of the 1930s.

If the Board of Trade project provided Edward Maxwell's entrée into the business community, and there is no doubt that it did, it was only indirectly responsible for his rapid success in establishing himself in the city. Early in January 1892, Henry Vincent Meredith, a member of the Board and at the time the assistant general manager of the Bank of Montreal, commissioned Maxwell to build him a new home.[2] Meredith was married to the niece of Sir Hugh Allan,

one of the most important capitalists in late nineteenth-century Canada. The large red brick mansion Maxwell designed for the Merediths, situated on the southwest corner of Pine and Peel kitty-corner to Allan's own "Ravenscrag", was widely acclaimed, and the young Maxwell would design five more buildings for members of the Allan family by 1897.

Important as the Allan family connection was, the Meredith commission was significant for other reasons. Vincent Meredith was a rising star in the firmament of Montreal business. For the next twenty years he would be a member of the tight-knit group of bankers and industrialists who charted the course for one of North America's most important financial groups, one that was based upon the Bank of Montreal and the Canadian Pacific Railway. More than any other single factor, it was the Maxwells' early and lifelong relationship with the families and firms composing this powerful financial group that influenced the pattern of their architectural careers.

Like the Board of Trade, the Bank of Montreal was an institution created in the pre-industrial age of merchant capitalism, and the bank's early growth was directly linked to short-term financing of mercantile activities within British North America and elsewhere in the Empire.[3] By the mid-nineteenth century, however, the Bank was showing signs of an increasing autonomy and had established itself as one of the leading banks in the New York currency and the Chicago commodity markets. In 1879 it was the first bank within the British Empire to float a government bond on the New York, as opposed to the London, bond market. In 1892 it became the London agent of the Dominion of Canada, another first for a "colonial" bank. During the years the Bank of Montreal was consolidating its role as the leading financial institution in Canada, it grew increasingly involved in the financing of industrial activity in the country. Without question, its most important investment was the Canadian Pacific Railway. Symbolically, in 1885, when the last spike of the country's first transcontinental railway was driven home, it was the bank's principal shareholder, vice-president, and soon-to-be president, Donald Smith, who wielded the sledgehammer.

This shift in focus from mercantile banking activities to a partnership in industry was the result of the maturation of industrial capitalism.[4] Although almost all of the industrial companies in the country remained firmly under the control of their founding families, the ability of these companies to expand rapidly to serve the developing pan-Canadian market depended increasingly on access to the domestic capital market. These changes were reflected in the composition of the Bank's board of directors. Of the thirty men appointed to the Bank's board between the start of construction of the CPR in 1882 and the outbreak of the Great War in 1914, twenty-two were industrial capitalists;[5] no fewer than thirteen of these would commission homes by Maxwell's firm.

The close and privileged relationship that the Maxwells enjoyed with the Bank of Montreal/CPR group was by no means limited to designing their city and country homes. The central element of the group's long-term strategy was the development of a resource-based hinterland in the Canadian West. Their plan involved leapfrogging over southern Ontario, which the main line of the CPR bypassed, in order to develop a "Tomorrow's Country"[6] centred in the wheat belt of Saskatchewan that would be dependent on, and to a significant degree controlled by, the transportation, banking and industrial firms headquartered in Montreal. In both the short and medium terms it was a highly successful strategy that invited imitation by the Grand Trunk Pacific and the Canadian Northern, the two transcontinental railways built just before the Great War. This basis for Montreal's dominant position in the Canadian economy would be severely shaken by the man-made ecological disaster of the Dust Bowl of the 1930s,[7] but this occurred long after the Maxwells' completion of the Saskatchewan Legislative Building and of many stations and hotels strategically located along the CPR's line.

The Maxwell practice therefore coincided with the rise of Montreal's leading industrialists and financiers to an almost unassailable position within the Canadian economy. More than forty percent of all the directors of the leading companies in Canada in both 1910 and 1930 lived in Montreal.[8] Although undoubtedly proud of their achievements, as the conspicuous consumption manifested by the mansions the Maxwells designed for them shows, they were not in fact members of a meritocracy. Upward social mobility was rare, for many of these men not only ran companies that served a pan-Canadian market, but also were members of the families who owned these companies. The relatively few business leaders who had not been born to wealth,

like J. B. Learmont, owed their success in no small measure to their marriages. Maxwell clients were therefore very different from the "hired guns" who manage modern-day corporate Canada.[9]

The Maxwell brothers worked in a business environment where family and firm, private club and private school, management and ownership were all interwoven. The result was a clientele comprising private individuals and corporations that were one and the same: with one major exception, the Bell Telephone Company of Canada,[10] all of Maxwell's important "corporate" clients were also major "private" clients. The CPR illustrates the connection well. During the 1890s, Edward Maxwell carried out at least twenty private commissions for R. B. Angus, Duncan McIntyre, T. G. Shaughnessy, William Van Horne, and James Ross – all prominent directors of the CPR – while at the same time his firm was working on no fewer than twelve different projects for the railway.

The Maxwell firm's work for the Bank of Montreal/CPR group was not limited to the companies associated with the group. There were also the important private houses that the brothers designed for capitalists who shared directly in the growth of the group, such as those for C. R. Hosmer and F. W. Thompson, co-owners of Ogilvie Flour; James Crathern and J. B. Learmont of the hardware wholesale firm of Crathern & Caverhill, later known as Caverhill & Learmont; Edward Clouston, general manager of the Bank of Montreal; Hartland MacDougall, a prominent stockbroker active in the underwriting of many of the group's issues; F. L. Wanklyn, R. B. Angus's son-in-law and the group's representative on the board of the Montreal Street Railway; Hal Brown, Canadian director of the London & Lancashire general insurance group; Henry and J. H. Birks, owners of the jewellery firm; Charles Smith, owner of the McCready shoe company; Alexander Ramsey, a paint and lead manufacturer; C. C. Ballantyne, owner of the Sherwin Williams Paint Company; and both Noah and Leo Timmins, owners of the Timmins, Ontario, gold mine.

If the private and public worlds of this upper stratum of the business community in Montreal were intertwined, they were also surprisingly narrow. Their unprecedented wealth combined with language and cultural barriers to cut them off from most of the middle stratum of bourgeois families in the city, who were French-speaking. Cocooned in their mansions in the Square Mile when not escaping to their country estates at Senneville and Saint Andrews, these men and women built a social life around the private clubs, schools and philanthropic societies they formed and funded. Quite early on, the Maxwell firm was commissioned to do work for three leading private clubs on the island of Montreal: the Mount Royal, the Saint James's, and the

Forest and Stream. The firm also supervised construction of the Montreal Stock Exchange, designed by George Post of New York. None of these buildings was open to the general public; nor were they the exclusive preserve of any particular financial group. Thus they served as advertisements to a broader cross section of the upper reaches of the business community.

In light of this club work and the partnership's later work for Trafalgar and Miss Edgar's private girls' schools and the Royal Victoria, Montreal General and Alexandra hospitals, it is surprising just how little work the firm did for families and companies that were not somehow connected with the Bank of Montreal/CPR group. Two prominent exceptions to this general observation should be noted, however. During the years the firm flourished, a second financial group was created around the Forget/Holt interests. In the two decades after the death of Louis-Joseph Forget in 1911, this group, centred around the Royal Bank of Canada and led by Herbert Holt, would successfully challenge the Bank of Montreal's hegemony within the city's business community.

L.-J. Forget represented one of the few cases of social mobility into the highest realms of finance and industry by a member of Montreal's French-speaking majority. He started out as an employee of James Crathern and later was financed in his early stock-broking activities by J. B. Learmont. Whether or not it was through them that Forget came to admire the Maxwells' work cannot be ascertained. It is clear, however, that he greatly favoured the architects, for the Maxwell Archive contains drawings of some fifteen private commissions for Forget, while two of his most important holdings, the Richelieu & Ontario Navigation Company and the Montreal Street Railway Company, were important corporate clients of the firm.

Herbert Holt, who had greatly expanded his family fortune as a CPR contractor along with James Ross, never had any private contracts with the Maxwell firm. However, when his newly acquired bank, the Merchants Bank of Halifax, began to expand into central Canada in the 1890s, Edward Maxwell was its architect of choice in Montreal for close to a decade. In 1901 the Merchants Bank of Halifax became the Royal Bank of Canada, and the Maxwell firm did no major work for them after 1904, when a heightened rivalry between the two Montreal-based financial groups often took on an architectural form. After all, Holt would explain his use of a Roman bath as the model for the Saint James (Saint-Jacques) Street headquarters of the Royal Bank, built in the late 1920s, when it finally surpassed the Bank of Montreal in total assets, on the grounds that the Romans conquered the Greeks. Holt characterized the porticoed head office of the Bank of Montreal as a Greek-inspired temple to wealth.

No survey of the Maxwells' clients would be complete without mentioning the Art Association of Montreal, a commission that resulted from a competition, wherein the brothers won out against the talented McGill architect Percy Nobbs.[11] One may doubt whether the playing field was level, for many of the prominent collectors in the city – those who played a leading role in the life of the Art Association of Montreal – lived in homes designed by the Maxwells.[12] What better way of publicly affirming their own discerning tastes than by having the centrepiece of the Montreal art world designed by their own architects?

Edward Maxwell died while overseeing the enlargement of the most famous of all the CPR buildings, the Château Frontenac in Quebec City, a fitting monument to his career. Hopefully it is evident from this essay that Edward and William Maxwell were what Gramsci termed "organic intellectuals", in that the significance of their work can best be understood as serving, and ultimately tied to, a particular social group, that being in this case, as most often, the dominant one.[13] Thus, the Maxwell brothers gave form and substance to both the public and the private dreams of the families and firms who controlled one of the most influential and powerful financial groups in Canada's history.

[1] All quantitative statements concerning the business of the Maxwell firm in this piece are derived from the MA as inventoried in *Edward & W. S. Maxwell: Guide to the Archive/Guide du fonds* (Montreal: Canadian Architecture Collection, McGill University, 1986).

[2] John Bland, "Edward Maxwell: Biography", in *ibid.*, p. 5.

[3] A somewhat romanticized history of the Bank of Montreal is Merrill Denison, *Canada's First Bank* (Toronto: McClelland and Stewart, 1966).

[4] A general history of this process is Brian Young and John Dickinson, *A Short History of Québec: A Socio-economic Perspective* (Toronto: Copp Clark, 1988).

[5] Robert Sweeny, *A History and Guide to the Records of Selected Montreal Businesses Before 1947* (Montreal: HÉC, 1978).

[6] At the turn of the century this phrase was commonly used to to describe Saskatchewan.

[7] John H. Thompson, *The Harvest of War* (Toronto: McClelland and Stewart, 1978).

[8] Gilles Piedalue, "Les groupes financiers au Canada (1900-1930)", *Revue d'histoire de l'Amérique*, vol. 30 (June 1976).

[9] The expression was used by Alf Powis, the longtime CEO of Noranda, to explain the difference between himself and people who owned their own firm, in Peter C. Newman, *The Canadian Establishment* (Toronto: McClelland and Stewart, 1976), p. 181.

[10] Bell Telephone, although headquartered in Montreal, was not owned by Montrealers. Its principal shareholders were the family of Alexander Graham Bell and their Canadian cousins, the Sises. It should be noted, however, that the president of Bell in the 1890s, when Maxwell started to work for the company, was John Grey, who, like H. V. Meredith, had married one of the Allan heiresses.

[11] Rosalind M. Pepall, *Construction d'un musée beaux-Arts/Building a Beaux-Arts Museum*, exhib. cat. (Montreal: Montreal Museum of Fine Arts, 1986).

[12] For a discussion of this milieu, see Janet M. Brooke, *Discerning Tastes: Montreal Collectors 1880-1920*, exhib. cat. (Montreal: Montreal Museum of Fine Arts, 1989).

[13] See Antonio Gramsci, *Selections from Prison Notebooks* (New York: International Publishers, 1971), p. 10, where the organic intellectual is seen as belonging to "historically formed specialized categories for the exercise of the intellectual function. They are formed in connection with all social groups, but especially in connection with the more important, and they undergo extensive and complex elaboration in connection with the dominant social group."

THE
"OLD CRAZE OF BUYING BOOKS"
THE LIBRARIES OF EDWARD
AND WILLIAM MAXWELL

Irena Murray

The impressive libraries that Edward and William Maxwell amassed throughout their lifetimes provided a source of architectural information and satisfied a marked penchant for collecting. It is fortunate that at least a part of their collections is preserved at the Blackader-Lauterman Library at McGill University through the generosity of Edward's widow, Elizabeth Ellen Maxwell; the family of his son, Stirling Maxwell; his grandson, Henry Yates; and William's daughter, Mary Maxwell Rabbani. Thus, four hundred and fifty volumes have been reunited with McGill's other Maxwell holdings of personal and business records and almost twenty thousand architectural drawings and photographs.

The importance of book collecting to the brothers and the bond it represented in their relationship is illustrated in a letter of March 1895 in which William described some of his recent purchases in Boston to Edward:

> ... I have caught my old craze of buying books ... Have subscribed to "Concours Publics" it being a magazine (monthly) giving plans Elevations Etc of the prize winning plans in the competitions held by the French Government Etc I was the first one to subscribe to it in our office, 5 others subscribed immediately after me. It is a splendid publication and costs $9.40 a year ...
>
> You asked me to look out for new books Etc I can confidently recommend the following. 1st A bargain. Nash's Elizabethian [sic] Houses, 5 vols, original Edition (same as those Mr. Learmont lent you) at Estes & Lauriat's. These vols are very scarce. Cost $16 or $17 I don't know which. There is one set out, if you want to let me know immediately. This work was published at $45.00.

> From Helburn (whom I see often) "L'Architecture Francais [sic]" 7 vols. 5 of plates. Cost $55. The firm bought this work and used it great deal on hotel. It is a magnificent work –
> From Helburn – "Hess Holzbauten" by Bickel contains 2 vols 80 plates cost $20 – This book is devoted to half timber work principally German ...[1]

This glimpse into the brothers' early collecting habits reveals some interesting details regarding their sources and underscores the twenty-one-year-old William's potential as a bibliophile.

While there were few Montreal bookdealers who never received a visit from the Maxwells, according to family testimony, they dealt with a number of specialized firms in particular. In Montreal, their mainstay was a branch of the Bruno Hessling company, "publisher & importer of books on science and art", at 51A McGill College Avenue. Hessling's headquarters were in Berlin and Paris; their New York branch was more narrowly specialized in "books on architecture and decorative arts". Another frequent source was Armand Guérinet, a Paris-based publisher and seller specializing in art and architecture, most likely first discovered by William during his studies in Paris.

Edward's Library

Both brothers were in the habit of writing their names in the books they acquired and often marked the year of purchase on the title page. The earliest recorded acquisition, a slim volume of selected works of Washington Irving (1880) inscribed "Ed. Maxwell, High School [of] Montreal", may have been part of the school's curriculum. The first architectural title in McGill's Maxwell Collection was probably a Christmas present to Edward from his family the year he first went to work in Boston. Inscribed December 25, 1886, *Notes and Sketches of an Architect* (1876) was an English trans-lation of a work by Félix Narjoux, a nineteenth-century French architect and travel writer who was a student of Viollet-le-Duc. The importance books on architecture held in the Maxwell family may be surmised from titles that had belonged to Edward and William's father, E. J. Maxwell, for example the fourth edition (1853) of Thomas Tredgold's *Elementary Principles of Carpentry*, originally acquired by Edward's grandfather and name-sake, and the fourth edition (1826) of the *Treatise on the Decorative Part of Civil Architecture* by Sir William Chambers. A large number of books were inscribed on special occasions; Howard Crosby Butler's *Scotland's Ruined Abbeys* was a Christmas gift from Edward to his wife in 1899, the year the book was published. Among the titles Edward acquired during his employment with Shepley, Rutan & Coolidge, and one he had listed in his sketchbook among "books to get", is Vignola's *Traité pratique d'architecture* (1865 edition).

Edward appears to have been a particularly active collector toward the end of the century. His journal for 1892 indicates that he twice attended a sale of the library of F. B. Matthews, a Montreal businessman and a charter member of the Art Association of Montreal.[2] Although no title can be traced to Matthews's library, other Maxwell purchases in this period have been linked to the library of the architect and designer Edward Colonna, namely part of the series of *Monographs on American Architecture* (1886-1898) issued as a supplement to *American Architect and Building News* to document projects of architect H. H. Richardson. Their original owner is clearly identifiable by the Colonna-designed bookplates. Colonna's work in Montreal from 1888 on and his projects for the Canadian Pacific Railway (see cat. entry 20) may ac-count for Edward's interest in Colonna's collection.[3] The inscribed dates indicate that Edward acquired the books at a sale on December 10, 1898, where he also purchased the first edition of one of the most influen-tial of eighteenth-century British architectural books, James Gibbs's *A Book of Architecture* (1728).

Periodicals illustrating buildings and decorative details also formed an important part of Edward's library. The McGill holdings include early volumes of the *American Architect, Architectural Record, The Architectural Review, L'Architecture d'aujourd'hui, The Brickbuilder*, the French series *Croquis d'architecture* and the influential Viennese review *Das Interieur*.

Edward's library encompassed titles on architec-tural and urban history, design and decorative arts, monographs on architects and artists, portfolios of competition drawings, books on building types, pam-phlets on building safety and construction, reference works of biographical and encyclopedic nature, and volumes on painting, drawing and geometry. Among

the authors represented are Jean-Charles Delafosse, Josef Halfpenny, Johann Karl Krafft, Batty Langley, Paul Marie Letarouilly, A. C. and A.W.N. Pugin, and E. E. Viollet-le-Duc. With his brother's invaluable assis-tance, Edward had built an outstanding office library – broad in scope, rich in example and easy to consult.

William's Library
It was Edward's younger brother William, however, whose prodigious interests, vast knowledge and analyt-ical mind – coupled with a lifelong passion for book buying – formed one of the most interesting and least-known Montreal collections of the first half of the twentieth century. William's daughter, Mary Maxwell Rabbani, remembers her father as "a man whose inter-est in every aspect of artistic expression in all ages and cultures was universal and profound" and who "collect-ed antiques as well as books, but later in life confined his collecting instincts to rare and limited editions mostly illustrated by famous modern artists".[4]

William Maxwell amassed an important collection of Japanese prints, gleaned clippings on the decorative arts from hundreds of periodicals, and developed a rich and broad-ranging personal library. A recent estimate of the total number of items in William Maxwell's library indicates holdings of between thirty-five hundred and four thousand volumes, surely a personal collection with few Canadian rivals in its time.[5] Although several of William's Montreal contem-poraries, such as David R. McCord, Gerald Hart and Joseph B. Learmont, may have amassed libraries com-parable or greater in size, none displayed such a passion for collecting rare and limited editions of European authors. J. B. Learmont and his brother W. J. Learmont may have influenced William's early collecting inter-ests;[6] be that as it may, book collecting quickly became the young architect's most absorbing avocation. "He had the true spirit of a student with all the interest and patience that implies and this characterized him until the end of his life," writes his daughter. "All my own feelings for and knowledge of art began when he would show me pictures in his wonderful books ..."[7]

More than one hundred titles on the history and techniques of the printed book, book collecting and bibliography attest to the seriousness of William's collecting: T. F. Dibdin's *Bibliographical Decameron*, R. B. McKerrow's *Introduction to Bibliography*, C. Ratta's *L'art du livre et de la revue* and A.S.W. Rosenbach's *Books and Bidders* convey but an inkling of the depth of his interest.[8] Furthermore, William served on the Library and Prints Committee of the Art Association of Montreal from 1919 to 1929, together with the McGill University Librarian Dr. G. Lomer.[9] The Association's annual reports also acknowledge several donations by William of Japanese prints and books on art.[10]

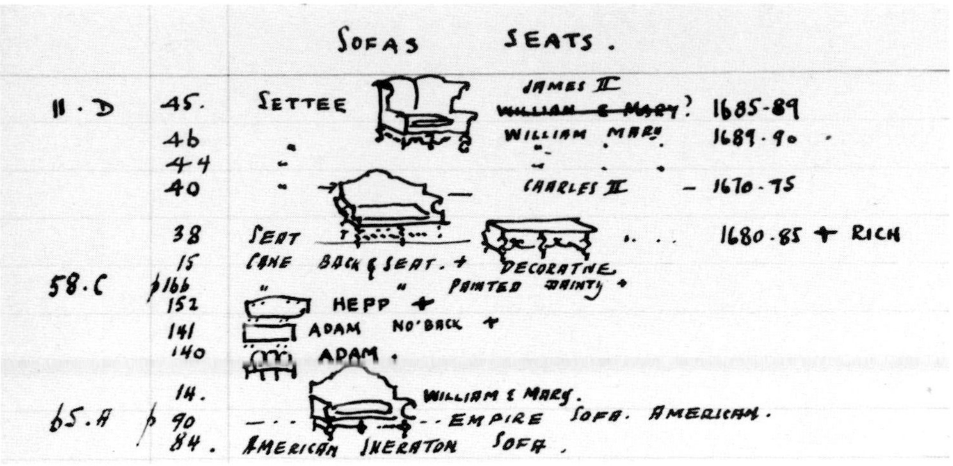

Fig. 5. *Iconographic index card to library of William S. Maxwell,*
undated. Montreal, McGill University, Canadian Architecture
Collection.

The pride of William's library was his collection of about eight hundred art books and a similar number of literary works illustrated by modern artists and often printed in limited editions by private presses. A random glance reveals titles such as *Les œuvres burlesques et mystiques de frère Matorel mort au couvent* by Max Jacob, published in 1912 by Henry Kahnweiler with wood engravings by André Derain, and others illustrated by such noted artists as Charles Émile Carlègle, Paul Colin, Raoul Dufy, Charles Guérin and Hermann-Paul. The Bodley Head, Cranach Press, Nonesuch Press and Golden Cockerel Press are among the houses whose work William especially sought out.

Among W. S. Maxwell's early and rare books donated to McGill are the first edition of Sir John Soane's *Designs in Architecture* (1778), the first edition of the first English translation of Alberti's *De re aedificatoria*, the 1716 London edition of Palladio's *The First Book of Architecture,* and A. C. Pugin's *Examples of Gothic Architecture* (1850) and *Ornamental Gables* (1839).

William's acumen as a bibliophile was matched by his desire to keep the office collection accessible; as it grew, he drew up a dictionary catalogue by author, title and subject, as well as an alphanumerical shelflist.[11] With the zeal of a true bibliographer, he also developed an iconographic index to plates and illustrations in his books and periodicals (fig. 5). William's encyclopedic interests covered nearly every aspect of art, architecture and the decorative arts; books in French, Italian and German are well represented.

The reassembling of the Maxwell libraries at McGill has taken place in spurts over a period of nearly thirty years. A first segment of Edward's collection,

consisting of both books from his former office on Beaver Hall Square and items from his personal library, was offered to McGill by Edward's widow in 1946, while the Maxwell's house at 3480 Peel Street was under renovation.[12] Additional books came to the University when Mrs. Maxwell subsequently offered the archive of Maxwell architectural drawings to the McGill School of Architecture. Of the architectural titles that remained in the possession of the Maxwells' heirs, many have since been given to McGill.[13] However, the original collection comprised a greater number of volumes than have been incorporated into the collections of McGill's Blackader-Lauterman Library; many titles mentioned in Edward's sketchbooks, daily journal and correspondence cannot be traced to the reassembled collection.

The route by which the books on architecture from W. S. Maxwell's library were acquired was a circuitous one. These were kept in the collection of the Maxwell firm until the early 1950s (art books and literature were in his home library at 716 [now 1548] Pine Avenue). After William's death in 1952, his daughter, Mary Rabbani, moved her father's collections to Haifa, where she has lived since 1937. A bibliophile, too, Mme Rabbani designed a library on the ground floor of her residence to accommodate the collection. Following the publication in Montreal of *Edward & W.S. Maxwell: Guide to the Archive,*[14] Mme Rabbani generously offered her father's architectural library to McGill. The repatriation of this collection reunited some widely dispersed Maxwell holdings in the spring of 1987. Along with the architectural drawings and photographs of the Maxwell projects in the Canadian Architecture Collection of the

Blackader-Lauterman Library and the personal and business records of the firm, the Maxwell libraries provide another frame of reference for these architects' education and work.

[1] Letter from W. S. Maxwell, Boston, to Edward Maxwell, Montreal, March 16, 1895, MA, Series H. (For a discussion of the date of this letter see "The Education and Training of William S. Maxwell", note 4, in the present catalogue.) The titles mentioned in the letter include *Les Concours publics d'architecture*, 16 vols. in 14 (Paris: Librairies-Imprimeries Réunies, 1895-1914); Joseph Nash, *The Mansions of England in the Golden Time*, 4 vols. (London: Willis & Sotheran, 1869-1872); *L'architecture française*, 12 vols. (Paris: Guérinet, 1891-1899); and Ludwig von Bickell, *Hessiche Holzbauten* (Marburg: Elwert, 1887-1891). Bibliographic information was obviously given from memory. Names of suppliers refer to Dana Estes and Charles E. Lauriat, prominent Boston booksellers and publishers of the late nineteenth century, and William Helburn, a New York publisher of art and architectural books, whose label appears in many volumes of the Maxwells' libraries. A comparison of the catalogues of the Joseph B. Learmont library (New York: Anderson Galleries, 1917-1918) and the 1910 William John and Agnes Learmont bequest of books on art and architecture to the AAM suggests that the lender of Nash's book could have been William J. Learmont. While rich in early Bibles, first and rare editions of literary authors, and Americana, Joseph B. Learmont's collection included virtually no titles on architecture. Finally, W. S. Maxwell is referring to Touraine Hotel in Boston, the work of Winslow & Wetherell.

[2] "Daily Journal, 1892", unpaginated, entry for February 23, 1892 and corresponding entries in the cash account section for February 23 and 25, 1892.

[3] Martin Eidelberg, *E. Colonna* (Dayton: The Dayton Art Institute, 1983), pp. 20-29.

[4] Letter from Mary Maxwell Rabbani, The Philippines, to Irena Murray, Montreal, July 23, 1989 (Blackader-Lauterman Library of Architecture and Art, McGill University, Montreal).

[5] Letter from Nell Golden, Haifa, to Irena Murray, Montreal, November 16, 1989 (Blackader-Lauterman Library of Architecture and Art, McGill University, Montreal).

[6] See note 1.

[7] Rabbani letter of July 23, 1989.

[8] "Partial List of W. S. Maxwell's Personal Library", August 11, 1989 (typescript; Blackader-Lauterman Library of Architecture and Art, McGill University, Montreal).

[9] AAM, *Fifty-eighth Report* 1919 (Montreal, 1920).

[10] *Ibid.*, pp. 19, 23, and AAM, *Fifty-ninth Report* 1921 (Montreal: 1922), pp. 16, 18.

[11] Letter from Nell Golden, Haifa, to Irena Murray, Montreal, August 10, 1989 (Blackader-Lauterman Library of Architecture and Art, McGill University, Montreal).

[12] For information on the early acquisitions I am grateful to Emeritus Professor John Bland and Henry Yates, grandson of Edward Maxwell.

[13] Edward's grandson Henry Yates has indicated that his sister, Mrs. Mary Walker, a resident of Bermuda since 1966, took a certain number of books on architecture for her husband, architect Jordy Walker. Unfortunately the books were destroyed by humidity and no record exists (interview by the author, June 20, 1989).

[14] *Edward & W.S. Maxwell: Guide to the Archive/Guide du fonds* (Montreal: Canadian Architecture Collection, McGill University, 1986).

VII

CRAFTSMEN AND
DECORATIVE ARTISTS

Rosalind M. Pepall

The quality of workmanship in the buildings of Edward and William Maxwell was outstanding. One reason for this was the wealth and taste of so many of their clients – people who could, and would, pay for handcrafted work by qualified artists and craftsmen in expensive imported materials. Another was the value the Maxwells placed on the collaboration between the architect and the craftsman or artist, a value that can be traced to the influence of H. H. Richardson and the École des Beaux-Arts on their education and training. Like their American and French teachers, the Maxwells worked closely with the artists upon whom they relied to execute the decorative aspects of their buildings.

The contributions of the woodcarver, stone sculptor, metalworker or stained glass maker are liable to go unidentified and unrecognized unless he happens to be an artist of particular repute. In the Maxwell account books, however, the names of the participating firms, contractors and artisans are noted for every building, along with the date, type and cost of the work commissioned. These records, which provide an invaluable and rare resource with which to pinpoint the role of craftsmen in an architectural practice, also reveal the degree of respect the Maxwells accorded their work.

Edward and William Maxwell were frequently called upon to supply furnishings, wall coverings, carpets, light fixtures, fireplace accessories and, in some cases, antiques to complete a room's interior decor. Designs for interior ornament and furnishings were carefully delineated in the elevation and detail drawings of their buildings.

Because of their interest in the arts and their social connections with the Montreal art community, the Maxwell brothers were in a position to commission architectural decoration from some of the best artists and craftsmen in Canada. Among their close friends were Maurice Cullen, George Hill, Clarence Gagnon,

William Hope and George Horne Russell.[1] William in particular belonged to a number of art organizations, including the Pen and Pencil Club, the Canadian Handicrafts Guild and the Arts Club.[2] Both brothers enjoyed painting and exhibited their canvases regularly at the Art Association of Montreal's Spring Exhibitions.

Hand-carved interior woodwork and sculpted stone exterior ornament lend elegance to a residence and indicate the prosperity of its owner. The Maxwells were fortunate to have had many prosperous clients and so sought out skilled craftsmen capable of executing this type of decorative work.

In the Maxwell records, frequent reference is made to the sculptor George Hill, with whom Edward enjoyed a long and fruitful collaboration. Born in Shipton, in the Eastern Townships of Quebec, Hill received his professional training in Paris from 1889 to 1894, where he studied at the Académie Julian and the École des Beaux-Arts.[3] Upon returning to Canada in 1894, he opened a studio in Montreal and immediately began his association with Edward. He created a plaque of the architect and his wife in 1897 to commemorate their marriage the year before.[4] Hill made models for the stone carving on some of Edward's early buildings, such as the Birks store and the Merchants Bank of Halifax, and his collaboration with the architects continued until the First World War.

At the turn of the century, ornate, richly carved furniture in various revival styles was the fashion for the formal rooms of a house, and the Maxwells were sometimes called upon to design furniture to harmonize with a room's architecture. George Hill was responsible for the carved decoration on all of the dining room furniture made for Charles Hosmer's residence,[5] and he and probably his assistants carved the linenfolds, the tiny grotesque animals and the leaf scrolls on the wooden panelling around the room

Fig. 6. Brian Merrett, *Detail of dining room panelling in Hosmer House*, 1991. Montreal, The Montreal Museum of Fine Arts.

(fig. 6). When Louis-Joseph Forget asked the Maxwells to carry out major alterations to his house on Sherbrooke Street, the architects designed a piano case for the drawing room (cat. 44e). The Louis XVI cartouches, trophies and garlands that adorned the wooden panelling of this room were carried over into the design of the piano, which was painted white to match the panelling. George Hill was asked to carve the decoration on the piano, which still retains its original gilt metal music rack and candle holders.[6]

Hill's reputation as one of Canada's foremost sculptors in the first decades of the twentieth century is based mainly on his public monuments and war memorials.[7] One of his greatest achievements is the Sir George-Étienne Cartier monument at the foot of Mount Royal Park, which he worked on from 1912 to 1914. The Maxwells designed the monument's base and laid out the square in which it stands.[8]

One of Hill's apprentices who later became a well-known sculptor in his own right was Elzéar Soucy. Born in Saint-Onésime, Kamouraska, he grew up in Montreal and studied sculpture there at the École du Conseil des Arts et Manufactures.[9] Then, in his own

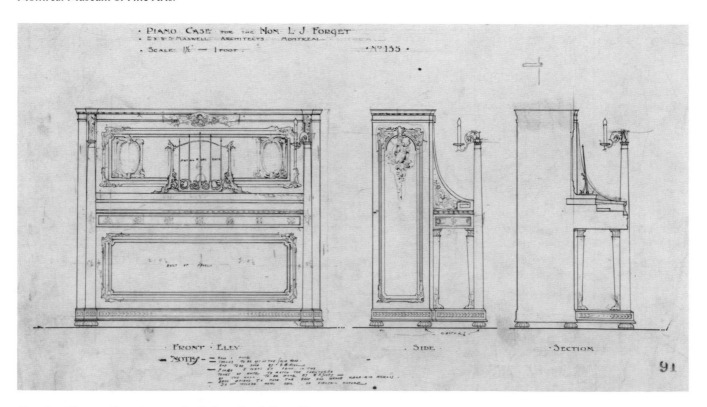

Cat. 44e. *Elevations for a piano case for the Louis-Joseph Forget House (Sherbrooke Street, Montreal)*

Cat. 39d. *Main hall and staircase, James T. Davis House*

words, "after three years of apprenticeship devoted to carving sitting-room armchairs in the styles of Victoria and Louis-Philippe", he joined Hill's workshop in 1898.[10]

Soucy was not given commissions directly by the Maxwell firm until the 1930s,[11] but he had previously worked under Hill in a number of the Maxwell buildings. The work in the Hosmer house, "un véritable petit Versailles", stood out in Soucy's mind as he reminisced in later years about the thirty craftsmen who had been engaged to carve the florid wood, stone and plaster decoration in the Drummond Street residence.[12] According to Soucy, young Quebec sculptors worked alongside about ten specialists from Italy and elsewhere in Europe who were brought to Montreal from New York, where they had been working on the John D. Rockefeller residence.[13]

A lesser-known sculptor who carried out carved decoration and made furniture for many of the Maxwells' major clients was Félix Routhier.[14] His name appears in the Maxwell office records from 1900 to 1911. Routhier executed the magnificent oak staircase

panels in the James T. Davis house for the extraordinary sum of $6,565 (cat. 39d). His skill is evident in the hand-carved pierced leaf scrolls and newel posts of the balustrade.[15]

Routhier's work for the office ended just at the time the brothers began to give large commissions to the Bromsgrove Guild (Canada) Limited, the Montreal branch of the Worcestershire-based Bromsgrove Guild of Applied Arts, which was linked with the Arts and Crafts movement.[16] The Montreal workshop opened in 1911 under the management of British architect E. Lance Wren. The Guild was no doubt encouraged to open the office by the Maxwells' commissions for the furniture and architectural sculpture for the Saskatchewan Legislative Building, the Art Association of Montreal's new gallery and the Dominion Express Company's offices on Saint James (Saint-Jacques) Street, all of which were under construction that year.[17]

The Maxwells designed the workshop for the Bromsgrove Guild on Clarke Street. The building included space for "plasterwork, carvers, cabinet-makers, upholsterers and polishers, a veneering room, kiln, and

Fig. 7. Photographer unknown, *Dining room table in Davis House*, undated. Private collection.

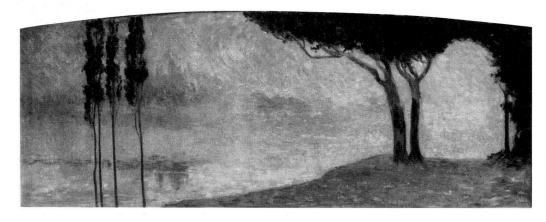

Fig. 8. Brian Merrett, *Mural by Maurice Cullen in billiard room of Davis House*, 1991. Montreal, The Montreal Museum of Fine Arts.

an office and draughting room for Mr. Wren".[18] The British firm continued for a number of years to supply the Maxwells with stained glass windows and draperies, whereas the Canadian branch executed furniture and plaster models for carving or casting. The Bromsgrove Guild (Canada) advertised that they had been responsible for "all the modelling for all ornamental work in wood, iron, bronze, plaster and stone ... as well as many items of special furniture" in the major additions to the Château Frontenac carried out by the Maxwell firm from 1920 to 1924.[19]

The men in the Bromsgrove Guild's Canadian workshop, most of whom were British, were considered to be the best and the most expensive cabinetmakers in Montreal.[20] Wren and his staff may have carried out some of their own furniture designs, but in their work for the Maxwells they generally followed plans supplied by the architects. Though based on historical English, French and Italian examples, the pieces were not slavish reproductions. The refined and often sumptuously carved ornament contrasted with the surfaces left undecorated to show off the wood's rich colouring and grain (fig. 7).

In addition to commissioning wood carving and furniture, the Maxwells asked artists to paint mural panels as an integral part of the interior decoration in some of their buildings. At the end of the nineteenth century, a number of Canadian artists endeavoured to promote mural painting in both public and private buildings, and a Society of Mural Decorators was formed in Toronto in 1894.[21] Its members encouraged mural painting in schools, libraries, churches and government buildings, as well as in private houses. Aware of these developments, the Maxwells commissioned artists to carry out a number of murals. These were painted not directly onto the wall, but on canvas and then glued in place. The favoured location for murals was above mantelpieces or set into the wall panelling.

Maurice Cullen was one of the Canadian artists who experimented with mural painting. Cullen had shared lodgings with William when they were both in Paris in 1899, and his studio on Beaver Hall Square was located very close to the Maxwells' architectural office.[22] The Maxwells called upon him to carry out murals in a number of their important city residences, notably the James T. Davis (fig. 8) and Richard R. Mitchell houses.[23] Cullen chose landscape scenes in subdued tones that harmonized with the rest of the interior decor. He did not sign his paintings, as they were considered decorations.

Frederick Challener was more prominent than Cullen as a mural painter. A founder of the Society of Mural Decorators, he promoted this art through his work and his writing. Challener understood the need for the architect and artist to "pull together" in order to integrate decorative painting with architecture.[24] He painted two murals for Maxwell houses and carried out decorations in the Royal Alexandra Hotel in Winnipeg.[25] Other artists, including Frederick Hutchison and Clarence Gagnon, also undertook the occasional commission for murals in Maxwell buildings.[26]

During the period when the Maxwell practice was in operation, stained glass windows were fashionable for both secular and religious buildings.[27] The Maxwell houses were often ornamented with stained glass, which added a touch of colour to transoms or cabinet cases. A few cartoon drawings for glass in William's hand remain among the Maxwell records. The firm of Castle & Son provided stained and leaded glass for a number of their houses. During the 1890s this firm was well known in Montreal – especially for its stained glass windows and church decoration. The company also developed a reputation for its fine cabinetmaking and interior furnishings. Between 1900 and 1912 the Maxwell brothers frequently ordered furniture, rugs, wallpaper and draperies from Castle & Son. A most important commission for stained glass was the two large windows the firm made in 1905-1906 for the billiard room of the L.-J. Forget house on Sherbrooke Street (cat. 44f).[28]

Cat. 44f. *Stained glass window from the Louis-Joseph Forget House (Sherbrooke Street, Montreal)*

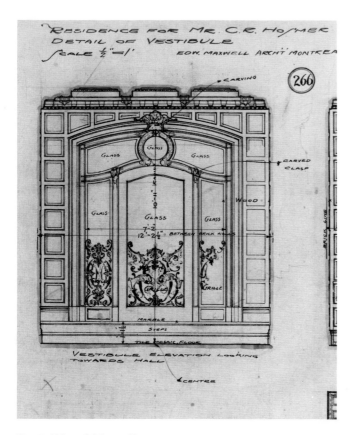

Fig. 9. Edward Maxwell,
Vestibule detail for Hosmer House,
undated. Montreal, McGill
University, Canadian
Architecture Collection.

For church windows, the Maxwells turned to the Bromsgrove Guild of Applied Arts. The British parent provided the series of thirteen stained glass windows for the Church of the Messiah in Montreal. These were designed and executed between 1907 and about 1917 by Archibald Davies, who ran the Guild's stained glass workshops from 1906 until his death.[29] These windows, all but two recently destroyed by fire, were inspired by British Arts and Crafts design, their backgrounds filled with naturalistic flowers and birds.[30]

Many of the Maxwells' buildings feature exquisite metalwork in the form of wrought iron entrance door grilles, balconies and gates. Instead of buying industrially produced metal wares, the Maxwells preferred to commission handcrafted metalwork, for example the grilles wrought in scrolled leaf forms on the vestibule doors of the Hosmer house (fig. 9). Many of the designs for this decorative ironwork were drawn by William Maxwell. His year of study in Paris had undoubtedly contributed to his enthusiasm for an art in which France had long excelled.

Another craftsman, Paul Beau, who began his career as an antique dealer, supplied Maxwell clients with his own fine hand-hammered brass and copper pieces as well as the occasional antique.[31] His work may be found in many of the residences, hotels and clubs designed by the Maxwell brothers.

Beau was one of the numerous craftsmen who were indebted to the Maxwells' support. William's daughter, Mary Maxwell Rabbani, recalls that her father had a close working rapport with these artisans, who "adored him".[32] By taking full advantage of the skill and dedication of trained craftsmen, Edward and William Maxwell ensured the superior quality of their architecture. In recent years the reassessment of Edwardian architecture has led to a renewed appreciation for the decorative work of these artists, which was so essential a component of the Maxwell buildings.

1 Hope and Horne Russell were clients as well as friends. The houses built for William Hope, one in Montreal and one in Saint Andrews, N.B., no longer exist. William Maxwell designed a summer house for Horne Russell in Saint Andrews in 1924.

2 Leo Cox, "Fifty Years of Brush and Pen: A Historical Sketch of the Pen and Pencil Club of Montreal" (unpublished manuscript, 1939, in the personal records of W. S. Maxwell). The club was founded in 1890, and among the members listed were William Brymner, William Van Horne, Robert Harris, George Hill and Percy Nobbs. W. S. Maxwell joined on December 21, 1907. In 1910 he served on the General Committee of the Canadian Handicrafts Guild, founded in 1906 to promote the revival of handcrafted arts. For his role in the Arts Club, see cat. entry 48.

3 Hill (1862-1934) studied under Jean-Antonin Injalbert and Henri Michel Chapu and finally with Alexandre Falguière at the École des Beaux-Arts (undated information form filled out by George William Hill, National Gallery of Canada, Ottawa, and scrapbook in the collection of the sculptor's daughter, Dr. Eleanor Venning).

4 In the late nineteenth century, a number of sculptors commemorated their friends and colleagues with medallions. For example, Karl Bitter made a portrait relief of his friend Richard Morris Hunt in 1895, and Augustus Saint-Gaudens presented his longtime collaborator, the architect Stanford White, with a marble relief portrait of Mrs. Bessie White as a wedding gift in 1884.

5 [Work Costs Book F, 1899-1904], p. 45, MA, Series C.

6 Ibid., p. 20, indicates that Hill was paid $627 for this commission on November 6, 1902. He was probably responsible for carving the wall panelling as well, for he was paid $1,369.22 in 1901 for, as noted less specifically in the account book (p. 23), "modelling and carving Sherbrooke St".

7 Venning scrapbook; see also Aline Gubbay, "Three Montreal Monuments: An Expression of Nationalism" (Master's thesis, Concordia University, 1978).

8 See the essay "City Planning and Urban Beautification" in the present catalogue.

9 Soucy (1876-1970) studied under Arthur Vincent and Louis-Philippe Hébert at the Conseil des Arts et Manufactures in Montreal, and apprenticed in the atelier of Alfred Lefrançois and Philippe Laperle. See "Elzéar Soucy : sculpteur sur bois", in Jean-Marie Gauvreau, Artisans du Québec (Montreal: Les Éditions du Bien Public, 1940), p. 142, and Msgr. Olivier Maurault, "Une famille de sculpteurs : Les Soucy", in Société Royale du Canada. Mémoires, 3rd series, vol. 36, section 1 (May 1942), pp. 71-76.

10 Huguette Cléroux, "A Study of the Works of Mr. Elzéar Soucy", with a preface by Elzéar Soucy (unpublished manuscript, Université de Montréal Library School, 1961), p. iii. Soucy acquired the workshop of George Hill between 1912 and 1914, and went on to establish his reputation in church sculpture and statues of prominent public figures. See Gloria Lesser, École du Meuble 1930-1950 (Montreal: Le Château Dufresne Inc., Musée des arts décoratifs de Montréal, 1989), pp. 45-49.

11 The Maxwells paid Soucy for a model of a Celtic cross for the J. T. Davis family on May 22, 1930 [Work Costs Book N, 1914-1915], p. 45, MA, Series C.

12 Gauvreau, 1940, p. 145.

13 Cléroux, 1961, p. iii.

14 In his parish registry, Félix Routhier is referred to as a sculptor on the occasion of his marriage in 1868 (ANQM, Paroisse Notre-Dame-de-Montréal ZQ0001-0026, Registre – Mariages, vol. 121, p. 131, no. 600, Félix Routhier and Julie Plante, November 23, 1868). It seems that he died in 1916, since the following year his wife is listed as a widow.

15 [Work Costs Book M, 1904-1914], p. 284, MA, Series C. Routhier was paid in various instalments from February 15 to December 11, 1911.

16 See Alan Crawford, By Hammer and Hand: The Arts and Crafts Movement in Birmingham (Birmingham: Birmingham Museums and Art Gallery, 1984), pp. 32-33.

17 For an account of the work of the Bromsgrove Guild (Canada) in the AAM Art Gallery, see Rosalind M. Pepall, Construction d'un musée Beaux-Arts/Building a Beaux-Arts Museum, exhib. cat. (Montreal: Montreal Museum of Fine Arts, 1986), pp. 75-82.

18 Project no. 46.0, "Bromsgrove Guild and Lumber", undated, MA.

19 Construction, vol. 18 (August 1925), p. 17.

20 Telephone interviews by the author with Hugh Illsley, April 15, 1985, and Richard Bolton, May 28, 1985.

21 For background on the Canadian mural movement, see Rosalind M. Pepall, "The Murals in the Toronto Municipal Buildings: George Reid's Debt to Puvis de Chavannes", The Journal of Canadian Art History, vol. 9, no. 2 (1986), pp. 142-160.

22 Maurice Cullen (1866-1934) returned to Montreal in 1902, and from 1906 his studio was at 3 Beaver Hall Square. The Maxwells' office was at 6 Beaver Hall Square.

23 See cat. entries 39 and 36. Cullen carried out a large decorative panel for the L. H. Timmins residence in Westmount in 1913 ([Work Costs Book M, 1904-1914], p. 351, MA, Series C).

24 See Frederick Challener, "Mural Decoration", CAB, vol. 17 (May 1904), pp. 90-92.

25 For the Maxwells, he undertook a major "Painting Decoration" for Dr. Milton Hersey's residence on Rosemount Avenue in Westmount (demolished) about 1910-1911 for which he was paid $300 ([Work Costs Book M, 1904-1914], p. 133, MA, Series C). For F. Howard Wilson's Sainte-Agathe house, Challener painted a mural over the mantel for $50 (August 22, 1911 [Work Costs Book M, 1904-1914], p. 297, MA, Series C).

26 Frederick W. Hutchison (1871-1953) painted a mural decoration on the ceiling of the "reception room" for Charles Hosmer in 1902 ([Work Costs Book F, 1899-1904], p. 42, MA, Series C). Clarence Gagnon is recorded as executing "2 decorative panels" for the Eugène Lafleur house on Peel Street, January 7, 1903 ([Work Costs Book M, 1904-1914], p. 141, MA, Series C), as well as stencilled decoration in the Clouston house, Senneville, and the chapel of the Forget house, also in that area, in the summer of 1903 ([Work Costs Book F, 1899-1904], pp. 24, 52, MA, Series C). William Clapp carried out a painted decoration in the Dominion Express Company Building in 1912 ([Work Costs Book M, 1904-1914], p. 168, MA, Series C).

27 See Alice Cooney Frelinghuysen, "A New Renaissance: Stained Glass in the Aesthetic Period", in In Pursuit of Beauty: Americans and the Aesthetic Movement, exhib. cat. (New York: Rizzoli, 1986), pp. 176-197.

28 The Maxwells paid Castle & Son $600 for the two windows, April 18, 1906 ([Work Costs Book M, 1904-1914], p. 189, MA, Series C).

29 The work of Davies (1878-1953) is mentioned briefly in Crawford, 1984, p. 126. Orders for the windows are listed in [Work Costs Book M, 1904-1914], p. 261, MA, Series C. See also Nevil Norton Evans, Memorials and Other Gifts in the Church of the Messiah, Montreal (Montreal, 1943).

30 Two illustrations of this major commission by Davies appeared in "British Stained Glass", in Studio Year Book of Decorative Art (London: The Studio, 1910), pp. 46, 111.

31 See Rosalind M. Pepall, Paul Beau (1871- 1949) (Montreal: Montreal Museum of Fine Arts, 1982).

32 Interview with Mary Maxwell Rabbani by France Gagnon Pratte and the author, April 1, 1989, Haifa.

VIII

CITY PLANNING AND
URBAN BEAUTIFICATION

Jeanne M. Wolfe and Peter Jacobs

The work of the Maxwells reaches beyond architectural design into the realm of city planning and beautification. In an attempt to achieve modern standards of urban design, the Maxwells collaborated with such important landscape architects as John C. Olmsted and Frederick Law Olmsted, Jr. (sons of Frederick Law Olmsted), Frederick Todd, and Rickson Outhet; and they were members of a number of municipal improvement committees.

One of the major factors that shaped urban planning theory at the turn of the century was the 1893 World's Columbian Exposition in Chicago. At least two Montreal architects are known to have visited the exposition: Andrew Taylor, a councillor of the newly founded Province of Quebec Association of Architects, and Edward Maxwell. Although Edward's favourable reaction is only briefly referred to in a letter from his father to his mother,[1] Taylor shared his impressions at length with the PQAA, extolling the beauties of the "Fair White City on the shores of Lake Michigan".[2] His speech, reported widely, helped spark an enduring interest among Montreal architects in city planning and the aesthetics of the urban landscape.

The town planning movement of the late nineteenth and early twentieth centuries represented the convergence of a number of reform initiatives aimed at ameliorating the urban squalor occasioned by extraordinarily rapid industrialization and urbanization. By the late nineteenth century, most North American cities had a league for public health reform, a parks and playgrounds association, a fledgling architectural association, usually fostering City Beautiful ideas, a municipal art movement and a lobby against corruption and illegal practices in city government.[3] Toward the end of the century, fuelled by the ideas of the Garden City movement in Britain and the urban park movement in North America, these groups advocated town planning as a remedy for the ills they addressed.

Montreal was no exception. The appallingly overcrowded workers' housing stimulated calls for public health reform.[4] The physical planning component of the reform movement focussed on proposals for improving sanitary conditions, structuring the city fabric with wide tree-lined streets and conserving natural environments. One important project was the recreational development of Mount Royal, which was acquired by the city in 1874 for the almost inconceivable sum of $1,000,000. Frederick Law Olmsted was retained to design the park and undertook the work between 1874 and 1876.[5]

The PQAA, founded in 1890, served as the platform from which the Maxwells and other leading Montreal professionals promoted the urgent need for urban reform. Early in the Association's history, architects proposed that there should be a municipal board to approve plans of all new buildings and to foster the coherence of streetscapes. Following his visit to the Chicago exposition, Andrew Taylor drafted a petition requesting that City Council appoint a Standing Art Committee to "examine and report on all plans, designs and models of monuments and embellishments of our public squares and avenues".[6] Despite the PQAA's continued insistence, a committee was never appointed.

Meanwhile, the City Beautiful movement had been gaining momentum. In the wake of Daniel Burnham's plans for Washington (1902) and San Francisco (1905), many cities embarked on studies, and in both Toronto and Montreal the local associations of architects assumed leadership.[7] At the urging of Percy Nobbs, in 1906 the PQAA set up a Civic Improvement Committee, and in 1907 William Maxwell became its chairman. Eleven meetings were held that year, with Mr. Pinoteau, Superintendent of Parks, and, among other groups, the Parks and Playgrounds Association. The committee applied to Montreal's Parks and Playgrounds Committee (then responsible for open spaces and recreation) for an annual grant of $500, which was received in 1907 and 1908.[8]

By early 1908 William Maxwell's Civic Improvement Committee had drafted an overall plan, and four subcommittees had been formed. Schemes were proposed for Lafontaine Park and the development of Duluth

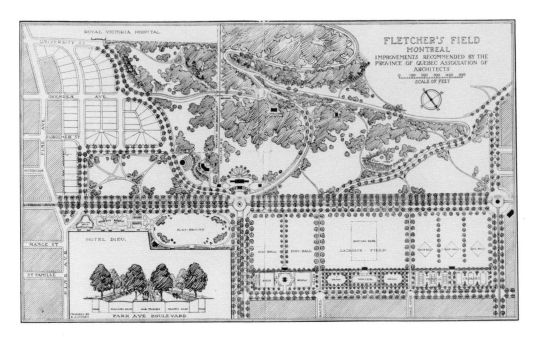

Fig. 10. Rickson A. Outhet, *Fletcher's Field,
Montreal: improvements recommended by the Province of
Quebec Association of Architects*, 1909. Montreal,
McGill University, Canadian Architecture
Collection.

Street into a boulevard connecting Fletcher's Field and Sherbrooke Street; for Park Avenue, with proposals to develop it as a boulevard with one side for pleasure driving and the other for heavy traffic; for Atwater Avenue and the riverfront as far as the Victoria Bridge; and for diagonal streets from the city centre outwards to the urban edge.[9]

The PQAA retained Rickson Outhet, Canada's first native-born landscape architect, to help develop the proposals. Outhet had trained in the Olmsted office, where he was assigned to work on Burnham's revision of L'Enfant's plan for Washington. This experience with the design of major transportation corridors, boulevards and avenues was essential in articulating the goals developed for Montreal under Maxwell's guidance. By June 15, 1908, the plans (fig. 10) were ready for submission to the city and for publication in brochure form.

Upon the founding of the Civic Improvement League in 1909 to act as a clearinghouse for civic betterment activities, the PQAA Civic Improvement Committee immediately became a member, and the new umbrella group took over the task of publicizing and trying to sell both the merits of the architects' plan and the need for an overall planning authority. In fact, in the report of the PQAA Civic Improvement Committee for 1910, William Maxwell explained that it had been less active that year because of the formation of the Metropolitan Parks Commission (which lasted a brief two years). He noted that the architects had offered their direct professional services to this commission but "were informed that ideas would be drawn in a broad way ... and that for purposes of criticism and advice they had decided to call in an American expert of 'international reputation'".[10] The original intent seems to have been to invite Daniel Burnham, or if not, F. L. Olmsted, Jr. This episode resulted in a spat between Percy Nobbs, Professor of Architecture at McGill, an ardent town planning advocate and active member of the PQAA committee, and Maxwell. Nobbs, apparently objecting to the fact that an American rather than a Canadian architect was to be called in for advice, tendered his resignation (soon withdrawn) from Maxwell's committee.[11]

In any event, F. L. Olmsted, Jr. did come to Montreal for three days in September 1910, and a copy of his report is to be found in the Maxwell Archive. It deals with rapid transit, the need for a hierarchical street plan, and recreation — Olmsted advocated a recreational centre not farther than one-quarter mile from every home in the city and proposed that at least five percent and not more than ten percent of new urban subdivisions be given over to open space.

Maxwell continued to work with the Civic Improvement League. W. D. Lighthall, the mayor of

Cat. 57d. *Model for the Sir George-Étienne Cartier Monument*

Westmount, became a convenor of its City Planning Committee, which included such notable citizens as Sir William Van Horne. The league "constantly promoted the study of city housing and advocated schemes for garden cities and for workingmen's dwellings, side by side with those for more parks, playgrounds, and open spaces as desired by all town planners".[12]

The Maxwell brothers collaborated extensively with urban planners and landscape architects, as they did with artists and craftsmen (cat. 57d). In Senneville alone, the firm worked with Olmsted Brothers on the

estates of E. S. Clouston (1899), R. B. Angus (1899) and L.-J. Forget (1900).[13] In Montreal they worked together on the properties of H. V. Meredith (1894) and James Ross (1899).[14]

The natural successor to the Olmsteds in Montreal was Frederick G. Todd. The quiet vision of Todd is little known despite his broad career spanning forty-five years in Canada.[15] Born in New Hampshire in 1876, Todd attended the Agricultural College in Amherst, Massachusetts, and then worked for four years in the Olmsted office before moving to Montreal in 1900. As

Cat. 58c. *Pavilion and "Lookout", Mount Royal Park*

an Olmsted apprentice, he worked on the landscape designs for Maxwell-designed houses in Montreal and later did others on his own, including the grounds of the Hosmer house on Drummond Street (1905), the L.-J. Forget estate in Senneville (1908) and the J.K.L. Ross house on Peel Street (1909). He soon became nationally known, publishing his seminal report on the parkway system for Ottawa in 1903.[16] Todd was also an active member of the Civic Improvement League and an ardent advocate of the Olmsted legacy.[17]

Todd had worked on the implementation of the Olmsted plan for Mount Royal when he was an apprentice in the firm in 1896. When he moved to Montreal, one of his first projects involved a proposed site plan and a substantial chalet for the lookout atop the mountain park.[18] Although it was never executed, Todd continued to be involved with the park site and collaborated on a subsequent chalet, designed by the Maxwells and Marchand & Haskell in 1906, which was built (cat. 58c). In accordance with Olmsted's earlier work on the park, the planting plan made rich use of native plants, and it complemented the elegant lines of the chalet as well.

In addition to their collaboration on civic design proposals, the Maxwells worked with Rickson Outhet on a number of private residences, including the D. McNicoll house on Côte-Saint-Antoine Road (1905), the E.T. Galt house on Simpson Street (1909), the Percy Cowans house on Ontario Avenue (now Avenue du Musée; 1910) and the Shirres house, also on Ontario Avenue (1911).

The Maxwell firm also collaborated with notable Canadian sculptors on several public monuments. These include the Strathcona Memorial on Dominion Square (1904), and the monuments to John Young on Youville Square (1906) and to Sir George-Étienne Cartier on Park Avenue (1913-1914; cat. 57a). The Young statue was sculpted by Philippe Hébert, those of Strathcona and Cartier by George W. Hill (fig. 11).[19]

The commitment of Edward and William Maxwell to urban reform and the enhancement of the built environment was most clearly expressed in their many noteworthy architectural projects. This commitment extended as well to the urban design, landscape and public monuments of the city they loved so well.

Cat. 57a. *Monument to Sir George-Étienne Cartier*

1 Letter from E. J. Maxwell to Johan Maxwell, August 12, 1893 (private collection, Montreal).

2 "Province of Quebec Association of Architects: Proceedings of the Annual Convention", *CAB*, vol. 6 (October 1893), p. 104.

3 Paul Rutherford, ed., *Saving the Canadian City* (Toronto: University of Toronto Press, 1974), and Gilbert A. Stetler and Alan F. J. Artibise, eds., *The Canadian City: Essays in Urban History* (Toronto: McClelland and Stewart, 1977).

4 Herbert Ames, *The City below the Hill* (1897; reprinted, Toronto: University of Toronto Press, 1972); Émile Nadeau, "Promenade mélancolique à travers les cimetières de Québec", *Le Bulletin médical de Québec*, vol. 15 (1913), pp. 248-271, 299-324; and Marie Adami, *J. George Adami: A Memoir* (London: Constable, 1930).

5 Frederick Law Olmsted, *Mount Royal* (New York: Putnam, 1881).

6 Walter Van Nus, "The Plan-Makers and the City: Architects, Engineers, Surveyors, and Urban Planning in Canada, 1890-1939" (Ph.D. dissertation, University of Toronto, 1975), pp. 154, 163.

7 Thomas S. Hines, *Burnham of Chicago: Architect and Planner* (Chicago: University of Chicago Press, 1979); James Lemon, "Plans for Early 20th Century Toronto: Host in Management", *Urban History Review*, vol. 18 (June 1989), pp. 11-31; "Montreal Notes", *CAB*, vol.19 (March 1906), p. 41; and Jeanne M. Wolfe, "Montréal: des plans d'embellissement", *Continuité*, vol. 31 (Spring 1986), pp. 24-27.

8 PQAA Archives, Box 06-P-124-2 (1908), Letter folder 6, "Report of the Civic Improvement Committee of the PQAA for 1907", January 3, 1908.

9 Edward Maxwell, "Parks and Parkways", *PQAA Yearbook* (1907); PQAA Archives, Box 06-P-124-2 (1908), Letter folder 6, "Report of the Civic Improvement Committee", May 12, 1908, and June 12, 1908; and Jeanne M. Wolfe, "Yesterday's Tomorrows: Some Early Plans for Montreal", *The Fifth Column*, vol. 2 (Winter 1982), pp. 6-11.

10 *PQAA Yearbook* (January 3, 1911).

11 PQAA Archives, Box 06-P-124-2 (1910), Letter folder 8 (December 6-7), and "Report of Mr. F. L. Olmsted to the Metropolitan Parks Commission" (typescript, 1910), MA.

[12] William H. Atherton, *Montreal (1535-1914)* (Montreal: S.J. Clarke, 1914), vol. 2, p. 673.

[13] On the Olmsteds' work, see John Taylor Boyd, Jr., "The Work of Olmsted Brothers", *Architectural Record*, vol. 44 (December 1918), pp. 502-521.

[14] Charles E. Beveridge, comp., *The Master List of Design Projects of the Olmsted Firm 1857-1950* (Boston: National Association for Olmsted Parks in conjunction with the Massachusetts Association for Olmsted Parks, 1987).

[15] Peter Jacobs, "The Quiet Vision of Frederick Todd", in *Roots: Landscape Architecture in Canada* (1976).

[16] Ottawa Civic Improvement Commission, *Report of Frederick G. Todd on the Parkway System of Ottawa* (1903).

[17] Peter Jacobs, "Frederick G. Todd and the Creation of Canada's Urban Landscape", in *Landscape Preservation*, special issue of *The Bulletin of the Association for Preservation Technology*, vol. 15, no. 4 (1983), pp. 27-37.

[18] Frederick G. Todd, "Character in Park Design", *Canadian Municipal Journal* (October 1905).

[19] Colin S. MacDonald, ed., *A Dictionary of Canadian Artists* (Ottawa: Canadian Paperbacks, 1968), pp. 442-443, and Agnes Joynes, "Sculpture of G. W. Hill", *Saturday Night* (May 14, 1938), p. 2.

Fig. 11. Photographer unknown, *George Hill in his studio*, undated. Montreal, The Montreal Museum of Fine Arts.

Pl. I. William Sutherland Maxwell, *Front elevation for a proposed "salle des fêtes"* (cat. 6b)

Pl. II. Edward Maxwell, *Ames Gate Lodge* (cat. 7b)

Pl. III. Edward Maxwell, *Perspective for Windsor Station Addition* (cat. 24)

Pl. IV. Edward & W.S. Maxwell, *Perspective for the Canadian Pacific Railway Winnipeg Station* (cat. 25b)

Pl. V. Edward & W.S. Maxwell, *Perspective for the Palliser Hotel* (cat. 26a)

Pl. VI. *Hosmer House* (fig. 32)

Pl. VII. Edward Maxwell, *Perspective for the Edward S. Clouston House* (cat. 32a)

Pl. VIII. Edward & W.S. Maxwell, *Perspective for the main house, Richard B. Angus Estate* (cat. 45a)

Pl. IX. Edward & W.S. Maxwell, *Perspective for the Legislative and Executive Building, Regina, Saskatchewan* (cat. 52a)

Pl. X. Castle & Son, *Stained glass window from the Louis-Joseph Forget House* (cat. 44f)

Pl. XI.
Maxwell memorial window, Church of the Messiah (cat. 54d)

CATALOGUE

Catalogue entries are numbered in accordance with the list of exhibits at the end of each section.

Dates of buildings indicate period of construction, when this is known.

Dimensions are given in centimetres, with height preceding width and depth.

Early Life and Training

The critical influences upon an architect's creative output are many and varied: the period and place of birth, childhood experiences and interests fostered within the family, educational opportunities (or lack of them), type and location of professional training, exposure to current architectural trends, readings, travels and works seen. Between about 1888 and 1900, the two Maxwell brothers, sons of a Montreal lumber dealer, had to leave their native city in order to receive architectural training of a quality not yet available in Canada. During these formative expatriate years, they were greatly influenced by the legacy of H. H. Richardson (particularly Edward) and, directly and indirectly, by the École des Beaux-Arts (particularly William). Throughout their student and working lives they depended heavily on architectural books and illustrated magazines and journals for information and inspiration.

1a. William Notman & Son
Edward Maxwell
1893 (printed 1991)
Gelatin silver print
38.1 x 48.3
Montreal, McCord Museum
of Canadian History, Notman
Photographic Archives

1b. William Notman & Son
William Sutherland Maxwell
1898 (printed 1991)
Gelatin silver print
38.1 x 48.3
Montreal, McCord Museum
of Canadian History, Notman
Photographic Archives

2a. J. Hampton Field
Agnes Reid Maxwell
Undated
Albumen silver print
14.5 x 10.5
Montreal, private collection

2b. J. Hampton Field
Edward Maxwell
Undated
Albumen silver print
16.5 x 11
Montreal, private collection

2c . Photographer unknown
*Edward John Maxwell family: Edward,
William, Johan MacBean Maxwell,
Amelia, Jessie Gertrude and Edward
John*
About 1899
Gelatin printing-out paper
11.5 x 15.6
Montreal, private collection

2d. Photographer unknown
*Elizabeth Ellen Aitchison
(Mrs. Edward Maxwell)*
Undated
Platinum print
22 x 14.2
Montreal, private collection

2e. Photographer unknown
*Edward Maxwell's children: Stirling,
Jean, Elizabeth and Blythe*
About 1910
Silver print
14.8 x 10.3
Montreal, private collection

2f. Photographer unknown
*Mrs. William S. Maxwell and daughter
Mary*
About 1913-1914
Silver print
21.5 x 16
Montreal, private collection

2g. Frederick William Hutchison
*Portrait sketch of William Sutherland
Maxwell*
1904
Charcoal and chalk on paper
33 x 40.6
Signed and dated on left:
F.W. Hutchison 1904
Haifa, Mary Maxwell Rabbani
collection

2h. Artist unknown
Portrait sketch of Edward John Maxwell
Undated
Charcoal and white chalk
on paper
59.7 x 52.1
Haifa, Mary Maxwell Rabbani
collection

3. George William Hill
*Portrait relief of Edward and Elizabeth
Maxwell*
1897
Plaster
27.5 x 21.7 x 2
Montreal, McGill University,
Canadian Architecture Collection

4a. Edward Maxwell
*Edward John Maxwell House
(Westmount, Quebec)*
1887
Watercolour, graphite and black
ink on paper
22.9 x 29.3
Signed and dated lower left: *Ed.
Maxwell. 1887./ 19th December 1887*
Montreal, private collection

4b. Edward Maxwell
*Saint-Jean-Baptiste Church (Mont-
Saint-Hilaire, Quebec)*
1890
Watercolour and graphite
21.5 x 15
Signed lower left: *EM*; dated
lower right: *18.8.90*
Montreal, private collection

4c. Edward Maxwell
*The Block House (Saint Andrews,
New Brunswick)*
1899
Watercolour
22.5 x 34 (by sight)
Inscribed, signed and dated lower
left: *St. Andrew's EM 13.8.99*
Montreal, private collection

5a. William Sutherland Maxwell
Beaupré (Quebec)
1900
Watercolour and graphite
22 x 28 (by sight)
Inscribed lower left: *Beaupré*;
signed and dated lower right:
W.S.Maxwell/1900
Montreal, private collection

5b. William Sutherland Maxwell
*Farm outbuilding at Senneville, P.Q.,
for Hon. L. J. Forget*
1906
Watercolour on paper
17 x 30 (by sight)
Signed and dated lower right:
W.S. Maxwell. 1906.
Haifa, Mary Maxwell Rabbani
collection

5c. William Sutherland Maxwell
*Harbour Scene, Seal Cove, Grand
Manan, N. B.*
1933
Watercolour on paper
22.8 x 28 (by sight)
Signed and dated lower left:
W.S. Maxwell. 1933
Haifa, Mary Maxwell Rabbani
collection

6a. William Sutherland Maxwell
Figure study
Undated
Charcoal on paper
62.5 x 48
Montreal, McGill University,
Canadian Architecture Collection

6b. William Sutherland Maxwell
*Front elevation for a proposed
"salle des fêtes"*
About 1900
Watercolour, ink and graphite
on light card
31.8 x 52.1
Montreal, McGill University,
Canadian Architecture Collection

6c. William Sutherland Maxwell
Side elevation for a proposed "salle des fêtes"
About 1900
Watercolour, ink and graphite on light card
32 x 60.8
Montreal, McGill University, Canadian Architecture Collection

6d. William Sutherland Maxwell
A State Barge
1900
Watercolour on paper
84.5 x 55.7 (by sight)
Signed and dated: *W.S. Maxwell 1900*
Haifa, Mary Maxwell Rabbani collection

6e. William Sutherland Maxwell
Sketches made in Venice
1900
Graphite on wove paper
17.6 x 26
Inscribed and dated upper right: *Venice/-1-9.1900.*
Montreal, McGill University, Canadian Architecture Collection

6f. William Sutherland Maxwell
Sketches made in France
1899
Graphite on wove paper
15 x 25
Signed and dated upper left: *W.S. Maxwell/ 1899*
Montreal, McGill University, Canadian Architecture Collection

6g. William Sutherland Maxwell
Sketch made in Angers
Undated
Graphite on wove paper
22 x 14
Montreal, McGill University, Canadian Architecture Collection

7a. Edward Maxwell
Lantern of Saint-Ouen, Rouen
1896
Watercolour and graphite on vellum paper
65.5 x 46.8
Inscribed, signed and dated lower left: *Lantern of St. Ouen./ Rouen-/ E Maxwell/ 1896*
Montreal, McGill University, Canadian Architecture Collection

7b. Edward Maxwell
Ames Gate Lodge (North Easton, Massachusetts, by Henry Hobson Richardson)
1891
Watercolour and graphite on vellum paper
35.5 x 47.9
Dated lower right: *30-5-91*
Montreal, McGill University, Canadian Architecture Collection

8a. *Page from Edward Maxwell's scrapbook, vol. 2, with sketch perspective of the Williams Institute (New London, Connecticut, by Shepley, Rutan & Coolidge) and various details*
1889-1894 (scrapbook)
Graphite, ink and watercolour on wove paper
50.5 x 37
Montreal, McGill University, Canadian Architecture Collection

8b. *Page from Edward Maxwell's scrapbook, vol. 2, with self-portrait and sketch elevations for the Edward S. Clouston House*
1889-1894 (scrapbook)
Graphite, ink and watercolour on wove paper
50.7 x 38
Self-portrait dated: *17.4.91*
Montreal, McGill University, Canadian Architecture Collection

9. *Edward Maxwell's drawing instruments*
1884
Walnut, brass, velvet, tape, metal, ivory
7.2 x 19.8 x 16.5
Montreal, McCord Museum of Canadian History

10. *Edward Maxwell's "Daily Journal" for 1892: pages with accounts for October and November*
1892
21 x 17 x 1.8
Montreal, McGill University, Canadian Architecture Collection

11a. *Edward Maxwell's travel sketchbook: page with First Baptist Church (Newton, Massachusetts, by Henry Hobson Richardson)*
1888-1889 (sketchbook)
Watercolour and graphite on vellum paper
14.6 x 9.6
Montreal, McGill University, Canadian Architecture Collection

11b. *Edward Maxwell's travel sketchbook: page with tower in Vicenza*
1895-1909 (sketchbook)
Graphite, wax chalk, pastel and ink on vellum paper
13.4 x 18.2
Page inscribed and dated lower right: *Vicenza 5.2.96*
Montreal, McGill University, Canadian Architecture Collection

12a. *William Maxwell's travel sketchbook (Italy)*
1900
Graphite on paper
18.8 x 27
Signed and inscribed: *W.S. Maxwell/ 83 Boul. Montparnasse, Paris/188 Cote St. Antoine Rd., Westmount, P.Q.*
Haifa, Mary Maxwell Rabbani collection

12b. *William Maxwell's travel sketchbook (France)*
1899-1900
Graphite on paper
12 x 19
Signed, dated and inscribed: *W.S. Maxwell/London 1899/203 Boulevard Raspail, Paris/83 Boul. Montparnasse* Haifa, Mary Maxwell Rabbani collection

12c. *William Maxwell's travel sketchbook (France)*
1899-1900
Graphite on paper
12 x 19
Signed, dated and inscribed: *W.S. Maxwell/ London 1899/ 83 Boul. Montparnasse, Paris*
Haifa, Mary Maxwell Rabbani collection

13a. *"EDBA Concours Godebœuf de 1896",
page 83 from "Croquis d'architecture,
1897"*
1897
Lithograph on wove paper
56 x 40 x 4
Montreal, McGill University,
Canadian Architecture Collection

13b. *Frontispiece and plate XII, "St. Ouen,
Rouen", from "Sketch Book, Boston
Architectural Club, 1890"*
1890
Black ink lithographs on wove
paper
38.1 x 30.5
Montreal, McGill University,
Canadian Architecture Collection

13c. *Cover of "Monographs of American
Architecture III, The Ames Memorial
Building, 1886"*
1886
41.4 x 34.5
Montreal, McGill University,
Canadian Architecture Collection

13d. *"F.L. Ames Gate Lodge, North Easton,
Massachusetts, 1880", plate XIX from
"Monographs of American Architecture
III, The Ames Memorial Building, 1886"*
1886
Black ink lithograph on wove
paper
33.5 x 41.1
Montreal, McGill University,
Canadian Architecture Collection

14. *Edward Maxwell's photograph album:
page with views of the World's
Columbian Exposition of 1893*
About 1890-1900 (album)
31.2 x 44 x 4
Montreal, McGill University,
Canadian Architecture Collection

From the very beginning, commercial work was an important component of the Maxwell practice. Edward's able supervision in 1891-1892 of the erection of the Montreal Board of Trade Building introduced him to the powerful Montreal business community, quickly leading to the kind of prestigious corporate and private commissions that would occupy the Maxwell firm for thirty years until Edward's death. Works from the first half of the nineties, such as the Henry Birks & Sons store, were – not surprisingly – strongly influenced by the Romanesque/Italian Renaissance designs of Edward's American employers, Shepley, Rutan & Coolidge. In the late nineties, William's influence came into play in the opulent Modern French-style London & Lancashire Life Assurance Company, on which the younger brother worked as a draftsman. By the end of the first decade of the twentieth century, the firm had designed the Dominion Express Company, moving on to the modern American method of skyscraper design, in which the grid of the supporting steel frame is clearly expressed.

Cat.15b. *Henry Birks & Sons Store and Office Building*

15
Edward Maxwell
Henry Birks & Sons Store and Office Building

620 Sainte-Catherine Street West
Montreal, Que.
1893-1894

The Birks store (cat. 15b), the first commercial building by Edward Maxwell, was a significant early commission that enabled him to leave Shepley, Rutan & Coolidge. In the spring of 1892, still in the early months of independent practice, he began discussions with Henry Birks while supervising construction of the Montreal Board of Trade Building for the Boston firm.

Birks's forebears had been cutlers since the sixteenth century. Born in 1840, eight years after his family had emigrated from England to Montreal, Henry Birks found employment at the age of seventeen with Savage & Lyman, then Montreal's leading watchmaker and jeweller. In 1878, when his employer was forced into liquidation, Birks used his savings to buy the stock

and in 1879 opened Henry Birks & Company in a rented shop on Saint James (Saint-Jacques) Street, the city's main retail street.[1]

Phillips Square, in Montreal's upper town, became the city's cultural centre that year with the opening of the Art Association of Montreal's new gallery on the northeast corner. Bordered by Sainte-Catherine Street and linked by Beaver Hall Hill to Saint James Street in the congested old city, it was destined to become the hub of a new uptown retail district. In 1889 Henry Morgan announced his decision to relocate his department store (now The Bay) from Saint James Street to Sainte-Catherine Street, facing Phillips Square. Three years later Birks met with Maxwell.

Fig. 12. Shepley, Rutan & Coolidge, *Perspective for Montreal Board of Trade*, about 1891 (reproduction). Montreal, McGill University, Canadian Architecture Collection.

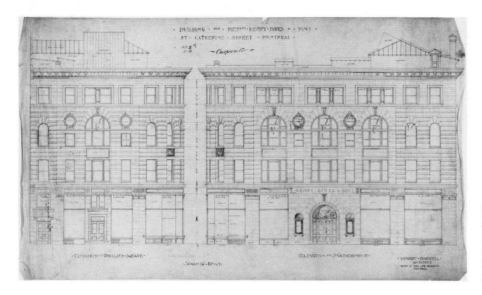

Fig. 13. Edward Maxwell, *Proposed elevation for Henry Birks & Sons Store and Office Building*, 1892 (photographic reproduction). Montreal, McGill University, Canadian Architecture Collection.

Early drawings dating from 1892 reveal how heavily Edward borrowed from the "transitional, half-Romanesque, half-Italian Renaissance"[2] Board of Trade design (fig. 12). A preliminary study (fig. 13) resembles a compressed version of the Shepley work: a tripartite composition marked by prominent round-arched windows and main doorway, the whole crowned by a boldly projecting cornice. Maxwell initially placed the greatest emphasis on the Sainte-Catherine Street front, while the east elevation, facing Phillips Square, was merely a stripped version of the façade.[3] As the design progressed it became more urbane, acknowledging the presence of the square. At the request of the client, a rounded corner was created.[4] The rather fussy ornament evident in the early study was reduced and more

evenly distributed across the wall surface as it curved around the corner to greet the square. This solution was to prove fortunate when the building was later extended to the south and around the corner along Cathcart Street.[5]

Construction of the four-storey structure commenced in 1893.[6] The ground floor windows have decorative cast-iron lintels that form a belt-course supporting the masonry of the superstructure and allowing for maximum display areas at street level. The buff-coloured Miramichi sandstone is laid in alternating narrow and wide courses. At the ends and on the rounded corner, the narrow courses project at the first- and second-storey levels, providing textural contrast. The entrance on Sainte-Catherine Street is treated as an ornamental frontispiece composed of an arch with a bold keystone, flanked by roundels and framed plaques. This motif is repeated in the second-storey windows above the entrance.

The rounded corner treatment evidently pleased Maxwell, for it reappears on two buildings he designed shortly afterwards. The first (fig. 14), erected in 1895, was an office building containing a branch bank commissioned by the Merchants Bank of Halifax (which later became the Royal Bank of Canada) at des Seigneurs and Notre-Dame streets in the expanding industrial working-class district bordering the Lachine Canal. Although a storey higher, the bank building's composition and ornament – especially the entrance treatment – is very similar to that of the Birks store, except that the entrance to the banking hall is on the corner. The other was the head office and main exchange for the Bell Telephone Company of Canada on Notre-Dame Street (fig. 15), designed in 1895. It was strikingly like the Board of Trade, within view just one block to the south. Round-arched openings, rusticated corners and richly profiled cornices – inspired by the Shepley, Rutan & Coolidge model – were trademarks of Maxwell's commerical work during the nineties.

ROBERT LEMIRE

1   Kenneth O. MacLeod, *The First Century: The Story of a Canadian Company* (Montreal: Henry Birks & Sons, 1979), and Ian Walker, "The Sterling Qualities of Henry Birks", *Montreal Star Weekend Magazine*, vol. 29 (February 24, 1979), pp. 4-7.

2   As described by J. D. Forbes, "Shepley, Bulfinch, Richardson & Abbott: An Introduction", *Journal of the Society of Architectural Historians*, vol. 17 (Fall 1958), p. 23.

3   A Notman photograph of this missing study is in the MA.

4   Maxwell's "Daily Journal, 1892" records several discussions with Henry Birks concerning the design. Within two days of their first meeting on April 18, Maxwell had prepared preliminary studies. At their April 20 meeting Birks suggested several changes including "a circular window on corner" and an additional storey that would accommodate offices and a photographic studio for William Notman & Son, who stood to benefit from the store's fashionable clientele.

5   In 1902 a fifty-six-foot (17.1 m) extension designed by the Montreal firm of Hutchison & Wood was added to the Phillips Square elevation. The contiguous property extending back to Cathcart Street was purchased in 1904, and a longer extension, also by Hutchison & Wood, was completed in 1907. The latter created a new main entrance from the square on axis with an interior stairway leading to a new mezzanine. Hutchison & Wood's work skilfully repeated the elements of the Maxwell's original design and featured the same materials. In the 1920s and 1930s various alterations were carried out by Nobbs & Hyde, including new glazing for the display windows and a wide balcony above the entrance from the square with the company name worked into the railing.

6   *Montreal Daily Star*, March 25, 1893, p. 3.

Fig.14. William Notman & Son, *Merchants Bank of Halifax*, 1896. Montreal, McCord Museum of Canadian History, Notman Photographic Archives.

Fig.15. Edward Maxwell, *Bell Telephone Company of Canada Head Office and Main Exchange*. Reproduced from *The Canadian Architect and Builder* (1897).

Fig. 16. William Notman &
Son, *London & Lancashire Life
Assurance Company Building*,
1899. Montreal, McCord
Museum of Canadian History,
Notman Photographic Archives.

16
Edward Maxwell
*London & Lancashire Life Assurance Company
Building*

244 Saint-Jacques Street
Montreal, Que.
1898-1899

This tall office building in the heart of the financial district was an important commission and an early instance of William Maxwell's participation (fig. 16). By the 1890s the intensely competitive life insurance companies were the fastest-growing financial institutions in Canada.[1] At the century's end, the insurance companies' buildings were among the most impressive in Montreal's financial district. Especially striking were the New York Life Building (1888) on Place d'Armes, Montreal's first "skyscraper", and the Standard Life and Canada Life Buildings (both designed by American architects) on Saint James (Saint-Jacques) Street. When a spectacular fire destroyed the Barron Block, the

London & Lancashire Life Assurance Company, which had been established in Canada since 1863, was able to purchase a prestigious corner lot having a forty-foot (12.2 m) frontage on Saint James Street and eighty feet (24.4 m) south along Saint John (Saint-Jean) Street. The sale of land took place in early April 1898, and by April 22 *The Gazette* reported that "Mr. Edward Maxwell, the well-known architect of the Bell Telephone building and other structures, has about completed the plans for the splendid new building ..."[2]

With one exception, the company's directors were important Maxwell clients: Lord Strathcona (the chairman), R. B. Angus, A. T. Paterson and E. L. Pease.

Another client, B. Hal Brown, was the company's general manager for Canada. He concurrently engaged Maxwell to design a country house in Saint-Bruno.

The Maxwell office must have been short-staffed at the time. Two valued employees, John S. Archibald and Charles J. Saxe, had left the previous year to form their own partnership. Edward was preoccupied with CPR work and several large country houses. William, who had been employed in Boston since 1895 as a draftsman, returned to work in his brother's office in early 1898. From the number of drawings for the London & Lancashire Life building initialed by William, it appears that the younger Maxwell was given considerable responsibility in the project. Moreover, the watercolour presentation drawing of the building (fig. 17) is signed *W. S. Maxwell '98*.[3] Although executed prior to William's studies in Paris, the design anticipates what awaited him abroad. For this commission William borrowed almost exclusively from Beaux-Arts sources, much as Edward had borrowed from Romanesque and Italian Renaissance models during his formative years. The sandstone (a light buff — probably from Miramichi) of which the building is constructed was well suited to the lavish ornament characteristic of the French Renaissance style, a manner in which William clearly delighted.

The ground floor was planned to house an important tenant, the Bank of Nova Scotia. The London & Lancashire utilized the first and sixth floors, while the remaining four floors contained rental office space.

The interior finishes were of excellent quality. The banking room had brass and marble fittings; the entrance vestibule and stair hall were finished in buff, green and grey marbles; and the London & Lancashire board room, which had tapestry-covered walls and oak trim, was lit by natural light filtered through a leaded-glass dome.

In 1909 the Maxwells proposed an addition that would have added two storeys by dismantling and reassembling the mansard roof. This proposal was abandoned, but at a later date dormers were crudely punched into the mansard as the board room was cut up into small offices. In 1979 the interior was entirely refinished in stark wallboard with contemporary trim.

ROBERT LEMIRE

Fig. 17. W. S. Maxwell,
*Perspective for London & Lancashire
Life Assurance Company Building*,
1898. Montreal, McCord
Museum of Canadian History,
Notman Photographic Archives.

---

1 Michael Bliss, *Northern Enterprise* (Toronto: McClelland and Stewart, 1987), p. 270. For a history of British insurance firms see *The British Insurance Business 1547-1970* (London: Heinemann, 1976).

2 *The Gazette* (Montreal), April 5, 1898, p. 2, and April 22, 1898, p. 3. Robert G. Hill kindly provided photocopies of these articles.

3 A photograph of this missing drawing is in the NPA.

Fig. 18. William Notman & Son, *Bank of Montreal, Westmount Branch,* about 1915. Montreal, McCord Museum of Canadian History, Notman Photographic Archives.

17
Edward & W.S. Maxwell
Bank of Montreal, Westmount Branch
Greene Avenue and de Maisonneuve Boulevard
(formerly Western Avenue)
Westmount, Que.
1904 (demolished)

In the fall of 1904 two new branch banks designed by the Maxwells − one for the Bank of Montreal (fig. 18), the other for the Royal Bank of Canada − were completed in Westmount.[1] Both were soon featured in an article in *The Architectural Review* on recent bank buildings written by the noted American bank specialist Philip Sawyer.[2]

The first of these commissions, the Bank of Montreal, stood on the northeast corner of Greene and Western Avenues.[3] The company had pioneered branch banking in the city with the erection in 1889 of its West End Branch at the corner of Sainte-Catherine and Mansfield Streets in the heart of the developing uptown retail area. Later, during the economically buoyant first decade of the twentieth century, the Maxwell firm was called upon to design not only the new branch in Westmount, Montreal's premier residential suburb, but also a second downtown branch, begun

in 1909 and located on Sainte-Catherine at the corner of Peel Street, near the busy West End Branch.[4]

The Canadian Architect and Builder's critic was somewhat less enthusiastic about the Maxwells' design for the Bank of Montreal than he was about the Royal Bank. He wrote: "A little further on in Green [*sic*] Avenue a small branch building of the Bank of Montreal has recently been erected by the same architects and shows the same quality and finish though not the same breadth and simplicity as the Royal Bank just described."[5] Constructed of grey Canyon Ohio sandstone and brick, the two-storey structure measured approximately seventy by thirty feet (21 x 9 m). It contained living quarters on the upper floor for the use of the bank's messenger (who also served as guard) and the caretaker.

The Bank of Montreal, in contrast to the Royal Bank, featured a corner entrance, a popular device of long standing in North American bank design, since it drew in traffic from two thoroughfares. Here the corner was rounded and this main entrance marked, as in the other bank, by an over-scaled rendition of the bank's coat of arms that rested on the cornice and projected high above the parapet. A pair of Ionic columns framed the doorway. An early published account described the exterior stylistic treatment, which is reminiscent of the recently completed Hosmer house, as "Louis XVI".[6] With its second, residential floor effectively an attic, the building appeared less monumental than its nearby two-storey rival. It advertises its presence more by the abundance and elegance of its architectural sculpture and detailing. The models for the sculpture were made by G. W. Hill and the carving executed by Henry Greene and Mr. J. Towne.[7]

Four development drawings for additions and alterations to the bank dated 1918 are preserved in the Maxwell Archive, but bank records indicate only that a one-storey extension and alterations were carried out in 1929-1930 with no indication of the architect involved. The building was ultimately demolished by the bank and replaced by an office building containing the branch.

SUSAN WAGG

[1] Maxwell drawings for the Bank of Montreal are dated 1904. Archival photographs of the completed building in the MA are dated September 1904.

[2] Philip Sawyer, "The Planning of Bank Buildings", *The Architectural Review*, vol. 12 (February 1905), p. 42.

[3] The first reference to the new Bank of Montreal branch appears in the Maxwell office records for September 1903, while that for the Royal Bank is in December ([Commission Book D, 1900-1904], pp. 125, 135, MA, Series C).

[4] Although a set of drawings, dated 1913, exists in the CAC for additions and alterations to the Bank of Montreal Ottawa Branch, it appears that the Maxwell firm did not design or alter other Bank of Montreal branches.

[5] *CAB*, vol. 17 (November 1904), p. 177.

[6] Robert Lemire kindly provided a photocopy of this article, cited as from the *Westmount News*, March 3, 1911.

[7] *Ibid.*

Cat. 18b. *Royal Bank of Canada, Westmount Branch*

18
Edward & W. S. Maxwell
Royal Bank of Canada, Westmount Branch

4192 Sainte-Catherine Street
Westmount, Que.
1904

This was one (cat. 18b) of two suburban branch banks one block apart designed by the Maxwells in the same year and illustrated by Philip Sawyer in his article on the planning of bank buildings in *The Architectural Review* of February 1905.[1] The Royal Bank of Canada was founded in Halifax in 1864 and federally chartered in 1869 under the name of the Merchants Bank of Halifax. As a result of the relative economic decline of the Maritimes after Confederation, the bank began looking for avenues for expansion outside their region, first establishing an agency in Bermuda in the early 1880s and, in 1887, a branch in Montreal, Canada's business and financial centre. It soon had three branches in Montreal. The original one at the corner of Saint-François-Xavier and Notre-Dame Streets was superseded in 1895 by a new main branch that occupied the entire ground floor of Edward Maxwell's Bell Telephone Company building. The third branch was opened in an expanding area of town in the Merchants Bank of Halifax building (1896), also designed by Edward Maxwell. By 1900 the aggressive bank had branches in seven Canadian provinces, as well as two in the United States and one in Cuba. To reflect the institution's national and international orientation, its name was changed to the Royal Bank of Canada in 1901, and in 1907 the head office was moved from Halifax to Montreal.[2]

Although the Royal Bank commissioned the American-born architect Howard Colton Stone to design its splendid head office on Saint James (Saint-Jacques) Street (1908), it retained Edward & W.S. Maxwell for some other branches and for additions and alterations from time to time. Notable was the new Westmount Branch, which was constructed during 1904 and still stands – although it no longer serves as a bank – on the corner of Sainte-Catherine Street and Greene Avenue. A branch had first opened in suburban Westmount in 1894, but these premises soon became too small and it was decided to erect a new building two blocks to the south. This was ready for occupancy in late 1904. The bank, a two-storey block, has façades of sandstone resting on a limestone base. The just-completed structure was reviewed in *The Canadian Architect and Builder* in November 1904; the pseudonymous reviewer, likely the Montreal architect Percy Nobbs, wrote:

> It is of no great size – the total height is probably less than 40 feet [12 m] – but it arrests attention by its appearance of compactness and unity. Any one who finds delight in stones of generous size may contemplate this building with great pleasure. The courses of the masonry are 21 inches [53 cm] deep and the blocking course on the top seems about 3 feet [90 cm] deep. This with the general air of breadth and simplicity about the little building comes upon one like a breath of fresh air after having to fill one's eyes with so much of niggled and unwholesome tawdriness that swarms around. As might be expected from an architect with an appreciation of good stone the details, the cornices and the quaint Ionic capitals are worked out in careful and even recherché manner. The main doorway and large front window mutually trespass on one another's domains in an audacious if picturesque way that must take the breath away from an ordinary law abiding citizen.[3]

The arrangement of the entrance front on Sainte-Catherine Street remarked upon by Nobbs, comprises wide, rusticated end piers framing two Ionic columns *in antis* (that is, set between the lateral walls and aligned

Fig. 19. Shepley, Rutan & Coolidge, *Perspective for New South Building & Loan Association Building.* Reproduced from *The American Architect and Building News* (1896).

with the front wall), with the intercolumniation given over primarily to glass. The ornate, pedimented stone doorway is set into the lower glass window area, the upper floor windows being set apart by a horizontal band of masonry. Thus do the main door and windows, as Nobbs so aptly put it, "mutually trespass on one another's domain". Crowning the Sainte-Catherine Street façade is a huge carved rendering of the insignia used by the bank from 1902 to 1962, which closely resembles the coat of arms of Great Britain.

The device of using powerful end piers and columns *in antis* – a motif inspired by the sacred treasuries of ancient Greece – to give a small bank building monumentality was in fact a very old one, having first appeared in the United States early in the Greek Revival period.[4] As a scheme for banks, it regained popularity around the turn of the century, the greater expanses of glass and the luxuriant, grandly scaled details differentiating the later versions from earlier ones. The extensive windows not only contribute picturesque audaciousness – and modernity – to the Royal Bank's façade, but admit needed light. The Maxwells may have drawn on a more ornate but less inspired design of this type by Shepley, Rutan & Coolidge, a building erected in 1896 for the New South Building & Loan Association in New Orleans (fig. 19), which was reproduced in *The American Architect and Building News* of May 30 that year and appears in a bound volume of architectural clippings that Edward Maxwell kept in his library.[5]

The secondary elevation fronting on Greene Avenue is five bays wide; the three central ground floor windows are the tallest and light the banking room. The windows of both floors on this simpler façade are set between pilasters that rise from the base to the entablature. A doorway leading to the floor above is located at the southwest corner.

After passing through a vestibule inside the entrance from Sainte-Catherine Street, the customer was flanked on the right by a door to the manager's office and on the left by the door leading to a room reserved for women. Beyond was the public banking room, which had continuous counters embellished with wood panelling running along the south and west perimeters and a handsome marble fireplace decorated with a prominent clock set into the west wall. The vault was located at the back of the room behind the counters. The upper floor was divided into offices. An undated set of linen working drawings for alterations and additions by Edward & W.S. Maxwell survives in the Maxwell Archive, which, although signed, were not executed in the manner indicated.[6] These would have enlarged the windows on the Greene Avenue elevation, relocated the main door to the bank at the northwest corner, and refurbished the offices on the upper floor, certainly for rental purposes.

The building, somewhat altered, is now used for retail purposes. However, it still adds "a breath of fresh air" – as it did in Nobbs's and the Maxwells' day – to a busy urban locale.

SUSAN WAGG

1 Philip Sawyer, "The Planning of Bank Buildings", *The Architectural Review*, vol. 12 (February 1905), pp. 42, 107.

2 A brief account of the institution's development, *The Royal Bank of Canada: A Chronology, 1864-1969* by Clifford H. Ince, can be consulted in the Royal Bank of Canada Archives, Montreal.

3 *CAB*, vol. 17 (November 1904), p. 177.

4 Solomon Willard used a pedimented version for the Boston Branch of the Second Bank of the United States in 1824-1825, while a more ingenious example, in which the pediment was omitted, was James Dakin's Bank of Louisville, designed in 1834.

5 Now in the Blackader-Lauterman Library of Architecture and Art at McGill University.

6 The publication *Architecture commerciale I : les banques*, published by the Communauté urbaine de Montréal (June 1908), notes on p. 128 that a permit for "agrandissement" was issued by the City of Westmount in 1930 and carried out by the contractor John Quinlan & Co. The extent of this work is unknown.

Cat.19b. *Dominion Express Building*

19
Edward & W.S. Maxwell
Dominion Express Building
201-215 Saint-Jacques Street
Montreal, Que.
1910-1912

The Dominion Express Building (cat. 19b) was the largest of the Maxwells' office buildings and shows their developed approach to "skyscraper" design. The composition was markedly different from the Romanesque/Italian Renaissance and Beaux-Arts office buildings designed by Edward Maxwell in the 1890s. Based on the American method (associated with Louis Sullivan) of dividing the elevation into a base, a shaft

and a crown, the design clearly expresses the grid of the supporting steel frame. In place of a heavy projecting cornice as at the Henry Birks & Sons Building and the London & Lancashire Life Assurance Company Building, a low parapet enlivens the roofline, and piers (plain in the midsection, rusticated in the end bays) provide a strong vertical emphasis. The base of the building, where the Dominion Express and Canadian Pacific

Cat. 19d. *Montreal Club dining room, Dominion Express Building*

Railway offices were located, is faced with light-coloured granite, while the upper storeys are clad in up-to-date white glazed terra-cotta.[1] The terra-cotta was manufactured by Doulton & Company using full-scale detailed drawings from the Maxwell office.[2]

Ornament serves to soften the building's spare geometry and stark white facing. Divisions between floor levels are marked by decorative spandrels, while in the two end bays between the base and shaft, large bronze shields bearing the emblems of the provinces are flanked by life-size female figures. The company's entwined initials are also used as an ornamental motif.

The Dominion Express Company, incorporated in 1873 as a parcel forwarding service, came under the control of William Van Horne in 1882, during his first

year as general manager of the Canadian Pacific Railway Company. Under his direction, Dominion Express developed an efficient forwarding system that anticipated the multimodal freight concept in use today.[3]

The first reference to the Dominion Express Company in the Maxwell office records appears in November 1909, when the company ordered studies for a ten-storey building to be located on the corner of Saint James (Saint-Jacques) and Saint-François-Xavier Streets and running through to Craig Street (now Saint-Antoine Street).[4] The sketch plans that the Maxwell firm subsequently prepared, dated December 1909, bear the title "Proposed Hotel at Corner of St. James and St. Francais [*sic*] Xavier for The Dominion

Express Company".[5] This project was apparently abandoned, for in March 1910 *Contract Record* recorded that the Maxwells were the successful competitors among six architects who submitted plans for a ten-storey office building on Saint James Street.[6]

Completed in 1912, the building stood in the heart of Montreal's financial district. On a site formerly occupied by a venerable landmark, the Saint Lawrence Hall, it is a prime example of the redevelopment activity then current in the area.[7] An article published in 1911 observed that "large commercial and high office buildings are replacing the older structures on St. James St., and on the very sites where once stood small houses and shop buildings, handsome and gigantic steel framed structures are fast becoming evident."[8] The lower portion of the new building comprised two main storeys facing Saint James Street and a basement on sloping Saint-François-Xavier; these three floors accommodated the Dominion Express Company and the CPR's steamship and general ticket offices. The basement also contained a large restaurant, which was entered from Fortification Lane. The second to eighth storeys were rented as offices. The top of the building was designed to accommodate the Montreal Club, an elegant private dining club that served the surrounding business and legal community (cat. 19d). Large segmental-headed windows embellished with carved foliage open onto two long balconies. An enclosed and heated pergola for the use of the club occupied the roof; in the summer it could be used as a roof garden.

An article in *Construction* (1912) indicates the superior quality of this "modern" office structure. The woodwork in the corridors and private offices was mahogany, and marble was used extensively. The sumptuous furnishings for the Montreal Club were supplied by the Bromsgrove Guild. The pergola on the roof must have been an especially delightful spot. Fifteen by seventy-five feet (4.6 x 22.9 m), with furniture "of cane with printed linen of black Chippendale design", it had large French windows "affording magnificent views of the surrounding mountains, city and harbor".[9]

ROBERT LEMIRE

1   Terra-cotta was used for the Ross Building in Saskatoon designed by the Maxwells in 1912. They also prepared plans in 1913 for a ten-storey building on Saint James Street facing Victoria Square, similar in design to the Dominion Express Building, which called for semiglazed terra-cotta, for the Marcil Trust Company. The project was abandoned.

2   "The Dominion Express Building, Montreal, Que.", *Construction*, vol. 5 (November 1912), pp. 46-54.

3   Omer Lavallée, *Van Horne's Road* (Montreal: Railfare Enterprises, 1974), p. 290.

4   [*Work Costs Book M, 1904-1914*], p. 303, MA, Series C.

5   Project no. 96.2, MA.

6   *Contract Record*, vol. 24 (March 2, 1910), p. 26. Ten storeys was the current height restriction in force. The site occupied by the Dominion Express Building was smaller than that of the Maxwells' proposed hotel of 1909, extending back only to Fortification Lane.

7   Long one of the city's finest hotels, Saint Lawrence Hall continued to operate in a portion of its premises at the southwest corner of Saint-François-Xavier and Craig Streets according to *Lovell's Montreal Directory* for 1913-1914.

8   *The Railway and Marine World*, vol. 15 (February 1911), p. 157. I am grateful to Robert G. Hill for bringing this article to my attention.

9   *Ibid.*, p. 54.

15a. Edward Maxwell
Elevations for the Henry Birks & Sons Store and Office Building
1893
Black and red ink and graphite on linen
59 x 101
Dated upper centre: 20-1-'93
Montreal, McGill University, Canadian Architecture Collection

15b. Photographer unknown
Henry Birks & Sons Store and Office Building
1894 (printed 1991)
Gelatin silver print
20.3 x 25.4
Montreal, McCord Museum of Canadian History, Notman Photographic Archives

15c. Hutchison & Wood, Montreal
Perspective for Henry Birks & Sons Store and Office Building Addition
1906
Watercolour and graphite
60 x 95.5 (by sight)
Delineator: W. J. Campbell
Inscribed lower left: *Hutchison & Wood/ Architects*; signed and dated lower right: *W.J. Campbell/1906*
Montreal, Henry Birks & Sons, Ltd.

15d. Brian Merrett
Henry Birks & Sons Store and Office Building
1990
Gelatin silver print
20.3 x 20.3
The Montreal Museum of Fine Arts

16a. Edward Maxwell
Elevation for the London & Lancashire Life Assurance Company Building
Undated
Graphite, black and red ink on linen
70.2 x 41.6 (by sight)
Montreal, McGill University, Canadian Architecture Collection

16b. Edward Maxwell
Dormer detail for the London & Lancashire Life Assurance Company Building
1898
Black, red and blue ink, watercolour and graphite on linen
62 x 74
Draftsman: W. S. Maxwell
Signed and dated upper left: *W.S.M: 26.9.98-*
Montreal, McGill University, Canadian Architecture Collection

16c. Brian Merrett
Dormer, London & Lancashire Life Assurance Company Building
1991
Gelatin silver print
35.6 x 35.6
The Montreal Museum of Fine Arts

17. William Notman & Son
Bank of Montreal, Westmount Branch
Undated (printed 1991)
Gelatin silver print
20.3 x 25.4
Montreal, McGill University, Canadian Architecture Collection

18a. Edward & W.S. Maxwell
Elevation for the Royal Bank of Canada, Westmount Branch
Undated
Black and red ink on linen
41.5 x 37.5
Montreal, McGill University, Canadian Architecture Collection

18b. William Notman & Son
Royal Bank of Canada, Westmount Branch
1911 (printed 1991)
Gelatin silver print
20.3 x 25.4
Montreal, McCord Museum of Canadian History, Notman Photographic Archives

18c. La Boîte du Pinceau d'Arlequin, under the direction of Jean-François Pinsonneault
Model of main doorway, Royal Bank of Canada, Westmount Branch
1991
Pine, hardboard, cement, plaster, paint
457.2 x 472.4 x 116.8
Courtesy of The Royal Bank of Canada, Montreal

19a. Edward & W.S. Maxwell
Perspective for the Dominion Express Building
1910
Sepia and graphite on wove paper
101.5 x 79 (by sight)
Delineator: D.A. Gregg
Signed and dated lower right: *D.A. Gregg. 1910*
Saint-Constant, Quebec, Canadian Railroad Historical Association

19b. William Notman & Son
Dominion Express Building
1912 (printed 1991)
Gelatin silver print
20.3 x 25.4
Montreal, McCord Museum of Canadian History, Notman Photographic Archives

19c. William Notman & Son
Entrance hall, Dominion Express Building
1912 (printed 1991)
Gelatin silver print
20.3 x 25.4
Montreal, McCord Museum of Canadian History, Notman Photographic Archives

19d. William Notman & Son
Montreal Club dining room, Dominion Express Building
1912 (printed 1991)
Gelatin silver print
20.3 x 25.4
Montreal, McCord Museum of Canadian History, Notman Photographic Archives

In 1897 the Canadian Pacific Railway became a client of Edward Maxwell, who also received many private commissions from its directors and its financier, the Bank of Montreal. Prompted by the upturn in the economy, as well as by competition from other railways, the CPR undertook an aggressive programme of replacing its original stations – most of them economical wooden structures built in the mid-1880s – with new buildings in more durable materials. These commissions proved to be mutually beneficial. the prestigious national work raised the stature of the Maxwell office outside Montreal, while the firm's designs contributed to the development of Canadian railway architecture.

Sir William Van Horne, the president of the CPR, was a talented artist and a knowledgeable amateur architect who chose his consultants with care, and so the large number of contracts he awarded Edward Maxwell in 1897-1898 may be taken as a sign of confidence. These were for a variety of stations and sites between New Brunswick and British Columbia – including an addition to the most significant station in the system, Windsor Station in Montreal (cat. 24, fig. 20), and a tourist hotel in the mountains of British Columbia.

Van Horne retired as president of the CPR in 1899 but soon became involved in the construction of a trans-Cuban railway, for which he solicited station designs from the Maxwell firm. His successor, Sir Thomas Shaughnessy, also retained the partnership (which became Edward & W.S. Maxwell in 1902) for a select number of particularly important hotels and stations. The shift in design – from Edward's Richardson-inspired medievalism to William's Beaux-Arts classicism – evident in these commissions is typical of the firm's work in general.

Cat. 24. *Perspective for Windsor Station Addition*

Fig. 20. William Notman & Son, *Windsor Station*, about 1904. Montreal, McCord Museum of Canadian History, Notman Photographic Archives.

Cat. 20. *Canadian Pacific Railway Vancouver Station and Offices*

20
Edward Maxwell
Canadian Pacific Railway Vancouver Station and Offices
Granville Street
Vancouver, B.C.
1897-1898 (demolished about 1913)

The station and office building (cat. 20) that Edward Maxwell designed for the western terminus of the transcontinental railway was an impressive, if short-lived, local landmark that helped to establish the Château style as the signature style for CPR architecture. This was the second Vancouver station; the first, a long and low frame structure built in 1887, was far too small for its purposes.[1]

Plans for a larger Vancouver station, with space for the CPR's regional offices as well as for operations, commenced about 1891. The initial designs were made by architect Edward Colonna; his drawings, which have been conserved together with Maxwell's, anticipate the main features of the executed building, and the foundations appear to have been laid according to Colonna's plans.[2]

Edward Maxwell revised the superstructure in 1897. The ground floor of the central portion, which featured a broad entrance arch, was faced in Calgary sandstone, and the remainder in buff brick. The tall central pavilion, sited at the foot of Granville Street, was flanked by a circular and a polygonal tower. The slate-covered hipped roofs were punctuated with gables and dormers topped by spiky finials. The Châteauesque allusions followed the precedents of the Banff Springs Hotel (1888) and the Château Frontenac (1893), both by Bruce Price. Edward used these castle-like elements on most of his other CPR designs of the time, including the similarly treated Broad Street Station in Ottawa (about 1900; see also cat. entry 21).[3]

The rapid growth in rail traffic soon rendered even this second building too small, just as the advent of Beaux-Arts taste made it look old-fashioned. In 1914 it was replaced by a third station (by Barott, Blackader & Webster), which is still used by the city for municipal marine and light rail transit.

HAROLD KALMAN and FRANCE GAGNON PRATTE

[1] The architect of the first station appears to have been P. Marmette. See Harold Kalman and John Roaf, *Exploring Vancouver* (2) (Vancouver: University of British Columbia Press, 1978), p. 79. Thomas C. Sorby also provided designs for the first Vancouver station, but his more elaborate scheme was not built (drawings in Sorby sketchbook, private collection, Vancouver).

[2] Project no. 59.3, MA. See John Bland, "E. Colonna's Contribution to the Château Style in Canadian Architecture", *AIBC Forum*, vol. 2 (January-February 1978), pp. 14-15.

[3] J. Edward Martin, *Railway Stations of Western Canada* (White Rock, B.C.: Studio E, 1979), p. 17, and Harold Kalman, *The Railway Hotels and the Development of the Château Style in Canada* (Victoria: University of Victoria Maltwood Museum, 1968), p. 26.

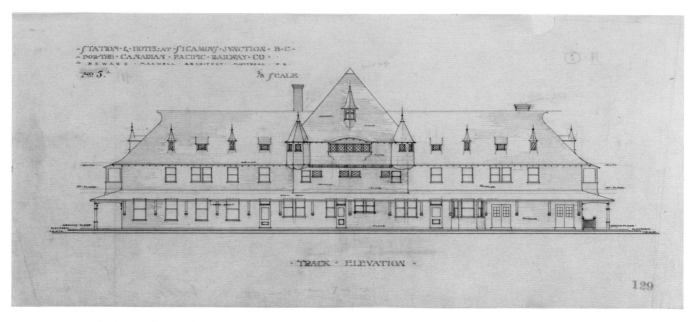

Cat. 21. *Elevation for the Canadian Pacific Railway Sicamous Junction Station and Hotel*

21
Edward Maxwell
Canadian Pacific Railway Sicamous Junction Station and Hotel
Sicamous, B.C.
1898-1899 (demolished about 1964)

The spectacularly sited Hotel Sicamous on scenic Shuswap Lake was a popular CPR attraction for more than half a century. Sicamous was the junction between the main line and the line south to Okanagan Landing, where one could board a CPR stern-wheeler and steam the length of Okanagan Lake to Penticton.

The farsighted Sir William Van Horne planned a series of hotels in the western mountains while the transcontinental line was being laid. These hotels served two purposes: their restaurants were substitutes for dining cars, which were too heavy to haul economically up the steep mountain grades; and they provided a base for tourism, which would generate lucrative passenger traffic. "Since we can't export the scenery," Van Horne declared, "we shall have to import the tourists."[1] Three small chalet-like "dining stations" designed by architect Thomas Charles Sorby were built in the British Columbia mountains in 1885-1886, and a large frame Châteauesque hotel by Bruce Price was built in

1888 at Banff Springs in the Alberta Rockies.[2] Price also prepared plans for a hotel at Sicamous in 1888, but nothing came of the project. Only when a fire destroyed the small original station in 1898 was action taken.[3]

The wood-frame hotel-cum-station was a long two-and-a-half-storey block with a tall central pavilion (cat. 21). A roof projecting from above the ground floor served to shelter the platform on the trackside and to cover a veranda, from which guests could admire the view of the lake. The shingle-clad building (fig. 21) was supported above the lake on wood girders and piles. Turrets at the corners of the pavilion and dormer windows with conical roofs provided the desired château-like appearance.[4]

The design was not unlike those of Edward Maxwell's large CPR stations for the divisional points at Moose Jaw, Saskatchewan (1898; cat. 22) and McAdam Junction, New Brunswick (1899), which were faced in

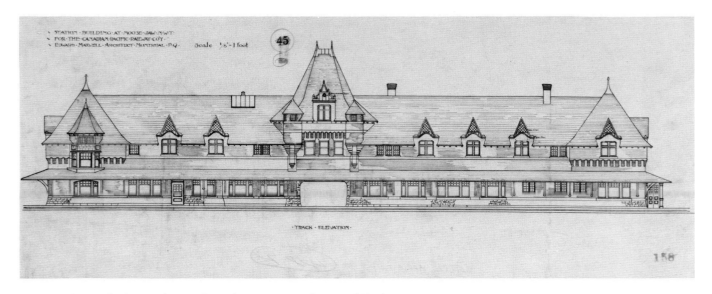

Cat. 22. *Elevation for the Canadian Pacific Railway Moose Jaw Station and Hotel*

brick and stone respectively, although both had pavilions at the ends as well as at the centre. The composition for Sicamous Junction may owe something to Shepley, Rutan & Coolidge's large station for the Boston & Albany Railroad at Springfield, Massachusetts (1888-1891), which had a massive central block linked to broad one-storey wings.[5]

The appearance of the hotel was considerably altered about 1910, when a full third storey was built, the central portion was given a gabled roof, and the ends were finished in half-timbering. This construction added twenty-five rooms to the original twenty-eight. The hotel operated until 1956, by which time reduced service into the Okanagan Valley had eliminated most of its market. After the station closed in 1964, the building was demolished.[6]

HAROLD KALMAN and FRANCE GAGNON PRATTE

Fig. 21. Photographer unknown, *Canadian Pacific Railway Sicamous Junction Station and Hotel*, undated. Ottawa, National Archives of Canada.

1   John M. Gibbon, *Steel of Empire* (Toronto: McClelland and Stewart, 1935), p. 304.

2   Harold Kalman, *The Railway Hotels and the Development of the Château Style in Canada* (Victoria: University of Victoria Maltwood Museum, 1968), pp. 6-11.

3   Kalman, 1968, p. 11, and J. Edward Martin, *Railway Stations of Western Canada* (White Rock, B.C.: Studio E, 1979), p. 19.

4   Project 59.12, MA. An alternative design (project 59.13, MA) with a chalet-like central pavilion was not executed.

5   Jeffrey Karl Ochsner, "Architecture for the Boston & Albany Railroad: 1881-1894", *Journal of the Society of Architectural Historians*, vol. 47 (June 1988), pp. 128-129; see cat. entry 23.

6   Martin, 1979, p. 19; Robert D. Turner, *West of the Great Divide: An Illustrated History of the Canadian Pacific Railway in British Columbia 1880-1986* (Victoria: Sono Nis, 1987), p. 44; and Roger G. Burrows, *Railway Mileposts: British Columbia (1)* (North Vancouver: Railway Milepost Books, 1981), pp. 56, 60.

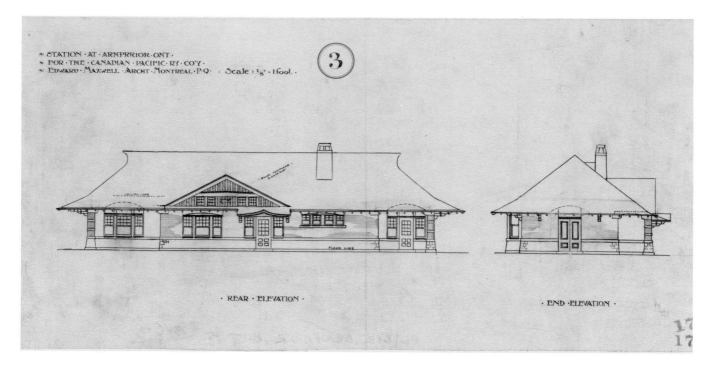

Cat. 23. *Elevations for the Canadian Pacific Railway Arnprior Station*

23
Edward Maxwell
Canadian Pacific Railway Arnprior Station
Arnprior, Ont.
1898 (demolished)

Several of Maxwell's commissions from the CPR were for medium-sized stations in established Ontario communities. The station at Arnprior, eighty kilometres west of Ottawa along the main line, was important for introducing a new approach to station design and being the prototype for several other CPR stations in the Ottawa Valley.

Maxwell's drawings for the station (cat. 23), one of which is annotated "approved Feb 10/98 by Sir Wm. V[an] Horne", proposed a larger and more complex structure than the one that was actually built (fig. 22).[1] As executed, the floor plan was a compact rectangle that contained the waiting room, ticket office, bagage/express room and washrooms. Its simple lines were interrupted only by the shallow projection of the operator's trackside bay window. Despite Van Horne's

approval, the proposed design was simplified for economy's sake, leaving out a ladies' waiting room and a gable on the street side (intended to illuminate the general waiting room). A broad hipped roof with flaring eaves, broken only by a shallow eyebrow dormer, covered the limestone building, clearly expressing its purpose as a shelter. As proposed, the plan was closer to the CPR stations at Galt and Woodstock, on the London subdivision in southern Ontario, which were also designed by Maxwell and built in 1898-1899.[2]

Both the proposed and the executed schemes for Arnprior were simpler in plan and profile than previous CPR station designs. They resemble several of the thirty-two stations designed between 1881 and 1894 for the Boston & Albany Railroad by H. H. Richardson and by Shepley, Rutan & Coolidge. The B & A depots were

Fig. 22. J. W. Heckman, *Canadian Pacific Railway Arnprior Station*, 1900. Montreal, Canadian Pacific Archives.

compactly massed with assertive stone walls and hipped roofs. Some roofs were elaborated with dormers (for example, Wellesley, Massachusetts, 1889), as in the working drawings for Arnprior, while others were uninterrupted (for example, Newton Lower Falls, Massachusetts, 1887), as Arnprior was built. The station at Riverside, Massachusetts, designed in 1893, has flaring eaves and an eyebrow dormer very similar to those at Arnprior. The simplicity, horizontality and dominant roofs of the B & A depots influenced station design throughout the United States and Canada.[3]

The CPR stations at Almonte, Pembroke, Renfrew – located like Arnprior on the Chalk River subdivision – and at nearby Perth were built to a design similar to that of Arnprior around 1899-1900. All were demolished in the 1970s and 1980s in response to decreasing passenger traffic and increasing maintenance costs.

HAROLD KALMAN and FRANCE GAGNON PRATTE

[1] Project no. 59.7, MA, and Harold D. Kalman *et al.*, "Arnprior Station: A New Use for the CPR Station", prepared for the Arnprior and District Historical Society, Ottawa, 1979.

[2] Drawings for the Galt and Woodstock stations are in the CPR Corporate Archives, nos. 33093-1 to 33093-5. See Commonwealth Historic Resource Management Limited, "A Study of Canadian Pacific's Heritage Railway Properties", prepared for the Ontario Heritage Foundation, Perth, Ont., 1989, pp. 43-45, 124-125, 207-208.

[3] Jeffrey Karl Ochsner, "Architecture of the Boston & Albany Railroad: 1881-1894", *Journal of the Society of Architectural Historians*, vol. 47 (June 1988), pp. 109-131. See also Matthew Kierstead, "H. H. Richardson and the Wellesley Farms Railroad Station", *Bulletin, Railroad Station Historical Society*, vol. 22 (March-April 1989), pp. 24-28.

Cat. 25b. *Perspective for the Canadian Pacific Railway Winnipeg Station*

25
Edward & W.S. Maxwell
Canadian Pacific Railway Winnipeg Station and Royal Alexandra Hotel
Fonseca and Higgins Avenues at Main Street
Winnipeg, Man.
1904-1906 (hotel demolished 1971)

The station and hotel that the CPR built in Winnipeg at the beginning of the century marked the company's conversion from the Château style to Beaux-Arts classicism and simultaneously indicated William's ascendancy as the Maxwell firm's principal design partner. Winnipeg was a busy transportation hub, serving not only the CPR but also the country's two new transcontinental lines – then under construction – and providing vital links to the United States. The headquarters of the CPR's western lines was located in the city. To keep up with the increased traffic and competition, the CPR redesigned its Winnipeg yards and shops between 1900 and 1904 and made plans to build a new station and a large hotel.

In 1899 Edward Maxwell had produced designs for a Château-style building to replace the first CPR Winnipeg Station, a two-storey buff brick structure dating from 1882. However, problems encountered acquiring land for a hotel and an underpass delayed the project for several years. By 1904 when the CPR was ready to build the station, architectural tastes had changed. Consequently the station and the hotel emerged in classical garb, reflecting current fashion and allowing William Maxwell to capitalize on his Beaux-Arts training.

Constructed during 1904 and 1905, the new Winnipeg Station was a suitably majestic monument. Its centrepiece is a grand portal formed by two pairs of

HOTEL · & · STATION · FOR · THE · CANADIAN · PACIFIC · AT · WINNIPEG
· EDWARD · & · W. S. MAXWELL · ARCHITECTS · MONTREAL · CANADA ·

Cat. 25a. *Perspective for the Canadian Pacific Railway Winnipeg Hotel and Station*

giant limestone columns *in antis*, or aligned with the front wall, that support a dentilled entablature and a parapet embellished with carved heads and a clock. Three doorways recessed behind the columns lead to the large public concourse and waiting room. Flanking wings contain additional public spaces and offices. The red brick walls are richly articulated with limestone trim, including quoins at the corners and shields above the third-floor windows (cat. 25b). The trackside elevation is similar, although lacking the colonnade.[1]

This classical precedent was followed in subsequent CPR rail terminals across Canada, including the third Vancouver Station (Barott, Blackader & Webster, 1914) and the Union Stations at Ottawa (Ross & MacFarlane, 1908-1912) and Toronto (Ross & Macdonald, Hugh G. Jones and John M. Lyle, 1914-1930). All adopted broad colonnades to create dignified porticos in a manner that reflects a familiarity with New York's Pennsylvania Station (McKim, Mead & White, 1906-1910) as well as the Winnipeg Station.

In 1906 the Royal Alexandra Hotel was completed immediately to the west of the station (cat. 25a), connected to it by a long express wing. The tightly composed seven-storey building continues the classical language and the materials. A brick superstructure rests on a high stone podium, with the ends slightly projecting on both principal façades. Many of the features of the

Royal Alexandra can be found at the Hotel Touraine in Boston, designed by Winslow & Wetherell and completed in 1897 while William was working for the firm. Both hotels were located on a corner site, were similarly composed, employed brick and stone, were capped by a prominent cornice, and displayed French-inspired exterior ornament.[2]

The Maxwells' foursquare classical design became a prototype for the CPR's later hotels in Prairie cities: the Palliser in Calgary (Edward & W.S. Maxwell) and the Hotel Saskatchewan in Regina (Ross & Macdonald, 1926-1927). Ironically, just as the CPR abandoned the Château style, the rival railroads adopted it, as at the Fort Garry Hotel (Ross & MacFarlane, 1911-1913) – the Royal Alexandra's chief competition as the most luxurious hotel in Winnipeg. The Royal Alexandra remained a popular spot for more than half a century, but after patronage declined, the CPR demolished it in 1971.

HAROLD KALMAN

---

1   Project no. 59.2, MA; J. Edward Martin, *Railway Stations of Western Canada* (White Rock, B.C.: Studio E, 1979), p. 33; and City of Winnipeg, Historical Buildings Committee, *1981: The Year Past* (Winnipeg: 1982), pp. 29-32.

2   I am indebted to Rosalind M. Pepall for bringing these similarities to my attention.

Cat. 26a. *Perspective for the Palliser Hotel*

26
Edward & W.S. Maxwell
Palliser Hotel

133 Ninth Avenue
Calgary, Alta.
1911-1914

The Palliser Hotel (cat. 26a), built adjacent to the CPR station in the heart of downtown Calgary, was a large, urbane building whose Beaux-Arts design provided a distinct contrast with the Château style that the railway used in scenic locations. This was acknowledged when the building was published in *Construction* in 1916: "Owing to the nature of the site, a picturesque solution of the problem, such as is evidenced in many of the company's hotels of the chateau type, was considered inadvisable."[1]

The three-hundred-and-fifty-room hotel was built in the European tradition of luxury hotels. The elegance of its design derived from the careful examination of models in the quest for an ideal solution. The complex organization of structure, public spaces and services has been given a simple geometrical order evident on the plans and elevations. This is seen, for example, in the cross-axes of the ground floor (cat. 26b), the arrangement of the ballroom and other public spaces on the first floor, and the E-shaped plan of the bedroom floors, making every bedroom an "outside" room. Intended to rise thirteen storeys and be crowned with a mansard roof, the Palliser had eight floors and a flat top when it opened in 1914. With the addition of four storeys and a full cornice in 1929, the Palliser became the tallest building in Calgary.

Cat. 26b. *Entrance hall, Palliser Hotel*

The exterior of the podium is finished in rusticated Indiana limestone (on a structural steel frame) and capped by a shallow cornice, its principal windows arched to provide an arcaded base. The upper floors are faced with Columbus brick, with a quoinlike treatment of the corners and the dentilled cornice. The interior design of the public spaces is traditional (cat. 26d) and refined (fig. 23), using rich materials such as Botticino marble (for the walls), Tennessee marble (for the floors), apple-green rugs, and tapestries decorating the walls of the main lobby.[2]

The interior underwent renovations in the 1980s, but the exterior has remained essentially unchanged since 1929.

JOHN BLAND and HAROLD KALMAN

1 "Hotel Palliser, Calgary, Alberta", *Construction*, vol. 9 (November 1916), p. 383.

2 Bryan Melnyck, *Calgary Builds* (Edmonton: Alberta Culture/Canadian Plains Research Center, 1985), pp. 146-147, and Heritage Files, Planning Department, City of Calgary, site no. 1-160.

Cat. 26d. *Drawing room, Palliser Hotel*

Fig. 23. Photographer
unknown, *Model for plasterwork
decoration for Palliser Hotel*, about
1912. Montreal, McGill
University, Canadian
Architecture Collection.

Cat. 27m. *Construction photograph showing Tower Block addition to the Château Frontenac Hotel*

27
Edward & W.S. Maxwell and Maxwell & Pitts
Château Frontenac Hotel (central tower and additional wings)

1 des Carrières Street
Quebec City, Que.
1920-1924

The crowning feature of the Château Frontenac, and the element that transformed the CPR's flagship hotel into a landmark of international stature, is the romantic central tower – the last project on which the Maxwell brothers worked together before Edward's death.

Perched on a spectacular site on the bluff at the edge of Quebec City's Upper Town, the Château Frontenac was begun in 1892-1893 to designs by Bruce Price. With its details paraphrased from the châteaux of the Loire Valley, it and Price's earlier Banff Springs Hotel (1888) established the Château style as the mode for the CPR's hotels. The original hotel, whose robust and compact composition reflected the work of H. H. Richardson, was enlarged with the addition of the Citadel Wing (by Price, 1897-1899), which formed a range of buildings around an enclosed courtyard; and

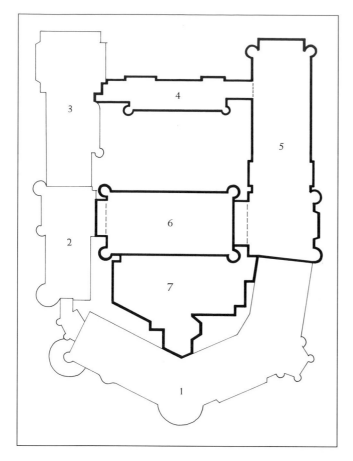

Fig. 24. *Simplified plan of the Château Frontenac Hotel in 1924.*
1. Original wing (B. Price 1892-1893); 2. Pavilion and Citadel Wing (B. Price, 1897-1899); 3. Mount-Carmel Wing (W.S. Painter, 1908-1909); 4. Service wing (Edward & W.S. Maxwell, 1920-1924); 5. Saint-Louis Wing (Edward & W.S. Maxwell, 1920-1924); 6.-7. Tower and tower block (Edward & W.S. Maxwell, 1920-1924).

the Mont-Carmel Wing (by W. S. Painter, 1908-1909), which projected toward the west.[1]

In 1919 the CPR commissioned the Maxwells to double the capacity of the hotel on its constrained site (fig. 24). Their solution was to remove Price's service wing and replace it with a seventeen-storey central tower (cat. 27m), another wing (the Saint-Louis Wing), and a low service wing, creating a plan in the form of the letter "A" above the first two floors. The high hipped roof that caps the tower provides a perfectly proportioned climax to the low cluster that surrounds it and dominates the striking Quebec City skyline. The dormers and turrets continue the château theme.

The lobby, public rooms, administration and elevator core were placed at the bottom of the tower, which was entered from the courtyard. Two grand staircases (cat. 27d), one of them oval (cat. 27e), lead guests from the lobby to the dining rooms, ballroom, palm room and other well-appointed public spaces on the first floor. A number of artists collaborated in their decoration, including Archibald Davies, Else Hower, Charles Kelsey and Adam Sheriff Scott. The upper floors of the tower and the Saint-Louis Wing contain bedrooms, bringing the number of guest rooms to six hundred and sixty. Edward spent three months in Europe searching for antique furniture (and some reproductions) for the rooms in the tower suites.[2]

Work continued from 1920 until 1924. Edward died in 1923, and William invited Gordon McLeod Pitts (1886-1954) to join him in partnership. Pitts had worked with the Maxwells in 1913 to supervise the construction of the High School of Montreal; he returned to McGill University to obtain a degree in architecture and once again joined Edward and William in 1919. He served as president of the Province of Quebec Association of Architects and subsequently represented McGill on the Montreal City Council. When Pitts died in 1954, he was vice chairman of the Executive Committee of the City of Montreal.[3]

In January 1926 a fire gutted part of the original wing, but it was quickly rebuilt.[4]

HAROLD KALMAN and FRANCE GAGNON PRATTE

[1] Harold Kalman, *The Railway Hotels and the Development of the Château Style in Canada* (Victoria: University of Victoria Maltwood Museum, 1968), pp. 11-13, 17, 32-37, and Luc Noppen, Claude Paulette and Michel Tremblay, *Québec: trois siècles d'architecture* (Montreal: Libre Expression, 1979), pp. 386-391.

[2] Project 69.0, MA; "Alterations and Additions to the Château Frontenac, Quebec, P.Q.", *Construction*, vol. 18 (August 1925), pp. 245-268; and "The Reconstructed Château Frontenac Hotel Quebec", *Contractor* (May 1924), pp. 2-13.

[3] John Bland, "Gordon MacLeod Pitts: Biography", in *Edward & W.S. Maxwell: Guide to the Archive/Guide du fonds* (Montreal: Canadian Architecture Collection, McGill University, 1986), p. 17.

[4] "Rebuilt Wing of the Château Frontenac", *Construction*, vol. 19 (July 1926), pp. 217-224.

Cat. 27d. *Staircase, Château Frontenac Hotel*

Cat. 27e. *Staircase, Château Frontenac Hotel*

20. Photographer unknown
Canadian Pacific Railway Vancouver Station and Offices
About 1900 (printed 1991)
Gelatin silver print (toned)
27.9 x 35.6
Montreal, Canadian Pacific Archives

21. Edward Maxwell
Elevation for the Canadian Pacific Railway Sicamous Junction Station and Hotel
Undated
Black and red ink on linen
30.7 x 70.4
Montreal, McGill University, Canadian Architecture Collection

22. Edward Maxwell
Elevation for the Canadian Pacific Railway Moose Jaw Station and Hotel
About 1899
Black ink on linen
28.5 x 72.5
Montreal, McGill University, Canadian Architecture Collection

23. Edward Maxwell
Elevations for the Canadian Pacific Railway Arnprior Station
About 1898
Black ink and graphite on linen
24.6 x 53.7
Montreal, McGill University, Canadian Architecture Collection

24. Edward Maxwell
Perspective for Windsor Station Addition
1899
Watercolour, gouache and graphite on wove paper
62 x 83
Delineator: W. S. Maxwell
Signed and dated lower right:
W. S. Maxwell 22-6-99
Saint-Constant, Quebec, Canadian Railroad Historical Association

25a. Edward & W.S. Maxwell
Perspective for the Canadian Pacific Railway Winnipeg Hotel and Station
1904
Watercolour, gouache and graphite on wove paper
59 x 99 (by sight)
Delineator: W. S. Maxwell
Signed and dated lower right:
W.S. Maxwell FEC 1904
Saint-Constant, Quebec, Canadian Railroad Historical Association

25b. Edward & W.S. Maxwell
Perspective for the Canadian Pacific Railway Winnipeg Station
1905
Watercolour and graphite on wove paper
41.5 x 68.5 (by sight)
Delineator: W. S. Maxwell
Signed and dated lower right:
W. S. Maxwell/1905
Saint-Constant, Quebec, Canadian Railroad Historical Association

26a. Edward & W. S. Maxwell
Perspective for the Palliser Hotel
1911
Watercolour and graphite on wove paper
76.5 x 132 (by sight)
Delineator: W. S. Maxwell
Signed and dated lower right:
W.S. Maxwell/1911
Saint-Constant, Quebec, Canadian Railroad Historical Association

26b. H. Pollard (Calgary)
Entrance hall, Palliser Hotel
Undated
Gelatin silver print
24 x 19
Montreal, McGill University, Canadian Architecture Collection

26c. H. Pollard (Calgary)
Ballroom, Palliser Hotel
Undated
Gelatin silver print
24 x 19
Montreal, McGill University, Canadian Architecture Collection

26d. H. Pollard (Calgary)
Drawing room, Palliser Hotel
Undated
Gelatin silver print
24.2 x 18.9
Montreal, McGill University, Canadian Architecture Collection

27a. Michel Bergeron
Model of the Château Frontenac Hotel
1991
Wood and plaster
99 x 114.3 x 172.7
Courtesy of Canadian Pacific Limited

27b. Edward & W.S. Maxwell and Maxwell & Pitts
Saint-Louis Street elevation for the Château Frontenac Hotel
Undated
Black ink on linen
69.5 x 91 (by sight)
Montreal, McGill University, Canadian Architecture Collection

27c. Edward & W.S. Maxwell and Maxwell & Pitts
Tower Block elevation for the Château Frontenac Hotel
1923
Black and red ink and graphite on linen
102.3 x 84
Dated lower left: *June 27. 1923*
Montreal, McGill University, Canadian Architecture Collection

27d. Photographer unknown
Staircase, Château Frontenac Hotel
1925 (printed 1991)
Gelatin silver print of half-tone reproduction
20.3 x 25.4
Montreal, McCord Museum of Canadian History, Notman Photographic Archives

27e. S. J. Hayward (Montreal)
Staircase, Château Frontenac Hotel
1925 (printed 1991)
Gelatin silver print
20.3 x 25.4
Montreal, McCord Museum
of Canadian History, Notman
Photographic Archives

27f. S. J. Hayward (Montreal)
Newel post, Château Frontenac Hotel
1925 (printed 1991)
Gelatin silver print
20.3 x 25.4
Montreal, McCord Museum
of Canadian History, Notman
Photographic Archives

27g. Photographer unknown
*Construction photograph showing
Maxwell additions to the Château
Frontenac Hotel*
January 11, 1921 (printed 1991)
Gelatin silver print
20.3 x 25.4
Montreal, McCord Museum
of Canadian History, Notman
Photographic Archives

27h. Photographer unknown
*Construction photograph showing
Maxwell additions to the Château
Frontenac Hotel*
February 22, 1921 (printed 1991)
Gelatin silver print
20.3 x 25.4
Montreal, McCord Museum
of Canadian History, Notman
Photographic Archives

27i. Photographer unknown
*Construction photograph showing
Maxwell additions to the Château
Frontenac Hotel*
April 19, 1921 (printed 1991)
Gelatin silver print
20.3 x 25.4
Montreal, McCord Museum
of Canadian History, Notman
Photographic Archives

27j. Photographer unknown
*Construction photograph showing
Maxwell additions to the Château
Frontenac Hotel*
May 10, 1921 (printed 1991)
Gelatin silver print
20.3 x 25.4
Montreal, McCord Museum
of Canadian History, Notman
Photographic Archives

27k. Photographer unknown
*Construction photograph showing
Maxwell additions to the Château
Frontenac Hotel*
July 26, 1921 (printed 1991)
Gelatin silver print
20.3 x 25.4
Montreal, McCord Museum
of Canadian History, Notman
Photographic Archives

27l. Photographer unknown
*Construction photograph showing
Maxwell additions to the Château
Frontenac Hotel*
September 30, 1921
(printed 1991)
Gelatin silver print
20.3 x 25.4
Montreal, McCord Museum
of Canadian History, Notman
Photographic Archives

27m. T. Lebel (Quebec City)
*Construction photograph showing
Tower Block addition to the Château
Frontenac Hotel*
May 25, 1923 (printed 1991)
Gelatin silver print
20.3 x 25.4
Montreal, McCord Museum
of Canadian History, Notman
Photographic Archives

27n. T. Lebel (Quebec City)
*Saint-Louis Street Wing and Tower
Block of the Château Frontenac Hotel*
July 10, 1923 (printed 1991)
Gelatin silver print
20.3 x 25.4
Montreal, McCord Museum
of Canadian History, Notman
Photographic Archives

27o. Edward & W.S. Maxwell
*Detail sketch for Jacques Cartier
Room, Château Frontenac Hotel
(white bear)*
May 6, 1922
Graphite on tracing paper
22.9 x 14.7
Montreal, McGill University,
Canadian Architecture Collection

27p. Edward & W.S. Maxwell
*Detail sketch for Jacques Cartier
Room, Château Frontenac Hotel
(hawk and shield)*
May 6, 1922
Graphite on tracing paper
19.6 x 25.4
Montreal, McGill University,
Canadian Architecture Collection

27q. Edward & W.S. Maxwell
*Detail sketch for Jacques Cartier
Room, Château Frontenac Hotel
(cock and crown)*
May 6, 1922
Graphite on tracing paper
29.3 x 16.9
Montreal, McGill University,
Canadian Architecture Collection

27r. Edward & W.S. Maxwell
*Detail sketch for Jacques Cartier
Room, Château Frontenac Hotel
(monkey, pine needles and cones)*
Undated
Graphite on tracing paper
27.1 x 16.4
Montreal, McGill University,
Canadian Architecture Collection

27s. Edward & W.S. Maxwell
*Frieze detail sketch for Frontenac
Room, Château Frontenac Hotel*
Undated
Graphite on tracing paper
22.9 x 7.6
Montreal, McGill University,
Canadian Architecture Collection

27t.   William Sutherland Maxwell
Sketch of chair from Hotel Statler,
New York
1915
Black ink on paper
20.5 x 17.1
Dated at right: *29.1.1915*
Montreal, McGill University,
Canadian Architecture
Collection

27u.   William Sutherland Maxwell
Sketch of café chair from Hotel
Gibson, Cincinnati
1915
Black ink on paper
24.1 x 15.2
Dated lower left: *29.1.1915*
Montreal, McGill University,
Canadian Architecture
Collection

27v.   William Sutherland Maxwell
Sketch of rotunda chair from Hotel
Statler, Detroit
1916
Black ink on paper
27.6 x 21.2
Inscribed and dated upper left:
Detroit 1916
Montreal, McGill University,
Canadian Architecture
Collection

27w.   Edward & W.S. Maxwell
Sketches for furniture for Jacques
Cartier Room, Château Frontenac
Hotel
1923
Black ink on linen
22 x 74
Signed and dated upper right:
W.S.M. 2 April. 1923
Montreal, McGill University,
Canadian Architecture
Collection

27x.   Maxwell & Pitts
Elevations and specifications for
sideboard and side table for the
Château Frontenac Hotel
February 4, 1925
Blueprint
33.9 x 25.4
Montreal, McGill University,
Canadian Architecture
Collection

27y.   Edward & W.S. Maxwell
Sketches of Tower Block and furniture,
Château Frontenac Hotel
Undated
Graphite on paper
15.1 x 23.4
Montreal, McGill University,
Canadian Architecture
Collection

27z.   Edward & W.S. Maxwell
Sketches for Palm Room, Château
Frontenac Hotel
Undated
Graphite on paper
15.2 x 23.5
Montreal, McGill University,
Canadian Architecture
Collection

27aa.   Edward & W.S. Maxwell
Sketches for treatment of Frontenac
Room, Château Frontenac Hotel
September 21, 1922
Graphite on tracing paper
38.4 x 36.7
Montreal, McGill University,
Canadian Architecture
Collection

27bb.   Edward & W.S. Maxwell
Sketch for pier, Château Frontenac
Hotel
Undated
Graphite on tracing paper
18 x 21.3
Montreal, McGill University,
Canadian Architecture
Collection

27cc.   Edward & W.S. Maxwell
Sketch for capital, Château Frontenac
Hotel
Undated
Graphite on tracing paper
13.5 x 10.5
Montreal, McGill University,
Canadian Architecture
Collection

27dd.   Edward & W.S. Maxwell
Sketch for capital, Château Frontenac
Hotel
Undated
Graphite on tracing paper
14.2 x 20.6
Montreal, McGill University,
Canadian Architecture
Collection

27ee.   Edward & W.S. Maxwell
Sketch for capital, Château Frontenac
Hotel
Undated
Graphite on tracing paper
23 x 11.9
Montreal, McGill University,
Canadian Architecture
Collection

27ff.   Edward & W.S. Maxwell
Sketch for capital and letter "F",
Château Frontenac Hotel
Undated
Graphite on tracing paper
29.4 x 18.6
Montreal, McGill University,
Canadian Architecture
Collection

CITY HOUSES

Important city houses figured among Edward Maxwell's earliest commissions and continued as a substantial portion of the firm's work. In the Square Mile, where Montreal's wealthy lived, the Maxwells designed more than thirty houses between 1892 – when Edward began his practice – and the onset of World War I. This prestigious quarter, bounded by Côte-des-Neiges Road, Pine Avenue, and University and Dorchester Streets, was where the two brothers eventually built houses for themselves. During this same period, the firm received commissions for more than twenty houses in the nearby suburb of Westmount, where many of the affluent built residences as the city core grew more crowded.

The Maxwells' houses ranged from grand mansions for some of Canada's richest men, such as Vincent Meredith, Edward Clouston and Charles Hosmer, to a modest semidetached pair in Westmount for the businessman George Plow. Stylistically conservative, the majority of these domestic commissions reflect clients' admiration for recently built homes of well-to-do Americans in Boston and New York.

Cat. 28b. *H. Vincent Meredith House ("Ardvarna")*

28
Edward Maxwell
H. Vincent Meredith House

1110 Pine (des Pins) Avenue West
Montreal, Que.
1894 (damaged by fire, January 7, 1990; exterior restoration, interior renovation with partial restoration of ground floor, Gersovitz Becker Moss Architects, 1991)

The H. Vincent Meredith House, on the northern edge of the Square Mile, was the first of more than fifty town and country houses Edward designed for prosperous Montrealers in the decade 1892-1902 (cat. 28b). In this picturesque red brick urban villa, he implemented current American ideas in style and planning learned during his apprenticeship in Boston.

The house, called "Ardvarna", was a gift from Andrew Allan, heir to the Allan shipping fortune, to his daughter Isobel Brenda and her husband, the financier Henry Vincent Meredith, who would succeed Sir Edward Clouston as the general manager of the Bank of Montreal in 1911 and would be honoured with a baronetcy by King George V in 1916.[1] The early progress of the project is recorded in Edward's journal where, in an entry for January 6, 1892, he noted that he had "Delivered plans to Mrs. Meredith".[2]

"Ardvarna" is magnificently sited on the steeply sloping southwest corner of Pine Avenue and Peel Street. Across the street and to the east rises "Ravenscrag", once the home of Isobel Meredith's uncle, Sir Hugh Allan. Nearby on Peel Street stood "Iononteh", her father's house, and not far away, on Stanley Street near Sherbrooke, Edward was building a house for her brother Hugh Andrew.

Although a city residence, "Ardvarna" emphasizes landscape and view, which are important aspects associated with a country house. Edward called upon the renowned landscape architects Olmsted, Olmsted & Eliot, of Brookline, Massachusetts, to develop the setting for the house. In a letter dated 1894, Edward wrote, "I have recommended one of my clients, Mr. H. V. Meredith, of Bank of Montreal, to communicate with you in regard to the laying out of his grounds ..."[3] Meredith subsequently corresponded with the firm until 1915. In the absence of extensive garden plans, a letter from Meredith provides some idea of the planting: "I have just returned to Montreal after an absence of several weeks and take the first opportunity to consult you with regard to replacing the dead shrubs and herbaceous plants at my grounds ... The terrace banks which were planted with vines ... have so far been very unsatisfactory ..."[4]

Edward intended to create a parklike setting and also carefully planned the views from within the house. The main façade faces north to Mount Royal Park (which had been designed by Frederick Law Olmsted, founder of the landscape firm) and the view from the south, or garden, front encompasses a panorama that includes the city, the Saint Lawrence River and the Green Mountains of Vermont.

The original Meredith house, as built in 1894, brought to Canada an architectural style that was popular on the American east coast in the 1880s. It is composed in the manner of a town house by H. H. Richardson. The reference here to the American architect is not surprising, since Shepley, Rutan & Coolidge, Edward's first employers, completed several houses designed by Richardson but which remained unfinished at his death and were in the office while Edward was working there.[5] Faced with red pressed brick, it is compact, boldly massed with semicircular and polygonal bays asymmetrically flanking a Romanesque porch with a segmental arch supported on robust columns and decorated with Byzantine leaf ornament.[6] The neo-Tudor chimney stacks, the most spectacularly picturesque aspect of the design, rise flamboyantly from the east and west elevations with multiple shafts and castellated chimney pots. The terra-cotta plaque below

Fig. 25. Edward Maxwell, *Detail from Trinity Church Rectory* (H. H. Richardson, architect), 1888. Montreal, McGill University, Canadian Architecture Collection.

the chimney stack on the east side clearly recalls the plaque on Richardson's Trinity Church Rectory in Boston, which Edward carefully recorded in his 1888 sketchbook (fig. 25).[7]

The *parti* is similar to that of the Oliver Ames house project, which Edward so admired that he pasted some of the Richardson floor plans in his scrapbook (fig. 26). The organizing principle of both houses is the same, the focus of each being a large central hall with the staircase located to one side and the main rooms disposed around the core (fig. 27).[8]

It was Richardson who first introduced the large living hall to America in the Codman house project between 1869 and 1871.[9] The Meredith house, like the Codman project, has a small vestibule that opens into a large hall. Each has an inglenook – a small, cozy fireplace alcove.[10]

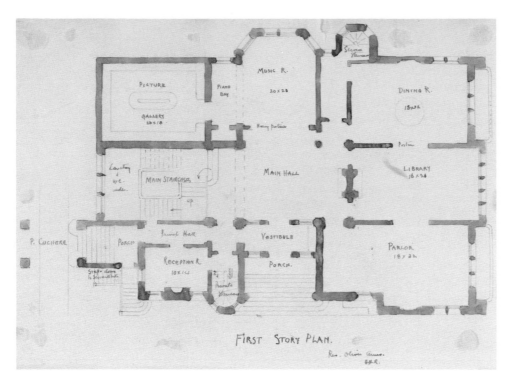

FIRST STORY PLAN.

Fig. 26. H. H. Richardson, *Ground floor plan for proposed Oliver Ames House*, 1880. Montreal, McGill University, Canadian Architecture Collection.

Precisely such spaces were described by Henry James in *The Other House*, which was published shortly after the Meredith house was built: "When Jean Martle ... was ushered into the hall ... she perceived it to be showy and indeed rather splendid. Bright, large and high, richly decorated and freely used, full of 'corners' and communications, it evidently played equally the part of a place of reunion and a place of transit."[11]

The Meredith hall is similarly large, measuring 38'10" by 11'2" (11.8 x 3.4 m) – and it is "full of 'corners' and communications". The inglenook is placed at the far right-hand side of the hall, and the grand staircase, to the right of the vestibule, spirals up through the semicircular turret to meet the landing on the first floor. The remaining rooms on the ground floor – the drawing room, the dining room and the library – open off the main hall and are oriented toward the south immediately overlooking the garden and in the distance, the river.

While the exterior details of the house are largely Romanesque and Gothic, the interior details are classical, reflecting an eclecticism typical of the time. The working drawings for the wainscotting and balusters used on the main staircase exhibit classical mouldings; details of plaster beams for both dining room and drawing room include winged cherubs. Some of the ornament was ordered from the catalogue of Elliott & Son, Toronto.

In 1914 the Maxwell brothers altered and added to the Meredith house. Three proposals were made, each incorporating an extension on the west side of the house. The second proposal was the most imaginative, including an open loggia pierced by three round-headed windows reminiscent of Venetian Gothic architecture. Ultimately the loggia was retained, but it was enclosed. Above the triple window a gabled dormer penetrates the roofline, continuing the picturesque profile of the original building. Changes included a re-disposition of the rooms: the billiard room was moved from the attic to the first floor of the new wing; the dining room was also moved to the addition.

By the time the Merediths occupied their house, an architectural revolution had begun in the midwestern United States: Frank Lloyd Wright, Edward's near contemporary, was working on the W. H. Winslow house (1893) in River Forest, Illinois. Here Wright began to alter the form of the American house, initiating a change that would not manifest itself in Canada until the eve of World War I.[12] Edward and his brother, trained in the academic manner, never introduced radical ideas into their work, but rather, together developed a conservative, traditional style.

ELLEN JAMES

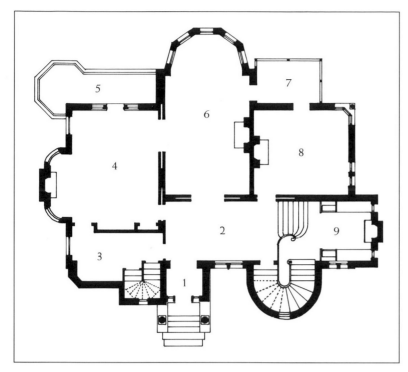

Fig. 27. *Simplified plan of ground floor of Meredith House.* 1. Vestibule 2. Hall 3. Serving pantry 4. Dining room 5. Veranda 6. Drawing room 7. Conservatory 8. Library 9. Alcove

[1] The house cost $36,862, and the architect's fee was 2 1/2 percent of the total [Commission Book C, 1892-1897], unpaginated, entry for Andrew Allan, MA, Series C. For more documentation on the house, including Lady Meredith's donation to the Royal Victoria Hospital, see Document No. 8977, September 12, 1941, MUA, RG 4 C495.

[2] "Daily Journal 1892", unpaginated, entry for January 6, 1892, MA, Series D.

[3] Letter, September 18, 1894, Olmsted Papers, Job no. 0231, Manuscript Division, Library of Congress, Washington.

[4] *Ibid.*, letter, August 27, 1896.

[5] See Mariana Griswold van Rensselaer, *Henry Hobson Richardson and His Works* (New York: Dover, 1969), reprint, pp. 104ff; and J. D. Forbes, "Shepley, Bulfinch, Richardson & Abbott, Architects: An Introduction", *Journal of the Society of Architectural Historians*, vol. 17 (Fall 1958), p. 20.

[6] The porch recalls Richardson's Adams House, Washington (1884-1886), illustrated in James O'Gorman, *H. H. Richardson and His Office: Selected Drawings* (Cambridge, Massachusetts: Department of Printing and Graphic Arts, Harvard College Library, 1974), pp. 81, fig. 8f.

[7] See O'Gorman, 1974, p. 71, fig. 5f. Trinity Church Rectory, Chimney Study, and [Sketchbook 2, 1888], unpaginated, "Trinity Parsonage", MA, Series I.

[8] See first-floor plan of Oliver Ames Project, 1880, in O'Gorman, 1974, p. 72.

[9] Vincent Scully, Jr., *The Shingle Style and the Stick Style*, revised edition (New Haven: Yale University Press, 1971), pp. 4ff.

[10] See Ann H. Schiller, "Charles F. McKim and His Francis Blake House", *Journal of the Society of Architectural Historians*, vol. 47 (March 1988), pp. 5ff, for the development of the inglenook in the work of Richard Norman Shaw.

[11] Henry James, *The Other House* (New York: Macmillan, 1896), p. 12.

[12] Francis C. Sullivan, who had worked briefly with Wright, built several houses in Ottawa reflecting the new style. See H. Allen Brooks, *The Prairie School: Frank Lloyd Wright and His Contemporaries* (Toronto: University of Toronto Press, 1972), pp. 272ff. I am indebted to David Rose, a graduate student at Concordia University, for bringing Sullivan to my attention.

Cat. 29. *Duncan McIntyre Jr.*
and Elspeth H. Angus Houses

29
Edward Maxwell
Duncan McIntyre Jr. and Elspeth H. Angus Houses

3674-3690 Peel Street
Montreal, Que.
1892-1894

The semidetached house, generally intended for the client of modest means, formed an important part of Edward's early practice. The first of his works of this type, however, is a mansionlike double house commissioned by Canadian Pacific Railway magnates Duncan McIntyre and Richard B. Angus for their respective children (cat. 29).[1]

McIntyre's son, Duncan Junior, and his wife Nellie were to live in the northern half of the pair, while Elspeth Hudson Angus and her husband Charles Meredith would occupy the southern half.

The commission initially involved Edward Seaborne Clouston, not Angus.[2] As it turned out, Clouston asked Edward to plan a freestanding house for him in 1893 (see cat. entry 32).

Edward designed a Châteauesque fortress of rough-hewn Miramichi sandstone with battered turrets and conical towers. The style was much favoured by clients associated with the CPR, and the railway adopted it for many hotels and stations across Canada.[3] Indeed Edward was working on the McIntyre-Angus houses while the American architect Bruce Price was supervising the construction of the first of the great Château-style hotels, the Château Frontenac in Quebec City.[4]

The main façade of each house is on the long side, taking advantage of the views of the river to the south and Mount Royal to the north. The façade elevations replicate each other and consist of the porch and turret balanced against a polygonal bay rising two stories and then terminating in a pinnacled gable. Medievalizing gargoyles spring from the cornice above the bay and a classicizing Palladian window lights the gable above, typical of the hybrid nature of the Château style.

The house is divided in two with the party wall marked by a large dormer let into the steeply sloping roof. The dormer, in keeping with the Château style, is decorated with elaborately carved pinnacles. The fundamental symmetry of the building is broken by the chimneys, dormers and gables that pierce the roofline and also, more subtly, by the difference in the two turrets: the polygonal south turret balancing in plan yet contrasting in elevation with the semicircular north turret.

The McIntyre-Angus houses are a reflected pair, an idea that evolved from the English terrace house and was meant to reduce costs. Edward was probably familiar with the house that Duncan McIntyre had built on Dorchester Street (now René-Lévesque Boulevard) in 1874-1875. Edward's father, E.J., was the carpentry contractor for this double mansion, which was designed by William Tutin Thomas using a mirror-image plan.[5] Edward also knew such plans firsthand from his Boston days. He included "a pair of floor plans – small Roxbury houses" in his scrapbook.[6] The floor plan is an "I"; the porch opens into a small vestibule that leads in turn to a reception hall. To the right of the hall (in the Angus half) is the drawing room, facing Peel Street. To the left of the hall, the dining room opens directly into the kitchen and pantry. The front and back stairs are arranged along the spine of the pair of houses. Access to the stairs is gained by crossing the reception hall.

Unlike many of Edward's later houses, the interiors here are dark, not only because the rooms are variously wainscotted with oak, cedar, mahogany and magnolia, but also because light is admitted only on three sides and through windows set in deep embrasures. A single skylight filled with stained glass panels filters light into the stairwell.

Two years after the McIntyre-Angus commission was completed, Edward designed two smaller and much less expensive semidetached houses using the reflected plan. Both projects are located in Westmount: one for Thomas Samuel at 35 Côte-Saint-Antoine

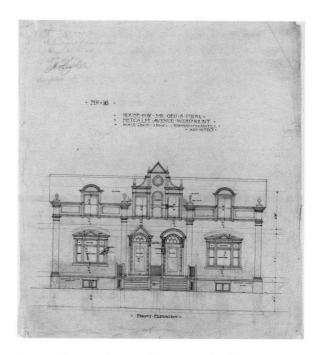

Fig. 28. Edward Maxwell, *Elevation for Plow House*, undated. Montreal, McGill University, Canadian Architecture Collection.

Road, the other for George Plow at 356 Metcalfe Avenue (fig. 28).[7] Although modest, the Samuel and Plow commissions share essential characteristics with the McIntyre-Angus houses, demonstrating Edward's ability to tailor the architectural requirements of the structure to the financial means of the client.[8]

ELLEN JAMES

1 McIntyre gave the property to his son on March 9, 1893 and Angus to his daughter on June 5, 1893. See MUA, RG 4, Folder "3660 Peel St", Declaration of Transmission of Immoveable Property No. 22922.

2 "Daily Journal 1892", entries for March 30, April 2 and 7, September 16 and 19; [Commission Book C, 1892-1897], unpaginated, entry for Duncan McIntyre, October 1892, MA, Series C; and [Scrapbook 1, 1894-1914], floor plan of semidetached residence on Peel Street with an indication of "Mr. and Mrs. Clouston's bedroom".

3 See Harold Kalman, *The Railway Hotels and the Development of the Château Style in Canada* (Victoria: University of Victoria Maltwood Museum, 1968), pp. 11ff.

4 See Russell Sturgis, "A Critique of the Works of Bruce Price", in *Great American Architects Series Nos. 1-6, May 1895-July 1899: The Architectural Record Co.* (New York: Da Capo, 1977).

5 The building is now part of the Canadian Centre for Architecture. For E. J. Maxwell's contract see ANQM, C. Cushing [notary] no. 7283, February 3, 1874.

6 [Scrapbook 2, 1889-1894], unpaginated, MA, Series F.

7 [Commission Book C, 1892-1897], unpaginated, Samuel and Plow entries, MA, Series F. Both Samuel and Plow lived elsewhere and rented out these properties.

8 Samuel's cost $11,800 and Plow's $9,000 — the masonry contract alone for the McIntyre-Angus houses was $28,246. [Tender Record Book P, 1892-1894], unpaginated, entry for April 18, 1893, J. H. Hutchison, masonry contractor, MA, Series C.

Cat. 30. *James Crathern House*

30
Edward Maxwell
James Crathern House

1572 Docteur-Penfield Avenue
Montreal, Que.
1892-1894

31
Edward Maxwell
Joseph B. Learmont House

1564 Docteur-Penfield Avenue
Montreal, Que.
1892-1894

These neighbouring houses on the western perimeter of the Square Mile built for two business associates are a pair of fraternal twins with similar plans but vastly different exteriors (cats. 30, 31). James Crathern, a founding member of Crathern & Caverhill, wholesale hardware merchants, and Joseph B. Learmont, who became a partner in the successor firm, Caverhill, Learmont & Company, called on Edward together on July 12, 1892 "and left instructions for two houses".[1]

Cat. 31. *Joseph B. Learmont House*

The plans are closely related and recall H. H. Richardson's N. L. Anderson house in Washington (1881).[2] For the ground floor plan of the Learmont house, Edward quoted the Anderson plan almost verbatim, using the stair hall as the organizing element, with the drawing room, music room, dining room and butler's pantry disposed around the core. For the Crathern house, Edward simply reversed the arrangement. At the beginning of his career Edward often borrowed a plan from Richardson's repertoire and adapted it to the particular demands of the site and the needs of the client. It is rare in Edward's work before the turn of the century not to find an asymmetrical plan using a central hall – no matter how small – as the organizing principle with the rest of the rooms opening out from it. Today, the ground floor of the Learmont house is one of the best preserved of Edward's interiors, retaining the mosaic floor of the vestibule, the golden oak woodwork in the stair hall, and the sycamore wainscotting in the drawing room, music room and dining room.

The contrasting exteriors of these houses disguise their close relationship. The distinctive character of the Crathern façade lies in the highly textured quarry-faced red sandstone, the turreted bay and the porch with its moulded semicircular arch and robust columns, whose details are reminiscent not only of H. H. Richardson's domestic architecture but also of the bold entrances of his civic and ecclesiastical buildings.[3] The Crathern house shares the stoniness, asymmetrically placed doorway and turreted bay of Richardson's

Fig. 29. Photographer unknown, *Gratwick House under construction* (H. H. Richardson, architect), about 1888. Montreal, McGill University, Canadian Architecture Collection.

Fig. 30. Brian Merrett, *Detail of entrance of Crathern House,* 1983. Montreal, Brian Merrett collection.

W. H. Gratwick house in Buffalo, New York (1888-1889), which Edward kept photographs of in his album (fig. 29).[4]

Sculptor Henry Beaumont contributed to the medieval spirit of the exterior with the carved foliate capitals and the abaci of the cloisterlike entrance (fig. 30), as well as the series of small corbels carved in bas-relief that enliven the space above the main arch and the decoration over the dormer window that frames the date of the building.

The Learmont exterior, in contrast, is far more restrained.[5] Faced with smooth grey limestone, the projecting bay is gently curved; above it is a large gabled dormer rather than a turret; the tympanum over the deeply recessed porch is decorated with ironwork (as in the Crathern house) and the sculpture is limited to classicizing bas-reliefs on the cornice, corbels and capitals.

The Crathern and Learmont houses, built not far from, but some distance below, the grand mansions designed for Meredith, Hosmer and Davis, represent the kind of sizable residences that Edward designed for clients of substantial, if not great, wealth.

ELLEN JAMES

1   See François Rémillard and Brian Merrett, *Demeures bourgeoises de Montréal : Le Mille Carré Doré 1850-1930* (Montreal: Éditions du Méridien, 1986; published in English as *Mansions of the Golden Square Mile: Montreal 1850-1930*), p. 136, where this is erroneously called Maxwell's first domestic commission. For the sequence of commissions see "Daily Journal 1892", unpaginated, entry for January 6, H. V. Meredith; March 30, Edward Clouston; July 12, J. B. Learmont and James Crathern, MA, Series D.

2   For the Anderson house plan, see Jeffrey Karl Ochsner, *H. H. Richardson: Complete Architectural Works* (Cambridge, Massachusetts: M.I.T. Press, 1982), p. 257.

3   For other Richardsonian houses of the period, see Virginia and Lee McAlester, *A Field Guide to American Houses* (New York: Knopf, 1984), pp. 301ff. The authors observe, "Because they were always of solid masonry construction ... Richardsonian Romanesque houses were much more expensive to build than were those Late Victorian styles which could be executed in wood. For this reason ... they were never common" (p. 302).

4   [Photograph Album, 1890-1900], p. 14, MA, Series A.

5   *Ibid.,* p. 15.

Cat. 32c. *Edward S. Clouston House*

32
Edward Maxwell
Edward S. Clouston House (also called "The House of the General Manager of the Bank of Montreal")
Peel Street
Montreal, Que.
1893-1894 (demolished about 1938)

The Clouston House was an elegant and efficiently planned mansion that *The Montreal Daily Star* deemed "the most elaborate ... erected in Montreal this year" (cat. 32c).[1] Financier Edward Seaborne Clouston, who was called the J. P. Morgan of Canada and who received

a baronetcy from King Edward VII in 1908, initially intended to build a semidetached house nearby with Duncan McIntyre Sr. (see cat. entry 29), but Clouston abandoned the project after he was appointed general manager of the Bank of Montreal in January 1893.[2] He

Cat. 32a. *Perspective for the Edward S. Clouston House*

asked Maxwell to design instead a freestanding residence suitable for the chief officer of a major commercial bank. It was to be located on upper Peel Street between the McIntyre-Angus site and the large James Ross house (1890-1892) by Bruce Price.

By the end of March 1893, Edward had prepared a perspective of the new residence showing the mansion of Duncan McIntyre in the background (cat. 32a).[3] Marjory Clouston, who was eleven years old and at school in Europe when proposals for the house were being studied, wrote to her father declaring, "I like the plans of our house very much, I'll stay at home ... if it is ever built."[4] The house was under construction in September; contracts amounted to $44,715.47, and the architect received two and a half percent of the total as his fee.[5]

Built of red sandstone trimmed with buff Ohio sandstone, the Clouston house was in the Château style as was the James Ross house. In the 1880s and 1890s this style, which consisted of freely combined elements of late Gothic and French Renaissance architecture found in the châteaux of the Loire Valley, was fashionable in the American northeast among wealthy clients of Price and Richard Morris Hunt, including W. K. Vanderbilt and John Jacob Astor IV.[6] Price, and the Maxwells, introduced the style to Canada in their houses and in buildings for the CPR.

The main façade of the Clouston house presented an elaborately ornamented entrance set to the right near the northern corner. The relief sculpture above the door included intertwined initials *BM* (Bank of Montreal) inscribed within a wreath supported by flanking angels. To the left and right of this central motif were two shields bearing the date *AD 1894*. Sculptor Henry Beaumont executed "all exterior stone carving in a first class and artistic manner".[7]

A turret – a prominent Château-style element – turned the south corner of the building. On the south elevation, which overlooked the city, a veranda joined the turret to a polygonal bay. These features and the rough-textured sandstone gave the structure a vigorous, picturesque character.

The three-storey residence was planned, like most grand Victorian city houses, with the servants' quarters and kitchen in the basement, formal rooms and a large hall on the ground floor, bedrooms and informal rooms for the family on the first floor, and additional bedrooms and storage space on the second floor.

The drawing room, dining room, billiard room and butler's pantry were organized around a central hall measuring 28'3" by 20'1" (8.6 x 6.1 m) which was described by *The Star* as "an imposing apartment ... finished in quartered oak with a handsomely carved stone mantel and a fine traceried window".[8] Perhaps it was in the hall, on December 27, 1895, that Clouston's daughters staged a comedy in one act, *Travellers Tell Fine Tales*, starring Marjory and Osla.[9]

Edward's detailed drawings for the ground floor include the mantel for the billiard room fireplace, which was enhanced by a splendid hood decorated with fleur-de-lys and rested on pilasters adorned with classical foliate ornament. George W. Hill produced the bas-reliefs in this room. A Renaissance overmantel for the drawing room was elaborately formal, with two niches (intended to contain classical Venuses) symmetrically arranged on either side of a mirror.

Clouston was evidently so pleased by Edward's work that in 1899 he commissioned him to make the alterations and additions to his country house, "Bois-Briant", in Senneville.

ELLEN JAMES

1. *The Montreal Daily Star*, November 3, 1894, p. 8.
2. "Daily Journal 1892", unpaginated, entries for March 30, April 2 and 7, September 16 and 19, MA, Series D; and [Commission Book C, 1892-1897], unpaginated, entry for McIntyre, October 1892, "Plans, specifications and tenders for Mr. Clouston and Duncan McIntyre, Jrs.' house. Total $40,589", MA, Series C. Deed of Sale from Duncan McIntyre, No. 5766, March 4, 1893, MUA, RG 4, C494, folder "3660 Peel Street". Land for this house was bought by the Bank of Montreal from Duncan McIntyre on March 4, 1893.
3. Project no. 74.23 [Perspective of the Edward S. Clouston House], MA.
4. Clouston Papers, N/A, "Letters to E. Clouston from daughters...", McCord Museum of Canadian History, Montreal.
5. [Commission Book C, 1892-1897], unpaginated, entry for September 7, 1893, MA, Series C.
6. Robert A. M. Stern, Gregory Gilmartin and John Massengale, *New York 1900: Metropolitan Architecture and Urbanism, 1890-1915* (New York: Rizzoli, 1983), pp. 316ff, and David Chase, "Superb Privacies: The Later Domestic Commissions of Richard Morris Hunt 1878-1895", in Susan R. Stein, ed., *The Architecture of Richard Morris Hunt* (Chicago: University of Chicago Press, 1986), pp. 151ff.
7. [Tender Record Book P, 1892-1894], unpaginated, MA, Series C.
8. *Montreal Daily Star*, November 3, 1894, p. 8.
9. Clouston Papers, N/A, invitation to Peel Street for the play, "Letters to E. Clouston from daughters...", McCord Museum of Canadian History, Montreal.

Cat. 33a. *Hugh A. Allan House*

33
Edward Maxwell
Hugh A. Allan House
3435 Stanley Street
Montreal, Que.
1894

The Hugh A. Allan House exhibits new ideas in planning, decoration and the use of materials that Edward brought from Boston to Montreal (cat. 33a). Hugh Andrew Allan, the eldest son of Andrew A. Allan and nephew of Sir Hugh Allan, commissioned Edward to design a residence on Stanley Street just above Sherbrooke, at the same time Edward was designing a house for his sister, Isobel Allan Meredith, at the corner of Pine Avenue and Peel Street (see cat. entry 28).[1] The house is an interpretation of the bowfront town house that is a distinctive feature of Boston's Back Bay.[2] The choice is not surprising since both the client and the architect lived in Boston in the late 1880s, Allan representing the family firm, the Allan Line Steamship Company Limited.[3]

The bowfront has been memorialized by Henry James, who in *The Bostonians*, published in 1885, described a "mansion which has a salient front"; and J. P. Marquand, in a novel set in the 1870s, wrote, "shortly before he purchased in Beacon Street he had been drawn, like so many others, to build one of those fine bow-front houses."[4] American critic Russell Sturgis observed in 1893 that the bowfronts "were essentially a Boston peculiarity" and rarely appeared elsewhere.[5] The picturesque character of the Allan house is enhanced by the jagged, stepped-back façade and the gable, which on the elevation drawing is flanked by pinnacles breaking the horizontality of the roofline. The smooth hemicycle of the bay projects vigorously from the wall plane, providing a foil for the polygonal oriel, which is juxtaposed to a whimsical small corner window. Into the stylistic mix Edward added Gothic ogival mullions, a crenellated parapet and Byzantine leafwork on the entrance archway.

In combining many stylistic elements, Edward illustrated critic Montgomery Schuyler's observation, quoted in the *Architectural Record* in the year the house was built, that "the repertory of the architectural forms of the past is the vocabulary of the architect."[6]

Edward chose a new and increasingly popular material, pressed brick, rejecting the traditional local grey limestone to explore the decorative potential of brick.[7] The smooth fabric of the bay contrasts dramatically with the roughness of the diapered brick of the top storey and with the basketweave pattern in the blind arcades. Three watercolour studies for the diaperwork were prepared by John Smith Archibald (1872-1934), who was apprenticing in Edward's office in May 1894 and who in 1897 established an independent architectural firm with another of Edward's draftsmen, Charles Jewett Saxe (fig. 31).[8]

Edward had more than a passing interest in the possibilities of brick. He subscribed to *Brickwork: An Illustrated Monthly Devoted to the Advancement of Brick Architecture*, a periodical first published in Boston in 1892. In the first number, which was in Edward's library, the editor declared: "Among the improvements ... which have characterized the architecture of this country during the last ten or fifteen years, perhaps none is more marked than the rapid advance that has been made in the use of brick and terra cotta. Until recently ... brick was used ... because it was cheaper than stone, and generally with little or no attempt at decorative effect."[9]

It was not only the decorative potential of brick that appealed to Edward, but also its colour. By combining brick with other materials, such as the fine cran-

Fig. 31. John S. Archibald, *Studies for diaper brickwork for Allan House*, 1894. Montreal, McGill University, Canadian Architecture Collection.

dalled sandstone used on the basement, Edward could achieve effective tonal contrasts in his architecture.

If the exterior owes much to ideas that Edward absorbed in Boston, so do the plan and the interior details. In New England, both the bowfront and the oval room were influenced by the architectural legacy of Charles Bulfinch (1763-1844), who had translated his experience of Robert Adam's London town houses into a Boston idiom.[10]

Here the bow occurs inside as a large semicircular niche in an otherwise rectangular drawing room. Continuing the theme of the oval, Edward placed a large elliptical dining room on the northeast side behind the drawing room. Clearly he liked the elegance and energy imparted by oval forms: he used them in his own house, built a little later, and in houses for other clients, including John McKergow and Charles Hosmer. The oval was particularly suitable for drawing rooms and dining rooms, especially since, in the words of an American socialite, "at parties no one likes to sit in a corner."[11]

Boldly eclectic on the exterior, the house is delicately classical on the interior. In the drawing room, for example, a broad cornice spans the opening above the juncture of the bay and the body of the room. The cornice rests on two fluted columns with composite capitals; its central panel is ornamented with a relief of garlands and urns. The classical details were ordered by catalogue from Elliott & Son, Toronto.

The dramatic stairwell with two sweeping flights to the first landing is announced by a lone, sentinel-like

Cat. 33b. *Stairhall, Hugh A. Allan House*

Ionic column (cat. 33b). A detail drawing delineates the elaborately turned newel posts and balusters arranged in groups of four, each with a different rope-like twist. In Edward's scrapbook, which in many ways served as his primer, there is a sketch of eight balusters, each with a different pattern, indicating his early interest in the smallest details of design.[12]

ELLEN JAMES

1 *Contract Record*, May 24, 1894, p. 2, notes that contracts were awarded for this house and the Meredith house.

2 The house cost $20,627. For the final account sent to Allan in July 1894 see [Commission Book C, 1892-1897], unpaginated, entry for Hugh A. Allan, MA, Series C. The architect's fee was 2 1/2 percent of the total, equalling $515.68.

3 There is a further Boston connection: in 1890 Hugh A. Allan's brother, Andrew A. Allan, commissioned the Boston firm of Rotch & Tilden to build the house just south of the site where Edward put up the house for Hugh. See *Répertoire d'architecture traditionnelle sur le territoire de la communauté urbaine de Montréal, Les résidences* (Montreal: CUM, Service de la planification du territoire, 1987), p. 16. See also Harry Katz, *A Continental Eye: The Art and Architecture of Arthur Rotch* (Boston: Boston Athenaeum, 1985). For a complete study of Back Bay architecture, see Bainbridge Bunting, *Houses of Boston's Back Bay* (Cambridge, Massachusetts: The Belknap Press of Harvard University, 1967).

4 Henry James, *The Bostonians* (New York: Penguin, 1984), p. 22, and J. P. Marquand, *The Late George Apley* (Boston: Little, Brown & Co., 1937), p. 25.

5 Russell Sturgis, *Homes in City and Country* (New York: Charles Scribners & Sons, 1893), p. 16.

6 William Jordy and Ralph Coe, eds., *American Architecture and Other Writings by Montgomery Schuyler* (Garden City, New York: Anchor Press/Doubleday, 1964), p. 73.

7 For the use of various building materials, including brick, in Montreal, see David Hanna, "Montreal, a City Built by Small Builders, 1867-1880" (Ph.D. diss., McGill University, 1986), p. 103.

8 See watercolour sketches by Archibald, initialled *J.S.A.*, dated 25.4.94 in [Scrapbook 2, 1889-1894], unpaginated, MA, Series F.

9 *The Brickbuilder*, vol. 1, no. 1 (January 1892), p. 1.

10 See William H. Pierson, Jr., *American Buildings and Their Architects: The Colonial and Neo-Classical Styles* (Garden City, New York: Anchor Press, 1976), pp. 218, 247, for more on Adamesque interiors in America. See Charles A. Place, *Charles Bulfinch, Architect and Citizen* (New York: Da Capo Press, 1988), p. 147, for a discussion of the Joseph Barrell house, which uses the bow, and Joseph and Anne Rykwert, *Robert and James Adam* (New York: Rizzoli, 1985), p. 156, for a discussion of the London town house of Sir Watkin Williams-Wynn with oval and polygonal rooms in the long, narrow format of the terrace house, and p. 169, Grosvenor House, London, for another house with a variety of room shapes.

11 Leonard K. Eaton, *Houses and Money, The Domestic Clients of Benjamin Henry Latrobe* (Dublin, New Hampshire: W.L. Bauhan, 1988), p. 26.

12 [Scrapbook 2, 1889-1894], unpaginated, MA, Series F.

Cat. 34. *Edward Maxwell House*

34
Edward Maxwell
Edward Maxwell House

184 Côte-Saint-Antoine Road
Westmount, Que.
About 1895-1896

An architect's house is an intimate revelation of his personal taste: witness Sir John Soane's house at Lincoln's Inn Fields, Frank Lloyd Wright's Taliesin East and West, and Ernest Cormier's residence in Montreal. Edward's first house combines features of a restrained Queen Anne cottage on the exterior and an exuberant, albeit scaled down, Georgian mansion on the interior (cat. 34). This stylistic pluralism permeates most of Maxwell's architecture.

Edward and his bride, Elizabeth Ellen Aitchison, moved into 184 Côte-Saint-Antoine Road shortly after their wedding on December 19, 1896. They lived there

until just after the turn of the century, when they moved to a house on Peel Street which Edward also designed.[1]

Edward's house is located on land owned by his father and is attached to his father's large Queen Anne residence. The site had originally been part of Metcalfe Terrace, the name given to four fieldstone farmhouses built in the 1840s. Two of these still stand just to the east of the Maxwell dwellings.

Facing north, Edward's house overlooks Murray Park, the former site of "West Mount", the home of William Murray. The site plan shows a narrow, irregular strip of land about ninety-six feet long on the east side, one hundred and eleven feet long on the west side and twenty feet wide across the front (29.3 x 33.8 x 6 m). Positioned obliquely the house is set well back from the street. It is red brick to match Edward's father's, however, the exterior is a simplified version of the Queen Anne style, which appears full-blown in his father's house.[2] Edward suppressed the exterior decorative elements on his house to permit the elaborately carved woodwork on the façade of his father's to stand out, appropriately announcing the lumber contractor's residence.[3] He limited the details to a few Queen Anne elements: a shaped gable dormer framing a Palladian window, a polygonal bay, Gothic mullions in the windows on the first floor and a shell niche over the front door.

The interior is another matter altogether. Here no deference was paid to his father's house; the young Edward gave free reign to his own taste. Many of the planning ideas incorporated here are reflected in his city-house commissions, including the combination of a variety of room shapes (not for the most part revealed on the exteriors) and a concern for brightening the interiors with skylights and well-lit stair landings.

The ground floor contains only two rooms disposed around a central hall. The dining room faces south and takes up the full width of the back of the house. Two steps lead down into the dining room from the hall, responding to the slope of the site. To the left, or east, of the hall is the staircase, the landing lit by a Palladian window on the east elevation.

The oval drawing room, an unexpected element, is discreetly set into the slightly projecting polygonal bay to the left of the entrance. Edward's interest in both the oval and the polygonal room, which lend an element of surprise and variety, was stimulated by town houses he saw while he worked in Boston. The remaining rooms are unexceptional.

The lush classical decoration of the interior conveys Edward's love of Greco-Roman forms, which he derived from both his training in Boston and his travels. The dining room cornice is enlivened by cherubs and the drawing room cornice is animated with a narrow egg-and-dart moulding resting on a wide band of alternating shells and swags. The overmantel of the dining room fireplace is supported by draped caryatids. Framed between these two figures is a plaster bas-relief with two putti, one holding a scroll, the other a lyre. The work was executed by the sculptor George W. Hill.

The architect left a more intimate portrait of himself in the extensive inventory of the contents of each room, and in a precise accounting of the costs. His itemized records show that he paid O. Deguise $675 for the brickwork; E.C. Mount & Co., $870 for plumb-

ing and heating; J. McLean $371 for plastering; Phaneuf $1,578.89 for carpentry; Hill $50 for the dining room fireplace; and Castle & Son $383.69 for painting.[4]

These prices become significant relative to the cost of other merchandise in the 1890s; Edward's daily journals show for instance that a corn plaster cost 15 cents; a hair cut, 20 cents; a suit, $25.65; a ticket to hear Paderewski play the piano, $1.50; and a turkey, $1.50.[5]

The list of objets d'art and household goods runs to twelve pages and discloses another aspect of Edward's personality: the collector. He surrounded himself with paintings, Oriental rugs, vases and plaster casts.[6] His art collection included paintings attributed to Sir Thomas Lawrence, Rubens, Jan Brueghel and Velázquez. In the hall Maxwell hung a print of one of his favourite buildings by Richardson – the Allegheny County Court House – as well as an engraving of the Roman Forum, two photographs of a Venus by Titian, an anonymous oil painting of York Cathedral and six of his own European sketches.

The drawing room and dining room were equally full of treasures, including watercolours of Saint Mark's and the Ducal Palace in Venice and the Roman ruins at Tivoli, an ivory miniature, two Pompeian bronze lamps, and four Chippendale chairs. In addition to an inventory of furniture and art, he also recorded the total cost of the books he owned – $2,054.40 – although he did not make a detailed list of his library until 1901.

Edward's first house reveals a cosmopolitan young man – artistic, literate and well travelled – whose eclectic taste was shaped by his apprenticeship in Boston and his voyages in Europe and the United States. All of this profoundly influenced his architectural design.

ELLEN JAMES

1   The exact date of the house on Côte-Saint-Antoine Road is difficult to determine, but there is a photograph of it dated about 1895-1896. [Photograph Album, 1890-1900], p. 41, "Cote St. Antoine Road, Montreal", MA, Series A.

2   The Queen Anne style has been well described by Mark Girouard in *Sweetness and Light: The Queen Anne Movement, 1860-1900* (Oxford: Clarendon Press, 1977), p. 1. See also Montgomery Schuyler, "Concerning Queen Anne", in W. H. Jordy and Ralph Coe, eds., *American Architecture and Other Writings by Montgomery Schuyler* (Garden City, New York: Anchor Press/ Doubleday, 1964), pp. 227-228.

3   The architect and date of the house are unknown. Edward made a painting of it dated 8/9/88 in which the picturesque aspects are emphasized. Watercolour roundel signed *E. Maxwell*, private collection, Montreal.

4   Maxwell notebooks, unpaginated, private collection, Montreal.

5   "Daily Journal 1892", unpaginated, "Cash Account", MA, Series D.

6   In 1948 when Maxwell's estate was appraised by Fraser Brothers, the paintings were largely listed as "attributed to". See Household Inventory, unpaginated, private collection, Montreal. However, Maxwell did own an authenticated painting by Pieter Brueghel the Younger, *Expulsion from the Inn* (about 1620). This was presented to the Montreal Museum of Fine Arts in 1955 by the Maxwell family in memory of Edward's wife (inv. 955.1122).

Fig. 32. Brian Merrett, *Main elevation of Hosmer House*, 1990. Montreal, The Montreal Museum of Fine Arts.

35
Edward Maxwell
Charles R. Hosmer House
3630 Drummond Street
Montreal, Que.
1901-1902

The Hosmer House (fig. 32), the most flamboyant of the Maxwells' grand city mansions, was designed for a former telegrapher, who by the age of thirty-five had become manager of the CPR's vast telegraph system. The site of the house, on the flank of Mount Royal, consisted of two parcels of land purchased by Charles Rudolph Hosmer in September 1899 and December 1900, augmented in 1909 by land purchased from the J. T. Davis family, neighbours to the north.[1] Maxwell office records show that preliminary studies for the house were accepted on March 3, 1900.[2] *Canadian Contract Record* for January 16, 1901, notes the granting of a building permit for the house.[3] In June 1902 carpets were being fitted, indicating that the building was nearing completion.[4]

Constructed of conspicuous red sandstone from the Moat Quarry near Galashiels, Scotland,[5] the house comprises three storeys – the third treated as an attic – and a basement. The main elevation, facing east toward Drummond Street, is three bays wide with a slightly projecting centre, the doorway sheltered by a columned and balustraded one-storey porch. The flanking windows are crowned by over-scaled triangular pediments embellished with cartouches and scrolls, and supported on consoles. The windows of the floor above have simpler rectangular surrounds decorated with scrolled keystone blocks. The attic storey is demarcated by a heavy cornice and balustrade, and is covered by a mansard roof. Here the windows are set in dormers featuring top-heavy segmental pediments,

Fig. 33. Brian Merrett, *North elevation of Hosmer House,* 1990. Montreal, The Montreal Museum of Fine Arts.

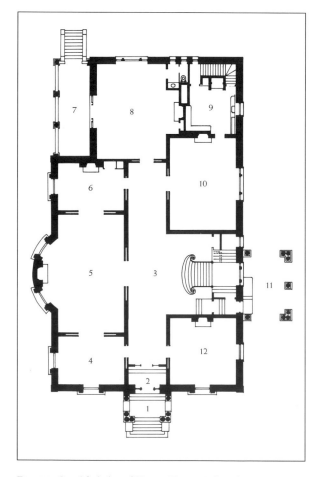

Fig. 34. *Simplified plan of Hosmer House.* 1. Porch 2. Vestibule 3. Hall 4. Reception room 5. Drawing room 6. Breakfast room 7. Veranda 8. Billiard room 9. Pantry 10. Dining room 11. Porte cochere 12. Library

which also rest on consoles and are ornamented with cartouches in their centres. The pediment that crowns the projection of the main elevation is larger than the rest and is set above an oeil-de-boeuf window, its surround a richly carved garland.

The south elevation, which overlooks downtown Montreal, is six bays wide, the centre breaking forward to form the elliptical bay of the drawing room. A recessed wing at the rear, accommodating a billiard room and pantry on the ground floor, has a veranda attached to its south face. The northern front, which faces up the mountain, is distinguished by a porte cochere, so that the house has, in effect, two formal, ceremonial entrances, a feature dictated by Montreal's harsh winter climate. The masonry treatment consists of a rusticated basement, heavy quoins at the four corners and smooth ashlar walls, setting off the lush, neo-Baroque carved ornament on the window heads, doorways and at cornice level. An exterior detail drawing contains the notation: "All carving to be modelled by Geo. W. Hill". That the ornament was intended solely to impress is evidenced by the fact that it was omitted on the north and west façades, which are not visible from the street (fig. 33).

The extravagant exterior ornament and the dual entrances hint at the arrangement of the interior, which was planned as a setting for grand social occasions (fig. 34). At the core of the ground floor is a long, spacious hall, which forms a main central axis extending west from the front door on Drummond Street and off which open the formal rooms. Located on a secondary axis are the porte cochere entrance, the main interior staircase and the drawing room, the doorway of which faces the stairs. The staircase divides at a landing lit by a window looking out over the porte cochere and then doubles back to reach the upper hall. The only ground floor room not entered from the main hall is the dining room pantry. It was furnished with a lift and dumbwaiter, since the kitchen, servants' hall and two servants' bedrooms were in the basement.

Because only working drawings for the house survive, it is difficult to determine how this luxuriously detailed, very French design developed. Although Edward Maxwell was associated with George Cutler Shattuck while the house was under way, most of the drawings are inscribed *Edward Maxwell, Architect, Montreal,* and only a few *Maxwell & Shattuck.* Two important Montreal commissions designed in 1898 in a similarly French manner predate the Shattuck partnership: the London & Lancashire Life Assurance Company, on which William worked as a draftsman, and the house for J. H. Birks.

It would seem that William collaborated to some extent with his brother, although he did not become a partner until 1902. An undated, unsigned, handwritten manuscript entitled "Notes on the Architecture and Decoration of the Residence of Mr. C. R. Hosmer, 302 Drummond St., Montreal", survives among Hosmer family records, and was likely provided by the Maxwell firm or written with the assistance of someone in the firm. The notes, describing the exterior of the house as a "free interpretation of Modern French Renaissance", record that "the designs after completion were submitted to M. Pascal, the eminent French Architect and Professeur at L'École des Beaux-Arts, Paris, whose criticism was of a very favorable nature". William, of course, went to Paris in the fall of 1899, entering Pascal's atelier, where he remained during the following year. Pascal had worked for three years for Charles Garnier on the Paris Opera (1862-1875), and there is something of the overblown Baroque scale and grandeur and the axial, ceremonial planning of this Second Empire showpiece in the Hosmer house. Edward, too, visited Paris; there is a ledger entry showing an account rendered to Hosmer in December 1901 in connection with Edward's expenses in New York, Paris, London and Toronto, where he would have been purchasing items for the house.[6] Further evidence of William's collaboration appears in an article on the house published in *Construction* in August 1911, which consistently attributes the design to "Messrs. E. & W. S. Maxwell".[7] From the time he returned from Paris in December 1900, and throughout 1901, William worked primarily on the Hosmer drawings.[8]

Domestic Modern French – the style used by Edward Maxwell's firm for the Hosmer house and more moderately for the earlier J. H. Birks house – had already been introduced in New York's "Billionaire District" by Carrère & Hastings early in the 1890s. In the hands of skilled graduates of the École des Beaux-Arts, writes Robert Stern, Modern French "combined the authority of historical example with a sense of modernity." As the style evolved, however, it exhibited two main tendencies, one relatively restrained, the other (called "Beaux-Arts Baroque" by Stern) so overwrought that it was referred to derisively in *The Architectural Review* as "Cartouche Architecture".[9] The cartouche-and-garland-laden Hosmer house clearly falls within the latter category, although as is typical of Canadian work generally, it is more modest in size and less excessively ornamented than its American counterparts. Still, it is the most brazenly ostentatious of all the self-made millionaires' homes that once abounded in Montreal's "Square Mile".

If the exterior of Charles Hosmer's house served as a highly visible statement of the client's new wealth, the interior did so to an even greater degree. The rooms on the ground floor, created for show and lavish entertaining, were a highly eclectic group – each very loosely based on a different historical period and furnished with a mixture of antiques, period reproductions and pieces designed by the architects. In addition to the handwritten notes and the article in *Construction*, an article by Evan Turner, a former director of the Montreal Museum of Fine Arts, written before the house's contents were dispersed, contains detailed descriptions of the extravagant main rooms and furnishings.[10]

Entering from Drummond Street, the visitor would have been shown into a reception room (cat. 35h) located to the left of the front door and from which the drawing room could be entered. Decorated in a French Rococo manner, this opulent little chamber had walls hung in green silk and furniture covered in Gobelins tapestry. It is distinguished by its intricate carved decoration and the most elaborate ceiling in the house – bedecked with profuse plasterwork and a ceiling panel and roundels painted by Frederick W. Hutchison (1871-1953). Like William Maxwell, the young painter had only just returned from a sojourn in Paris, where he studied at the Académie Julian.

The reception room and the much larger but slightly more restrained drawing room were treated as an ensemble, the "graceful but effeminate elegance of the days of Louis XVI" of the reception room "gradually blending" into the "really Royal manner of the 'Regence' and of the early Louis XV" of the drawing room. In the latter chamber the furniture was Louis XV in period, and the walls were covered in rose silk. The design and colouring of the woven Savonnerie carpets were chosen after the wall coverings had been selected, the colour scheme being inspired by the pièce de résistance of the room, a portrait of a pink-robed figure by Sir Joshua Reynolds, painter of the English aristocracy. This was placed strategically over the fireplace facing the door to the hall, in a frame designed by the architects.

Set in a wholly different key, the great hallway, too, was a place of parade, where fashionably dressed guests could "make entrances" and "progress" from drawing room to dining room and thereafter to the library or billiard room. The decor was intended as "a blending from the restrained Renaissance of the exterior, to the more florid and free type of the main staircase reminiscent of the period prevalent in 1600-1620, but broadly treated in a modern spirit. The wood work is of quarter-cut American white oak deepened in tone. The ceiling beams are bound with straps of hand-forged iron in a half-polished finish. A feature in the staircase worthy of study is the antique Dutch stained glass, which is fine in quality, some of it exquisite. The subjects in this window are mostly Biblical."[11] The hall's dark tones were offset by the old Flemish tapestries in a red and green woolen weave which hung on the walls.

Another extraordinary room is the library, located to the right of the front door. Here the ornament is

Cat. 35h. *Reception room, Charles R. Hosmer House*

heavy and masculine and so profuse that it overwhelms the modestly sized room that contains it. The intent was "to recall the Italian Renaissance during its richest and most highly decorated period of the 16th century".[12] Rich, dark tones predominate, the fireplace being made of Connemara green marble, with rosewood used for elaborately carved door and window surrounds, chimneypiece, frieze, and sumptuous ribbed and panelled ceiling. The walls are covered with a silk and velvet fabric consisting of a wine-red figure on a dull gold ground reproduced from one of the Renaissance period.

The dining room was given a French Gothic flavour. A powerful chimneypiece of Ohio sandstone, embellished with allegorical figures in the style of the thirteenth century (cat. 35c), dominates the room, which also features a carved mahogany wainscot, a beamed-and-plaster panelled ceiling, and walls covered with a blue hand-woven tapestry by William Morris. The furniture was designed by the architects as an inte-

gral part of the scheme. "The andirons were executed in the City, and have the medieval flavor pure and simple, while the fire tools are by one of the best English Crafts men."[13] The rug was antique Persian.

While the treatment of the breakfast room and billiard room "were unfettered by the restrictions and limitations of any set style", their materials and furnishings were nevertheless lavish, with tiger wood used for the breakfast room panelling and quarter-cut English oak for the billiard room. These two rooms, in particular, set off the work of contemporary craftsmen and designers.

Although different historical periods provided themes for most of the aforementioned rooms, historical accuracy was not a concern: it was the overall impression that counted. A dominant feature of the drawing room, for example, is the electric lighting arrangement in the ceiling, which, to modern eyes would seem more suitable in a turn-of-the-century ocean liner.

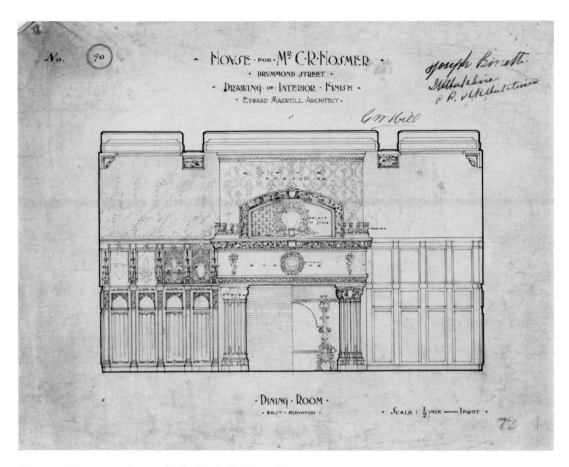

Cat. 35c. *Dining room elevation for the Charles R. Hosmer House*

Six family bedrooms are situated on the floor above. Two, with southern exposures, were arranged as a suite for Mr. and Mrs. Hosmer. There are also three bathrooms and a sewing room on this level. The attic contains ten other bedrooms, two bathrooms and a storage area.

SUSAN WAGG

1 Property records, including deeds of sale, relating to the Hosmer house are preserved in the MUA.

2 [Commission Book G, 1899-1903], p. 29, and [Commission Book D, 1900-1904], p. 24, MA, Series C. An entry for July 1900 records the cost of the house according to the contracts as $67,594, and of the stable as $1,689.86, with the architect's fee being 2 1/2 percent of the total.

3 *Canadian Contract Record*, vol. 12 (January 16, 1901), p. 3.

4 [Work Costs Book F, 1899-1904], p. 43, MA, Series C.

5 "Notes on the Architecture and Decoration of the Residence of Mr. C. R. Hosmer, 302 Drummond St., Montreal". Undated, unsigned manuscript from the files of Murray Vaughan, transcribed by Georgina Lucas (in the author's possession).

6 [Commission Book D, 1900-1904], p. 78, MA, Series C.

7 "A Montreal Residence in Renaissance Design by E. & W. S. Maxwell", *Construction*, vol. 4 (August 1911), pp. 49-55.

8 [Draftsmen's Hours per Client Book K, 1894-1901], pp. 177ff, MA, Series C.

9 Robert A. M. Stern, Gregory Gilmartin and John Massengale, *New York 1900: Metropolitan Architecture and Urbanism, 1890-1915* (New York: Rizzoli, 1983), p. 329.

10 Evan H. Turner, "Living with Antiques: The Hosmer House in Montreal", *Antiques*, vol. 92 (July 1967), pp. 91-93. There are entries in the Maxwell office record books that name many of the suppliers and craftsmen.

11 "Notes...", pp. 1-2. The antique stained glass, now removed for safe-keeping, has been discussed in an article in *Montreal Scene* (February 25, 1978), pp. 5-6, 31. An entry in the Maxwell office work cost book records the purchase in August 1900 of "antique stained glass" from M. Van Straaten.

12 "Notes..." and the *Construction* article disagree as to the style of the library, the former referring to it as Italian Renaissance, the latter as French Renaissance.

13 "Notes...", p. 5.

Cat. 36a. *Richard R. Mitchell House*

36
Edward & W.S. Maxwell
Richard R. Mitchell House

4103 Sherbrooke Street
Westmount, Que.
1907-1908

The Richard R. Mitchell House is a striking town house, unusual for its reliance on New York sources and the unexpected effects in the interior. The unfamiliar composition of its façade immediately attracts attention, with its large central bay window resting on columns to form a porch over the entrance door (cat. 36a). It was rare in Montreal to place a front door directly at ground level, without a flight of steps leading to it. This arrangement, recently referred to as the "American basement plan",[1] was the latest fashion in turn-of-the-century New York town houses. They had no front stoop, and the receiving rooms were located on the upper floor.

The Mitchell residence shows a balanced composition, divided in three horizontally by the floors and vertically by the windows. The architects took care to achieve these and other subtle visual effects. The smooth cut stone is coursed in such a way that each

Cat. 36c. *Staircase, Richard R. Mitchell House*

level of the façade has its own pattern. The decorative carved stone cartouches, the finials and the undulating frame of the window – a delightful Art nouveau touch – counter the predominant straight lines and flat planes.

The skill at creating arresting visual effects is carried through to the interior of the house, with the ascent from the entrance door to the main reception room intended to create an impression of ceremony. Upon entering, the visitor passed from the vestibule into a spacious chestnut-panelled hall (painted over in the 1950s). Servants' quarters and, at the back the kitchen, occupied this floor, where the visitor merely left his coat before proceeding up the prominent staircase at the far end. On the way up, a mural painting could be seen reflected in the mirrored panels of a false door on the first landing (cat. 36c). On the way down the

stairs, the mural, artificially lit, could be viewed directly (cat. 36b). It was set into a semicircular panel in the arch of the stairway ceiling. True to the Arts and Crafts ideal, it was physically integrated into the architecture of the building. The painting, commissioned from the Maxwells' friend Maurice Cullen,[2] depicts a landscape with sheep grazing beside a stream.

Other features also reflect the Maxwells' and the Mitchell family's interest in Arts and Crafts design, among them the stained glass in many window transoms, the handsome vestibule door,[3] the handwrought metalwork in lighting fixtures and a hand-hammered copper fireplace hood.

One floor above the ground level, the staircase separates the large, well-proportioned living room across the front from the dining room at the back. The understated newel posts and flat, tapered balusters with

Cat. 36b. *Mural by Maurice Cullen, Richard R. Mitchell House*

pierced decoration – devoid of abundantly carved decoration – emphasize simplicity and fine craftsmanship. Similar treatment may be found in many of the Maxwells' summer houses, which also display Arts-and-Crafts-inspired design.[4]

An interest in British craftsmanship had been a tradition at Robert Mitchell & Company, founded in 1851 by Richard Mitchell's father, which specialized in wrought iron and brass metalwork.[5] The younger Mitchell took over the company when his father died in 1897. He bought the Sherbrooke Street property in 1907, and the house remained in the Mitchell family until 1978.[6] The relation between client and architect must have been good, for afterwards the Mitchell company supplied electrical fixtures and other metalwork for many Maxwell clients.

ROSALIND M. PEPALL

1 Robert A. M. Stern, Gregory Gilmartin and John Massengale, *New York 1900: Metropolitan Architecture and Urbanism, 1890-1915* (New York: Rizzoli, 1983), p. 348.

2 According to the Maxwells' [Work Costs Book], M. Maurice Cullen was paid $80 for this mural decoration on October 8, 1908. The mural was removed in the 1980s.

3 The leaded glass of the vestibule door and sidelights was by G. and J. E. Grimson, as was the "upper hall window" ([Work Costs Book M], p. 299, MA, Series C).

4 See, for example, the interior of the Charles Hosmer summer residence in Saint Andrews, New Brunswick, in France Gagnon Pratte, *Country Houses of Montrealers, 1892-1924: The Architecture of E. and W. S. Maxwell* (Montreal: Meridian Press, 1987), pp. 160-161.

5 "The Late Mr. Robert Mitchell", *CAB*, vol. 10 (October 1897), p. 195, and "Notes", *JRAIC*, vol. 3 (January-February 1926), p. 44.

6 The title deeds to the property state that Richard R. Mitchell bought the land from James Robinson on January 21, 1907. I am grateful to Mr. and Mrs. Edward W. Wilson for showing me these deeds.

Fig. 35. W. S. Maxwell,
Proposal for J.K.L. Ross House,
1903. Montreal, McGill
University, Canadian
Architecture Collection.

37
Edward & W.S. Maxwell
J.K.L. Ross House

3647 Peel Street
Montreal, Que.
1908-1909

The J.K.L. Ross House is an important Montreal example of the Edwardian Baroque manner that flourished briefly in the urban centres of Canada before the outbreak of World War I. John Kenneth Leveson Ross must have been one of the Maxwells' more exasperating clients. The earliest of five different schemes for Ross's house that survive is dated 1903; yet constuction was not undertaken until 1908. Unlike many of the firm's clients, Ross was not a self-made millionaire, but the son and heir of one. His father, James Ross, was the contractor who, in 1883, had taken control of construction of the CPR west of Winnipeg, completing the line through the Rocky Mountains, the Selkirks and the Gold Range. The younger Ross, born in 1876, had lived with his parents in a railway car while the line was being constructed. In 1902, the year of young "Jack" Ross's marriage, the father purchased land on the east side of Peel Street opposite his own imposing Château-style house (1890-1892), designed by New York architect Bruce Price, who was the designer of the CPR's

Château Frontenac.[1] Office records reveal that Edward Maxwell had been instructed to go to New York in 1898 to consult with Price about alterations Edward's firm carried out to the elder Ross's house,[2] and it is therefore not surprising that Edward & W.S. Maxwell received the commission for the son's house, since Price died in 1903.

The earliest sketch for the house, an exterior perspective signed and dated *W.S.M. 1903* (fig. 35), indicates that the Maxwell brothers initially attempted to please the senior Ross, whose gift the house was.[3] Replete with turrets and dormers, the exterior is not unlike James Ross's house in composition and massing, although it has a marked curvilinear Art nouveau quality, suggesting that the Maxwells were simply updating a successful formula. The house that was finally built, however, is quite different. While the subsequent sketch plans are undated, it is possible to follow the evolution of the design as first the disposition of the main elevation and then the interior plans became

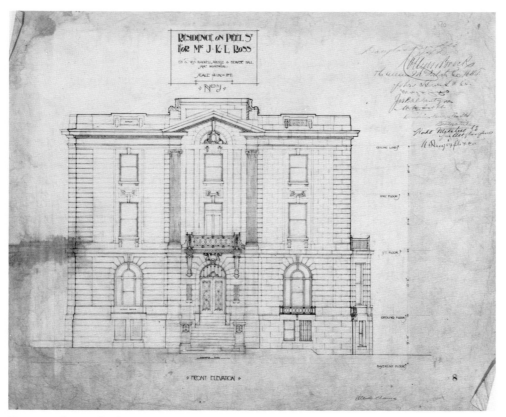

Cat. 37a. *Elevation for the J.K.L. Ross House*

Fig. 36. Photographer unknown, *End pavilion of Saskatchewan Legislative Building*, undated. Montreal, McGill University, Canadian Architecture Collection.

more orderly. The executed façade (cat. 37a), unlike that shown in the early sketch, is a perfectly symmetrical exercise in Edwardian Baroque classicism. It closely resembles the scheme used by the Maxwells for the splendid neo-Baroque end pavilions that terminate the long east/west axis of their Saskatchewan Legislative Building in Regina, designed in 1907 (fig. 36). Although it is not known exactly when the final version of the house façade was conceived, a cross section of the steel frame, provided by the Dominion Bridge Company, survives and is dated June 4, 1908.[4] It seems likely that the larger Regina scheme preceded the Montreal project.

In essence the main front (cat. 37b) of the J.K.L. Ross house is a chastened, more delicate version of the end pavilions at Regina, with their boldly projecting centre embellished with a colossal order comprising a broken pediment supported by paired Doric columns. The house has a shallower pediment resting on single fluted Ionic pilasters to frame a barely projecting central bay. In both designs there is a balcony supported by ornate consoles at the base of the order. In the house, lacy wrought iron, rather than heavy stone, is used for the balcony. There are fewer bays in the house – three instead of seven – and the fenestration and masonry are

Cat. 37b. *J.K.L. Ross House*

treated somewhat differently; still the correspondence between these two diversely functioning but contemporaneous elevations is striking. One can almost hear the Maxwells breathing a sigh of relief when they finally hit upon a formula grand enough to please J.K.L. Ross, who lived so lavishly that he went bankrupt in 1926.

The composition of the façade is ultimately Palladian in its derivation, consisting of a high basement and rusticated ground floor, above which are two floors, whose windows grow smaller and less elaborate as they ascend. The elevation is terminated by an emphatic cornice, with a parapet masking the roof and a projection rising above the pediment to give even greater importance to the centre. The house is faced with a buff limestone, which is rusticated on the ground floor and quoins, but treated as smooth ashlar on the upper two storeys. On the north and east elevations, which are not visible from the street, the detailing is reduced or eliminated altogether (fig. 37), and the east or rear façade is constructed of economical yellow brick.

The ground floor plan of the J.K.L. Ross house consists of a central axis composed of entrance vestibule, hall and breakfast room, and a secondary axis created by the main stair, which rises off the north side

Fig. 37. Brian Merrett, *North elevation of J.K.L. Ross House*, 1991. Montreal, The Montreal Museum of Fine Arts.

Cat. 37c. *Drawing room, J.K.L. Ross House*

of the hall near its centre. The device of placing the stairway to the side recalls the Hosmer house plan, although the J.K.L. Ross stair does not divide into two flights. Despite Ross's celebrated extravagance, the interior of his house (cat. 37c) is far more restrained than that of the parvenu Hosmer, although an early set of plans included a squash court on the top floor. (This client was a dedicated athlete.) The Ross house contains neither the extreme opulence nor the amazing variety of period decor that is so striking in the Hosmer house.

The hall features chamfered corners, warm-toned classical panelling, a welcoming fireplace and fluted pilasters, in the severe Tuscan order, that echo the pilasters of the façade. The soaring staircase in white marble has a handrail of oak, and supports and newel in cast iron, the newel fluted with a knob ending in a serpentine female form. The dining room, subdued and wood-panelled, accords nicely with the hall, while the

drawing room has a refined, feminine character, with an exquisite plaster ceiling and an elegant fireplace framed by fluted pilasters. J.K.L. Ross's daughter recalled that this gracious room was painted in the palest of pale greens[5]. The other notable room on the ground floor is the delightful little breakfast room at the centre rear, which has its own fireplace backing on to that of the hall. Placed to catch the morning sun, it has a bay window set within an arched semi-elliptical recess and a barrel-vaulted ceiling decorated with floral bands of plasterwork. Also striking is the front door's splendid bronze grille, executed by the firm of Hutchison & Sticht.

The house provides a highly unusual and original rendering of the Edwardian Baroque style. Whereas English, French and American architects could look to their past for native examples upon which to base a contemporary domestic Baroque, English Canada had no such tradition. The Anglophile Ross, who raced with the exclusive Royal Yacht Squadron at Cowes, England, might have been expected to favour a more derivatively English design. His architects were not so familiar (or so comfortable) with English examples as they were with American and French, but complied by giving the façade a firm Palladian basis and using features reworked from their competition-winning Saskatchewan Legislative Building, of which they must have been exceedingly proud. The translation from the public to the private realm is not entirely successful, however. The proportions of the façade are somewhat clumsy; the main elevation has an uncomfortably compressed look. It is not altogether surprising that when J.K.L. Ross inherited his father's larger house in 1913, he chose to live in it and sell his Maxwell-designed one.

Susan Wagg

1 Deeds relating to the J.K.L. Ross property, which has belonged to McGill University since 1976, are in the MUA.

2 [Commission Book I, 1895-1899], p. 101, MA, Series C.

3 Although initially in the original roll of drawings for the house, which came to McGill in 1954, this sketch was subsequently affixed in [Scrapbook I, 1894-1914], p. 110, MA, Series F.

4 Copy of plan of structural steel given to author by MacKenzie McMurray, Chairman of the Board, Dominion Bridge Company Limited, April 7, 1976. The Dominion Bridge Company, Inc., founded in 1883, supplied bridges for the CPR. James Ross, who had a controlling interest in the company, had been elected president in 1890, and in 1907 J.K.L. Ross was elected a director.

5 Mrs. Duncan Hodgson, interview by the author, 1976.

Cat. 38. *William S. Maxwell and Edward M. Renouf Houses*

38
Edward & W.S. Maxwell
William S. Maxwell and Edward
M. Renouf Houses
1548-1550 Pine (des Pins) Avenue West
Montreal, Que.
1909-1911

William Maxwell, like his brother, built a residence for himself in the Square Mile (cat. 38). It is one-half of an unassuming semidetached brick house on a choice site on Pine Avenue. His neighbour was Lieutenant-Colonel Edward M. Renouf, who ran a publishing business.[1]

The two houses are brought together under a rectangular, steep-pitched, slate hipped roof. One is virtually a mirror image of the other, the division marked simply by a downspout. The most striking feature of the two houses is the yellow brick walls, in colours varying from a light beige to a dark scorched orange laid out in a distinctive chequerboard pattern that contrasts with the smooth sandstone dressings. This decorative brickwork appears to have been a unique and personal experiment by William.

The front elevations differ slightly in certain details, such as the entrance doors, and the Maxwell façade (at the left) has fewer windows to correspond to the plan; this gives the full effect of the chequered wall pattern. The plans and rear elevations of the two houses have likewise been adapted to suit the different requirements of the occupants.

Although William's four-bedroom house is compact, the rooms on the main floor are spacious. The large formal living room and connecting dining room are laid out across the back and originally had a superb view of the city.[2] The room that provided the focus of William's activities was the library. It lies to the right of the entrance hall, behind the projecting bay. A cosy room and one of the most appealing in the house, it retains some of the original furniture, ornaments and fittings. William's daughter, Mary Maxwell Rabbani, recalls that her father frequently spent his evenings in the library working on his designs or clipping articles from magazines.[3] The high wood panelling of the library walls and the leaded window panes inset with antique European stained glass panels contribute to its warmth and charm. Another notable feature of the room is the prominent mantelpiece of hand-carved animal and plant forms in dark wood which contrasts with the smooth grey of the English marble fireplace surround, with just a touch of carved ornament (fig. 38).[4] The mural that was planned for above the mantelpiece was not executed. But in the living room, an Impressionist-inspired mural painting by French artist Henri Martin (1860-1943) was incorporated into a panel over the mantelpiece.[5] William also worked in a studio on the third floor, which had a skylight facing east and ample built-in drawer space.

William and his family moved from Westmount to Pine Avenue about 1911. They were members of the Bahá'í Faith, and the house has since become a national Bahá'í shrine because of the several days spent there in 1912 by 'Abdu'l-Bahá, son of the Bahá'í Faith's Founder.

Rosalind M. Pepall

Fig. 38. Brian Merrett, *Library fireplace in William S. Maxwell House*, 1991. Montreal, The Montreal Museum of Fine Arts.

---

1 Henry James Morgan, *Canadian Men and Women of the Time* (Toronto: W. Briggs, 1912), p. 936.

2 A modern high-rise apartment building on Docteur-Penfield Avenue now blocks the city view that William enjoyed.

3 Interview with Mary Maxwell Rabbani by France Gagnon Pratte and the author, Haifa, April 1, 1989. W. S. Maxwell kept meticulously catalogued files of clippings and articles on many aspects of decorative design. These files have been given to the Maltwood Art Museum and Gallery, University of Victoria, Victoria, B.C. by Mary Rabbani.

4 [Work Costs Book M, 1904-1914], p. 427, MA, Series C, records payment on April 4, 1911, to Félix Routhier for the "mantels and wardrobes" in W.S. Maxwell's house, so that he may have been responsible for the wood carving of the library mantelpiece, although for the Renouf house, George Hill received payment on October 16, 1909 (p. 385) for the "carving of library, drawing and bedroom mantels".

5 Martin was well known in Paris for his mural paintings in French public buildings; he won a "Grand Prix" at the 1900 Paris Exposition Universelle.

Cat. 39g. *Billiard room, James T. Davis House*

39
Edward & W.S. Maxwell
James T. Davis House
3654 Drummond Street
Montreal, Que.
1909-1911

The imposing residence built by James Thomas Davis has the scale and grandeur of a country house yet is set in the middle of the city on Drummond Street, at the foot of Mount Royal (fig. 39). Davis, a prominent building contractor, chose to build his house in the most fashionable residential area of the rapidly expanding city. His father, William Davis, had started the family business in Ottawa, where he prospered largely from government commissions for building railway bridges and major sections of the Lachine Canal. James and his eldest brother Michael maintained the high reputation of the firm after their father's death and continued to build many large works of civil engineering.[1]

The lot that Davis chose for his house had originally belonged to sugar magnate John Redpath, the masonry contractor for the original Lachine Canal. The site, on the west side of Drummond Street, was narrow and deep, with an impressive view toward the Saint Lawrence River. The Maxwells placed the main entrance on the broad south elevation, creating a grand façade facing the river.

The exterior design follows that of Edwardian country houses which were built in England at the turn of the century. The generation of architects who followed Richard Norman Shaw, such as Ernest Newton, William Lethaby and Mervyn E. Macartney, were designing large country residences whose style referred to the classical as well as the medieval vernacular heritage of English building.[2] These architects favoured traditional brick, which had the added advantage of being economical. The Davis house, also brick, combines Tudor and classical elements: finialed gables and tall chimneys, together with a classically inspired entrance porch and Palladian window above. Taking into account Canadian winters, the Maxwells used limestone foundation and a steeply pitched roof. A combined stable and coachman's residence, a substantial brick structure, was built on the southwest corner of the site.

The central entrance is flanked by gabled bays and wings. However, the symmetry is put slightly off balance because the western gable wing projects farther and has a bow-fronted window to accommodate the oval breakfast room. The principal rooms extend along an east-to-west axis. On the east side (toward Drummond Street) are the reception areas, and to the west are the rooms for meals.

The Davis house interior was decorated by some of Montreal's finest craftsmen and artists. The fittings and furnishings reflected the most fashionable taste found in grand North American city residences. Each room had its own stylistic character conveyed through its colour, furniture design and architectural motifs.[3] Eighteenth-century French elegance was considered most appropriate for the formal drawing room, which was highly ornamented with carved wooden wreaths and garlands, fluting, and a decorative cartouche enframing two painted cherubs over the door. The walls were painted and decorated in tones of white and gold, and the Louis XVI furniture matched the decor. In contrast the breakfast room was inspired by the English Regency period; the furniture was specially designed with curved backs to harmonize with the oval shape of the room. Heavier, more elaborate mahogany furniture was deemed suitable for the dining room, where almost every wood and plaster surface was profusely ornamented with carved panels and decoration that referred to seventeenth-century English models.

Other surprises awaited the visitor behind the restrained façade. Removed from the extravagant excesses of the dining room decor and from the formality of the drawing room was the billiard room (cat. 39g). Its decoration offered one of the best Canadian examples of the ideals of the British Arts and Crafts movement, which emphasized handcraftsmanship, the use of simple materials, reference to local traditions and the integration of the crafted arts with architecture. The billiard room entrance is approached from the main hall through a small door, with a stained glass panel depicting a squirrel. The natural chestnut wall panelling is decorated with hand-carved designs of Canadian flora and fauna, as was the large billiard table; originally there was a hand-stencilled frieze above the panelling. The brass door handles and plates were hammered by hand into Art nouveau leaf shapes. Even the fireplace tiles were handcrafted by the Pewabic Pottery in

Fig. 39. Photographer unknown, *Davis House*, undated. Montreal, McGill University, Canadian Architecture Collection.

Detroit.[4] Especially noteworthy are the three murals by Maurice Cullen incorporated into the panelling of the room.[5] The Art nouveau references in the sinuous trees and flat forms of Cullen's landscape scenes are in keeping with the design of the wood carving, stained glass and metalwork around the room. The architects collaborated with the sculptor, the cabinetmaker, craftsmen and artist to form a true union of the arts.

Another unusual room is the private oratory of Mrs. Davis, hidden away from public view on the first floor (cat. 39e).[6] The chapel was built in 1915, after the rest of the house was completed. It was the work of William Maxwell, who kept notes and drawings for every aspect of the design among his personal papers. These records, which include swatches of drapery material, are evidence of William's love for drawing intricate architectural ornament and of his care in choosing the exact furnishings and colours for interior decoration. In a space no larger than the linen cupboard the room was originally intended to be, William Maxwell created a resplendent jewel of an oratory. The walls have high panels of natural oak that match the large, richly carved altarpiece. The upper walls and vaulted ceiling are stencilled overall with silver, royal blue and white floral motifs on a ground of Japanese grasscloth. The whole decoration creates a shimmering silvery effect, highlighted at one end of the chapel with a stained glass window of the Virgin and Child.

William Maxwell worked here in collaboration with the Bromsgrove Guild (Canada) Ltd., who carried out the intricate carved Gothic trefoils and leaves, the linenfold panels, and animal motifs on the altar and panelling (after the architect's drawings). Archibald

Cat. 39e. *Oratory, James T. Davis House*

Davies, a stained glass craftsman connected with the British parent branch of the Bromsgrove Guild, created the window.[7] William painstakingly attended to every detail – the velvet window curtains, the prie-dieu, the overhanging lamp and the rug – woven especially in Ireland – in his effort to integrate the colour and design of the chapel.

The rich effects of architectural sculpture and decoration are evident throughout the Davis house. The balustrade of the main staircase, inspired by seventeenth-century English examples, was carved in large oak panels of boldly pierced leaf scrolls by Montreal sculptor Félix Routhier.[8] George Hill modelled some of the architectural decoration, and a number of the most impressive pieces of the family's furniture were made by the Bromsgrove Guild (Canada) Ltd. The client's taste for decorative ornament offered the city's craftsmen a unique opportunity to work with the Maxwells and to display their skill and technique, which were all but lost after the First World War.[9]

Rosalind M. Pepall

1   William Wood, ed., "James Thomas Davis: Builder and Contractor, Montreal", in *The Storied Province of Quebec* (Toronto: Dominion Publishing Co., 1931), vol. 4, pp. 493-494. Davis earned praise for stepping in after the disastrous collapse of the Quebec bridge in 1907 and built the sub-structure for the new bridge.

2   Gavin Stamp and André Goulancourt, *The English House 1860-1914* (Chicago: University of Chicago Press, 1986).

3   For a description of the house in its day, see J. Alfred Gotch, "Residence on Drummond Street, Montreal", *Construction*, vol. 7 (July 1914), pp. 267-274.

4   For information on the Pewabic Pottery, see Wendy Kaplan, *"The Art That Is Life": The Arts & Crafts Movement in America, 1875-1920* (Boston: Museum of Fine Arts, Boston, 1987), pp. 255-256.

5   Cullen was paid $350 on October 5, 1911, for "Decoration in Billiard Rm" ([Work Costs Book M, 1904-1914], p. 284, MA, Series C).

6   "An Oratory in a Montreal Residence", *Construction*, vol. 13 (September 1920), pp. 269-275.

7   For reference on Archibald Davies (1878-1953), see the essay "Craftsmen and Decorative Artists" in the present catalogue.

8   [Work Costs Book M, 1904-1914], p. 284, MA, Series C.

9   Mrs. James T. Davis lived in the house until her death in 1955. The house was acquired by McGill University in 1956 and is now occupied by the Physical and Occupational Therapy Department.

28a. Edward Maxwell
Elevation for the H. Vincent Meredith House ("Ardvarna")
Undated
Black and red ink, graphite and watercolour on linen
53 x 56
Montreal, McGill University, Canadian Architecture Collection

28b. William Notman & Son
H. Vincent Meredith House ("Ardvarna")
1906 (printed 1991)
Gelatin silver print
20.3 x 25.4
Montreal, McCord Museum of Canadian History, Notman Photographic Archives

28c. Brian Merrett
H. Vincent Meredith House ("Ardvarna")
1988
Gelatin silver print
17.7 x 22.9
The Montreal Museum of Fine Arts

28d. William Notman & Son
Mrs. H. Vincent Meredith
1897 (printed 1991)
Gelatin silver print
12.7 x 17.8
Montreal, McCord Museum of Canadian History, Notman Photographic Archives

28e. William Notman & Son
Henry Vincent Meredith
1898 (printed 1991)
Gelatin silver print
12.7 x 17.8
Montreal, McCord Museum of Canadian History, Notman Photographic Archives

29. Brian Merrett
Duncan McIntyre Jr. and Elspeth H. Angus Houses
1989
Gelatin silver print
20.3 x 20.3
Montreal, Brian Merrett collection

30. Brian Merrett
James Crathern House
1991
Gelatin silver print
20.3 x 20.3
The Montreal Museum of Fine Arts

31. Brian Merrett
Joseph B. Learmont House
1991
Gelatin silver print
20.3 x 20.3
The Montreal Museum of Fine Arts

32a. Edward Maxwell
Perspective for the Edward S. Clouston House
1893
Watercolour, brown ink and graphite on vellum paper
40.7 x 35.8
Delineator: Edward Maxwell
Signed and dated lower left:
E. Maxwell 93
Montreal, McGill University, Canadian Architecture Collection

32b. Edward Maxwell
Detail for the Edward S. Clouston House
Undated
Black ink and wash on linen
72.5 x 49.5
Montreal, McGill University, Canadian Architecture Collection

32c. William Notman & Son
Edward S. Clouston House
1892 (printed 1991)
Gelatin silver print
20.3 x 25.4
Montreal, McCord Museum of Canadian History, Notman Photographic Archives

32d. William Notman & Son
Edward Seaborne Clouston
1904 (printed 1991)
Gelatin silver print
12.7 x 17.8
Montreal, McCord Museum of Canadian History, Notman Photographic Archives

32e. William Notman & Son
Mrs. Edward S. Clouston
1894 (printed 1991)
Gelatin silver print
12.7 x 17.8
Montreal, McCord Museum of Canadian History, Notman Photographic Archives

32f. William Notman & Son
Osla Clouston
1895 (printed 1991)
Gelatin silver print
12.7 x 17.8
Montreal, McCord Museum of Canadian History, Notman Photographic Archives

32g. William Notman & Son
Marjory Clouston
1895 (printed 1991)
Gelatin silver print
12.7 x 17.8
Montreal, McCord Museum of Canadian History, Notman Photographic Archives

33a. Brian Merrett
Hugh A. Allan House
1982
Gelatin silver print
22.9 x 17.8
Montreal, Brian Merrett collection

33b. Brian Merrett
Stairhall, Hugh A. Allan House
1983
Gelatin silver print
22.9 x 17.8
Montreal, Brian Merrett collection

34. Photographer unknown
Edward Maxwell House
Undated (printed 1991)
Gelatin silver print
20.3 x 25.4
Montreal, McGill University, Canadian Architecture Collection

35a. Edward Maxwell
Elevation for the Charles R. Hosmer House
Undated
Black ink on linen
50.9 x 89.4
Montreal, McGill University,
Canadian Architecture Collection

35b. William Notman & Son
Charles R. Hosmer House
Undated (printed 1991)
Gelatin silver print
20.3 x 25.4
Montreal, McCord Museum
of Canadian History, Notman
Photographic Archives

35c. Edward Maxwell
Dining room elevation for the Charles R. Hosmer House
Undated
Black ink on linen
31.6 x 37.2
Montreal, McGill University,
Canadian Architecture Collection

35d. Edward Maxwell
Drawing room elevation for the Charles R. Hosmer House
Undated
Black ink on linen
29.2 x 59
Montreal, McGill University,
Canadian Architecture Collection

35e. Edward Maxwell
Library ceiling plan for the Charles R. Hosmer House
Undated
Black ink on linen
37.7 x 38.6
Montreal, McGill University,
Canadian Architecture Collection

35f. William Notman & Son
Drawing room, Charles R. Hosmer House
Undated (printed 1991)
Gelatin silver print
20.3 x 25.4
Montreal, McCord Museum
of Canadian History, Notman
Photographic Archives

35g. William Notman & Son
Library, Charles R. Hosmer House
Undated (printed 1991)
Gelatin silver print
20.3 x 25.4
Montreal, McCord Museum
of Canadian History, Notman
Photographic Archives

35h. William Notman & Son
Reception room, Charles R. Hosmer House
Undated (printed 1991)
Gelatin silver print
20.3 x 25.4
Montreal, McCord Museum
of Canadian History, Notman
Photographic Archives

35i. William Notman & Son
Charles Rudolph Hosmer
About 1895 (printed 1991)
Gelatin silver print
12.7 x 17.8
Montreal, McCord Museum
of Canadian History, Notman
Photographic Archives

35j. John Williams for the J. Walker Hardware Company, Montreal
Ornamental ironwork from vestibule doors, Charles R. Hosmer House
1902-1903
Wrought iron
Middle part: 97 x 84 x 4
Side parts: 90.5 x 38.8 x 4 (each)
Saint Andrews, N.B., private collection

35k. George W. Hill (attributed to)
Door panel from the dining room, Charles R. Hosmer House
1901-1902
Mahogany
196 x 81.3
Montreal, McGill University

36a. Brian Merrett
Richard R. Mitchell House
1984
Gelatin silver print
18.4 x 18.4
Montreal, Brian Merrett collection

36b. Brian Merrett
Mural by Maurice Cullen, Richard R. Mitchell House
1984
Gelatin silver print
18.4 x 18.4
Montreal, McGill University,
Canadian Architecture Collection

36c. Brian Merrett
Staircase, Richard R. Mitchell House
1984
Gelatin silver print
18.4 x 18.4
Montreal, McGill University,
Canadian Architecture Collection

36d. Brian Merrett
Upper staircase, Richard R. Mitchell House
1984
Gelatin silver print
18.4 x 18.4
Montreal, McGill University,
Canadian Architecture Collection

37a. Edward & W.S. Maxwell
Elevation for the J.K.L. Ross House
Undated
Black ink on linen
52.3 x 64.7
Montreal, McGill University,
Canadian Architecture Collection

37b. Brian Merrett
J.K.L. Ross House
1990
Gelatin silver print
20.3 x 20.3
The Montreal Museum
of Fine Arts

37c. Brian Merrett
Drawing room, J.K.L. Ross House
1982
Gelatin silver print
17.8 x 22.9
Montreal, Brian Merrett collection

37d. William Notman & Son
John Kenneth Leveson Ross
1914 (printed 1991)
Gelatin silver print
12.7 x 17.8
Montreal, McCord Museum
of Canadian History, Notman
Photographic Archives

37e. William Notman & Son
Mrs. J.K.L. Ross
1915 (printed 1991)
Gelatin silver print
12.7 x 17.8
Montreal, McCord Museum
of Canadian History, Notman
Photographic Archives

38. Brian Merrett
*William S. Maxwell and Edward
M. Renouf Houses*
1990
Gelatin silver print
20.3 x 25.4
The Montreal Museum
of Fine Arts

39a. Edward & W.S. Maxwell
Elevation for the James T. Davis House
1909
Black ink on linen
64.2 x 98.1
Dated upper centre: *September/1909*
Montreal, McGill University,
Canadian Architecture Collection

39b. Edward & W.S. Maxwell
*Ground floor plan for the
James T. Davis House*
Undated
Black ink on linen
63.7 x 98.1
Montreal, McGill University,
Canadian Architecture Collection

39c. William Notman & Son
James T. Davis House
About 1921-1924 (printed 1991)
Gelatin silver print
20.3 x 25.4
Montreal, McCord Museum
of Canadian History, Notman
Photographic Archives

39d. William Notman & Son
*Main hall and staircase,
James T. Davis House*
1912 (printed 1991)
Gelatin silver print
20.3 x 25.4
Montreal, McCord Museum
of Canadian History, Notman
Photographic Archives

39e. William Notman & Son
Oratory, James T. Davis House
1916 (printed 1991)
Gelatin silver print
20.3 x 25.4
Montreal, McCord Museum
of Canadian History, Notman
Photographic Archives

39f. Edward & W.S. Maxwell
*Oratory detail for the James T. Davis
House*
Undated
Graphite, watercolour, gouache
and wax chalk on vellum paper
46.5 x 62.8
Montreal, McGill University,
Canadian Architecture Collection

39g. Photographer unknown
Billiard room, James T. Davis House
Undated (printed 1991)
Gelatin silver print
20.3 x 25.4
Montreal, McGill University,
Canadian Architecture Collection

39h. Edward & W.S. Maxwell
Jardinieres for the James T. Davis House
Undated
Graphite on tracing paper
38.6 x 75
Montreal, McGill University,
Canadian Architecture Collection

39i. Bromsgrove Guild (Canada)
Limited
Clock from the James T. Davis House
1915
Carved and gilt wood
162.6 x 71.1 x 71.1 (approx.)
Private collection

39j. Edward & W.S. Maxwell
*Sketch perspective and elevation for clock
and stand for the James T. Davis House*
1915
Graphite drawing
26.7 x 15.3
Montreal, McGill University,
Canadian Architecture Collection

40. Duncan Swain with Gerald
Laforest
Model of the "Square Mile" in 1912
1991
Pearwood and copper
27.9 x 180.9 x 118.9
The Montreal Museum
of Fine Arts

The Maxwells' host of wealthy clients also called on the firm to design their vacation homes, on or just south of the island of Montreal, in the Laurentian Mountains, and in Saint Andrews, New Brunswick. Some of these, such as those for Messrs. Forget and Angus, were among Canada's grandest country estates, while others were less ostentatious, though still substantial, summer villas by the sea. Such commissions began in the nineties and continued until the time of Edward's death. The country houses demonstrate the versatility of the Maxwells, showing their ability to turn their hand to the major stylistic fashions that were popular in the eastern United States in the late nineteenth and early twentieth centuries and adapt these to a Canadian context. The American Shingle Style of Richardson and his followers, which Edward studied and sketched during his Boston sojourn, was a particularly strong design source for Maxwell rural houses through the years, although those for Forget and Angus were in the palatial Château style. Interestingly, the Forget commission – the earlier of the two – represents an unusual blending of the two influences. Also notable are two log cottages in the Laurentians dating from the late nineties, which relate to the rustic Adirondack Style that had developed in northern New York State in the previous decade in response to American millionaires' desire for comfort in the wilderness.

Fig. 40. Edward Maxwell, *Perspective for Hodgson Cottage*, about 1896. Montreal, McGill University, Canadian Architecture Collection.

41
Edward Maxwell
Thomas Hodgson Cottage
Sainte-Agathe, Que.
1896-1897

Among the numerous and stylistically varied vacation houses commissioned from the Maxwell firm over the years are two log houses designed by Edward in the 1890s that overlook Lake Brûlé in the Laurentian Mountains north of Montreal. One of these, built for Thomas Hodgson and called "Château du Lac", survives relatively unaltered (fig. 40).

Rustic summer cottages and fishing camps for the wealthy, situated on northern forest lakes and rivers and built of logs, are a phenomenon of the last quarter of the nineteenth century, as railways made wilderness areas more accessible. Although further research is needed, this type of rustic design appears to have arisen initially in the wild Adirondack region of New York and beside the lakes and salmon rivers of Quebec.[1] The use of logs as a basic building material for these camps was a distinctive feature. Other components might include natural stone, shingled roofs and – most especially – "rustic work": decorative elements composed of roughly dressed tree limbs and roots, or wood sheathing in which the bark is left intact. First built for Canadian and American industrialists, financiers and railroad builders, these camps or fishing lodges fit beautifully into their natural surroundings and satisfied romantic notions of the simple life in the wilderness.[2]

Edward Maxwell's lodge for Thomas Hodgson epitomizes the notion of rustic elegance. In addition to the log walls, roughly dressed tree trunks and branches form the posts and railing of the veranda, which surrounds the house on three sides. In the original working drawings, moreover, twigs were to be the finials crowning the shingled roof. Together with these rustic details are a sophisticated Palladian window, which illuminates the upper part of the two-storey living room, and leaded windows.

The interior, too, is a blend of the simple and the sophisticated. The living room is dominated by a large fieldstone fireplace, decorated with Delft tiles and surmounted by a glass-fronted china cabinet. The decor is marked by both coziness and elegance, featuring a wooden balcony, dark wood floors and high ceilings with exposed beams.[3]

In Quebec the democratization of hunting and fishing clubs was the death warrant of the great private preserves and of such sophisticated log constructions. Today, there remain few reminders in Quebec's provincial parks and forests of this architectural type. The log cottage for Thomas Hodgson is a rare example of such rustic architecture and a rarity in the Maxwell practice. It is unfortunate that Edward's other log house in Sainte-Agathe, for James Gardner, was covered with shingles when it was enlarged in 1910.[4]

FRANCE GAGNON PRATTE

---

[1] See Harvey H. Kaiser, *Great Camps of the Adirondacks* (Boston: David R. Godine, 1982); Paul R. Baker, *Stanny: The Gilded Life of Stanford White* (New York: Free Press, 1989), pp. 123-124; and Paul Louis Martin, *La chasse au Québec* (Montreal: Éditions du Boréal, 1990). Kaiser notes (p. 65) that advice about building camps was published in 1888 by William S. Wicks in *Log Cabins: How to Build and Furnish Them*, although Calvert Vaux had earlier recommended the artistic treatment of log buildings for rural sites in his *Villas and Cottages* (New York: Harper, 1864).

[2] Kaiser, 1982, p. xiii.

[3] See France Gagnon Pratte, *Country Houses for Montrealers, 1892-1924: The Architecture of E. and W. S. Maxwell* (Montreal: Meridian, 1987), pp. 113-127.

[4] Project no. 115.1, MA.

Cat. 42d. *Postcard view of the main house ("Covenhoven"), William C. Van Horne Estate*

42
Edward Maxwell, Maxwell & Shattuck,
Edward & W.S. Maxwell, and William
Cornelius Van Horne
William C. Van Horne Estate
Minister's Island, near Saint Andrews, N.B.
About 1898 – about 1902

In 1890 William Cornelius Van Horne, the president of the CPR, purchased the five-hundred-acre (200 ha) Minister's Island in Passamaquoddy Bay near the resort town of Saint Andrews, New Brunswick.[1] Here he embarked on an ambitious building programme that would ultimately include a large, rambling summer house and a working farm (cat. 42d). He named the house "Covenhoven" in tribute to his father, Cornelius Covenhoven Van Horne, and his Dutch forebears. Here Van Horne could devote himself to two favourite leisure activities: painting and stockbreeding.

According to Maxwell family history, Van Horne began designing his summer cottage himself but ran into difficulties with the local contractor and called Edward Maxwell to Saint Andrews to assist him.[2] A set of unsigned and undated plans in the Maxwell Archive shows the original house to be a modest one-and-a-half-storey building with a shingled roof extending to cover the veranda.[3] The walls and veranda piers are of red sandstone quarried from the southern tip of the island,[4] with shingles used for the shed dormer and roof. How much of the design of this original house and its various additions and outbuildings is attributable to Van Horne and how much to Edward Maxwell will perhaps never be known, since Van Horne liked to collaborate closely with his architects.[5] The first addition to the house appears to have been designed in 1899, for there are several drawings by Maxwell & Shattuck – one dated October 10, 1899 – that involve an extension at the northwest corner accommodating a dining room and a studio on the ground floor, with bedrooms above; and a smaller addition at the east by the kitchen.[6] This work added a second gable to the western flank and included a porte cochere that extended out from the veranda.

A later set of drawings, which are undated but signed Edward & W.S. Maxwell, expanded this second

Cat. 42a. *Preliminary elevation for barn, William C. Van Horne Estate*

gable and added a third one to the western flank, which provided accommodation for servants.[7] At this time – possibly in 1902 – it seems that the dining room was re-modelled, for there are drawings for interior decor such as a beamed ceiling treatment, wall panelling and corner fireplaces. Subsequently, further additions were undertaken, since there is now an extension at the east that includes a towerlike element, and the dining room and studio have been combined to form a larger dining room, with one large fireplace replacing the corner ones.[8] These various modifications to the original modest cottage resulted in the creation of a more imposing and picturesque summer home.

On this island retreat there are also a number of farm buildings that Edward Maxwell designed for (and perhaps with the help of) Van Horne.[9] The most imposing is the magnificent barn (cat. 42a) that housed the CPR president's prize herd of Dutch-belted cattle. The timber framing for this vast building is remarkable. Drawings and sketches for certain of these outbuildings, such as an icehouse and water tower and forcing house, are dated 1899 and are all signed by Edward, who was concurrently designing farm buildings for Van Horne in Selkirk, Manitoba.[10] There is also a round tower that overlooks the bay, where Van Horne had a painting studio. Whether the Maxwell firm was involved in the design of this fascinating structure is

not known, since there are no drawings for it in the archives.

After Van Horne's death in 1915, the property remained in the family until 1961. It was bought and sold several times before it was finally purchased by the Province of New Brunswick in 1982.

FRANCE GAGNON PRATTE

---

1 Richard Wilbur, "Minister's Island", *Canadian Geographic*, vol. 104 (June-July 1984), p. 30.
2 On Van Horne's suggestion Edward Maxwell purchased land on Bar Road in Saint Andrews on which to build himself a house. A notary's letter to Edward Maxwell dated September 8, 1899, concerning this land purchase is in the possession of Maxwell descendents.
3 Project no. 322.0, MA.
4 Wilbur, 1984, p. 30.
5 See Harold Kalman, *The Railway Hotels and the Development of the Château Style in Canada* (Victoria: University of Victoria Maltwood Museum, 1968), pp. 14-15.
6 Project no. 322.2, MA. An earlier undated sketch signed by Edward Maxwell called for an extension to the kitchen area that would have added a dining room on the ground floor and a billiard room above. This proposal was not carried out.
7 Project no. 322.2, MA.
8 The dates and those responsible for this later work are unknown, as there are no drawings in the MA. Based on local recollections, Richard Wilbur believes that construction and modifications continued until the time of Van Horne's death in 1915. Telephone interview by Susan Wagg, March 30, 1990.
9 Project no. 322.2, MA.
10 Project no. 322.4, MA.

Cat. 43c. *Main house ("Bois de la Roche"), Louis-Joseph Forget Estate*

43
Edward Maxwell, Maxwell & Shattuck, and Edward & W.S. Maxwell
Louis-Joseph Forget Estate
Senneville, Que.
1899-1903

The most original of the early Maxwell country houses is "Bois de la Roche", which still stands in Senneville. It was built for Louis-Joseph Forget, president of the Montreal Stock Exchange and founder of the stock brokerage house L.J. Forget & Company. Forget owned a summer home on the shores of Lake Saint-Louis – a Notman photograph dated 1888 shows the old house to have been an imposing rubble-stone structure with a prominent tower.[1] After a fire destroyed this house, Forget called on Edward Maxwell to design a new residence, which would be much more elaborate than the first.[2] Drawings for this summer home are variously signed Edward Maxwell and Maxwell & Shattuck.[3]

The new house (cat. 43c) was an essay in the Château style, which Edward had already employed in the early nineties in his houses on Peel Street for the children of Duncan McIntyre and Richard B. Angus and for the banker E. S. Clouston. In all these projects the architect employed circular towers, while in the Forget house, the use of an octagonal and a round tower and of triangular pinnacled dormers on the garden front particularly resembles the Peel Street elevation of the McIntyre-Angus houses.

"Bois de la Roche" is a small château of rugged stone with a high copper roof – a Canadianized version of a Loire château. The main component of the building is colourful fieldstone – a material which H. H. Richardson loved and which Edward Maxwell often used for his country houses. It is not, however, typical of the American Château style, where smooth ashlar was customary, and its use here was surely Edward's creative response to the site. The drawings even call for split boulders to be used for window surrounds, but in fact Scotch random-pick masonry was used around the windows as well as the band courses. The decorative elements – corbels, finials, mouldings – are of cut stone. The earthy colour of the boulders, the paler cut stone details and the green copper roofs harmonize admirably with the surrounding landscape.

The interior plan centres on a panelled hall that gives access to the library, drawing room and dining room. Drawings signed by Edward Maxwell exist for wooden fireplace mantels for all these rooms, although drawings for some of the wainscotting are signed Maxwell & Shattuck. Various elements suggest the holiday function of the house: windowed recesses in the towers, two spacious verandas, and a terrace onto which the French windows of the dining and drawing rooms open. The estate grounds were also an important part of the ensemble. Five drawings for landscaping by the Olmsted Brothers, dated March 1900, survive as well as two by Frederick Todd, dated 1908. The estate also contains several fieldstone-and-shingle outbuildings design by the Maxwell firm as well as a charming chapel of wood designed by Edward & W.S. Maxwell in 1902.[4]

FRANCE GAGNON PRATTE

[1] The Notman photograph is reproduced in France Gagnon Pratte, *Country Houses for Montrealers, 1892-1924: The Architecture of E. and W. S. Maxwell* (Montreal: Meridian Press, 1987), p. 72.

[2] [Commission Book I, 1895-1899], p. 148, MA, Series C. A photograph of the new house appears on p. 465 of Desiré Girouard, *Lake St. Louis Old and New* (Montreal, 1893; suppl., 1903); the 1893 edition has a photograph of the old house following p. 216.

[3] Project no. 113.0, MA.

[4] [Commission Book G, 1899-1903], p. 33, MA, Series C.

Cat. 45a. *Perspective for the main house ("Pine Bluff"), Richard B. Angus Estate*

45
Edward Maxwell and Edward & W.S. Maxwell
Richard B. Angus Estate
Senneville, Que.
1902-1903 (house demolished)

Of all the summer estates built by the Maxwells for their Montreal clients, the grandest and the most spectacular was "Pine Bluff", the Château-style summer residence of Richard Bladworth Angus at Senneville (cat. 45a). An active member of the Montreal business community and one of the original financiers of the CPR, Angus had first built a house on his Senneville property designed by the firm of J.W. & E.C. Hopkins in 1886.[1] This stone-and-shingle house, also named "Pine Bluff", was remodelled and expanded in 1898-1899 by Edward Maxwell, who transformed it into a large Tudor Revival composition. Wings were added to the original structure as well as a multitude of decora-

tive details: pepper-pot towers, pinnacled gables, a romantic staircase turret and some half timbering. The overwrought design is best explained as the work of a zealous young architect eager to please his client. Included among the drawings for this project is one for a rustic arbour by the Olmsted Brothers, dated October 1899, indicating that the noted American landscape architects were involved with the laying out of the grounds.[2]

This house was soon destroyed by fire, although the wrought iron entrance gates (designed by Maxwell & Shattuck) survived. In November 1901 Angus ordered the ruins cleared away, and studies for a new

Cat. 45c. *Peach house, Richard B. Angus Estate*

house were begun by Edward and William.[3] The new "Pine Bluff" was an even more imposing residence, a design in the Château style so admired by the men connected with the CPR. It displayed a formality and cohesion that was lacking in Edward's earlier houses in the style, such as L.-J. Forget's "Bois de la Roche"(see cat. entry 43). The main front was symmetrically organized: the two towers that flank the entrance portal were identical, as were the end bays with their dormers piercing the hipped roof. The rock-faced masonry was more regular in its coursing and colour than the fieldstone used for Forget's house. Early photographs show an austere building, its formal composition and rugged stone walls producing a forbidding appearance (fig. 41). This should have been moderated by the presence of Art nouveau elements – the strange, sharply

pointed dormers and odd segmental arched window heads. An unsigned watercolour drawing shows a striking curvilinearity in the forms, although this is less apparent in the executed work. This rendering bears a similarity to an unexecuted proposal drawn by William for the J.K.L. Ross house on Peel Street, dated 1903, in which a Château-style urban house is given an up-to-date Art nouveau flavour. While William absorbed Beaux-Arts classicism in Paris, he must also have seen examples of this current fashion.

Behind the austere façades there must have been a very refined and elegant interior, now alas destroyed. Entries in a Maxwell office ledger noting costs for furniture, rugs and curtains suggest that the architects were – as with the Hosmer house – heavily involved in the decorating of this client's home.

Fig. 41. William Notman & Son, *Main house ("Pine Bluff"), Angus Estate*, undated. Montreal, McGill University, Canadian Architecture Collection.

Happily, a number of the estate's outbuildings designed by the Maxwell firm were not demolished with the main house. Among them are a peach and potting shed – a delightful rustic composition with boulder walls and a shingled roof (cat. 45c) – and cottages trimmed with half timbering and decorative bargeboards.[4]

FRANCE GAGNON PRATTE

---

1   An elevation drawing in ink on linen signed *J. W. & E. C. Hopkins* and
    dated 1886 is in the CAC.

2   Project no. 11.1, MA.

3   [Commission Book G, 1899-1903], p. 71, MA, Series C.

4   Project no. 11.7, MA.

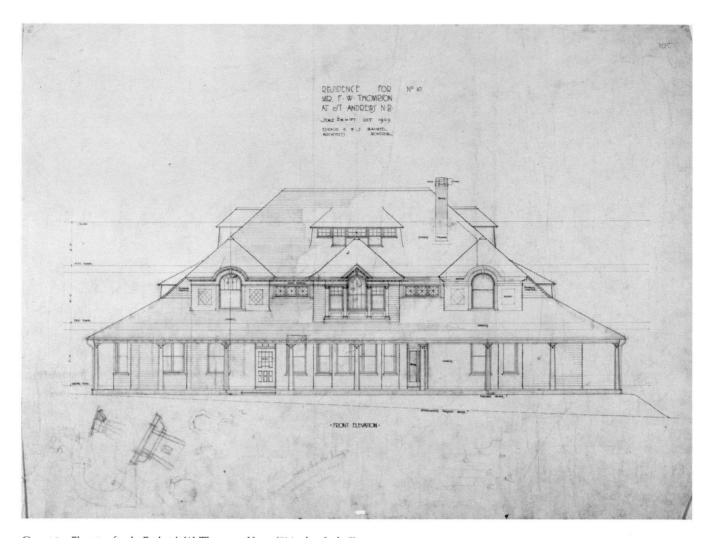

Cat. 46a. *Elevation for the Frederick W. Thompson House ("Meadow Lodge")*

46
Edward & W.S. Maxwell
Frederick W. Thompson House
Saint Andrews, N.B.
1909-1910

In June 1889 the Algonquin Hotel was opened in Saint Andrews, New Brunswick, confirming the resort status of the seaside community. While William Van Horne had distanced himself somewhat on Minister's Island, other Montrealers built large summer homes in the town – several designed by the Maxwell firm.[1] Edward Maxwell had first come to Saint Andrews in 1899 to help Van Horne in the construction of "Covenhoven". The next year Edward built a shingled summer house for his own family, extending it many times as his family grew.

An album of photographs collected by Edward in the late eighties and early nineties reveals his interest in what architectural historian Vincent Scully later named the "Shingle Style". Among the well-known examples are H. H. Richardson's Ames Gate Lodge in North Easton, his M.F. Stoughton House in Cambridge, Peabody & Stearn's "Kragsyde" in Manchester-by-the-Sea (all in Massachusetts), and McKim, Mead & White's Casino at Naragansett Pier, Rhode Island. By the time William joined the firm in 1902 and the two brothers embarked on other Saint Andrews commissions, the

Fig. 42. *Sketches for wicker furniture for Thompson House*, about 1909.
Montreal, McGill University, Canadian Architecture Collection.

picturesque style had become more formal, thanks in part to the classicizing influence of McKim, Mead & White.

"Meadow Lodge", the summer home (cat. 46a) designed in 1909 for Frederick William Thompson, managing director of Ogilvie Flour Mills and a friend of Charles Hosmer, exhibits this new formality.[2] The basic rectangle of the house is interrupted symmetrically by four projections containing the living room, the dining room, the main bedroom and the kitchen wing. On the façade, a major feature is the Palladian window of the central dormer. In the flanking dormers, the semicircular headed windows are also classical in feeling, and their arched surrounds are decorated with keystones. Under the eaves the moulding is denticulated, and the posts supporting the veranda roof suggest classical columns.

The surviving drawings indicate the involvement of the architects in all aspects of the design and furnishing of the house. Two drawings show driveways and planting and the location of a tennis court and stable, the latter also designed by the Maxwells and shingle-covered. More interesting, however, are a multitude of unsigned sketches in pencil on tracing paper of all kinds of furniture (fig. 42) and two plans of the two principal floors showing the arrangement of furniture in the house. These plans were prepared by Castle & Son, the Montreal decorators, "following instructions of Messrs. E. & W. S. Maxwell."[3] Especially notable are a set of dining room chairs incorporating a wheat motif on their backs, alluding to Thompson's connection with Ogilvie Flour Mills.

FRANCE GAGNON PRATTE

1   Willa Walker, *No Hay Fever & A Railway* (Fredericton: Goose Lane Editions, 1989), pp. 11, 13.
2   The linen working drawings for the house are dated October 1909, while details for the kitchen and pantry fittings are dated February 22, 1910. Project no. 315.0, MA.
3   *Ibid.*

41a. Edward Maxwell
Elevation for the Thomas Hodgson Cottage ("Château du Lac")
Undated
Black ink on linen
38.9 x 55.4
Montreal, McGill University,
Canadian Architecture Collection

41b. Edward Maxwell
Fireplace elevation for the Thomas Hodgson Cottage ("Château du Lac")
Undated
Black ink on linen
33.7 x 38.7
Montreal, McGill University,
Canadian Architecture Collection

41c. Brigitte Ostiguy
Thomas Hodgson Cottage ("Château du Lac")
1982
Gelatin silver print
17.7 x 25.4
Quebec City, France Gagnon
Pratte collection

41d. Brigitte Ostiguy
Fireplace, Thomas Hodgson Cottage ("Château du Lac")
1982
Gelatin silver print
17.1 x 25.4
Quebec City, France Gagnon
Pratte collection

42a. Edward Maxwell
Preliminary elevation for barn, William C. Van Horne Estate
Undated
Black ink on linen
37.3 x 71.5
Montreal, McGill University,
Canadian Architecture Collection

42b. Brigitte Ostiguy
Barn, William C. Van Horne Estate
1982
Gelatin silver print
22.2 x 35.6
Quebec City, France Gagnon
Pratte collection

42c. Brigitte Ostiguy
Water tower, William C. Van Horne Estate
1982
Gelatin silver print
23.6 x 35.6
Quebec City, France Gagnon
Pratte collection

42d. Photographer unknown
Postcard view of the main house ("Covenhoven"), William C. Van Horne Estate
About 1910 (printed 1991)
Chromogenic colour print
7.6 x 12.7
Montreal, McCord Museum
of Canadian History, Notman
Photographic Archives

42e. Photographer unknown
Postcard view of the main house ("Covenhoven"), William C. Van Horne Estate
About 1910 (printed 1991)
Chromogenic colour print
7.6 x 12.7
Montreal, McCord Museum
of Canadian History, Notman
Photographic Archives

42f. Photographer unknown
Postcard view of CPR Bar Road Station, Saint Andrews, New Brunswick
About 1910 (printed 1991)
Chromogenic colour print
7.6 x 12.7
Montreal, McCord Museum
of Canadian History, Notman
Photographic Archives

42g. Photographer unknown
Postcard view of entrance to the William C. Van Horne Estate
About 1910 (printed 1991)
Chromogenic colour print
7.6 x 12.7
Montreal, McCord Museum
of Canadian History, Notman
Photographic Archives

42h. William Notman & Son
Sir William Cornelius Van Horne
1901 (printed 1991)
Gelatin silver print
12.7 x 17.8
Montreal, McCord Museum
of Canadian History, Notman
Photographic Archives

42i. William Notman & Son
Lady Van Horne
1920 (printed 1991)
Gelatin silver print
12.7 x 17.8
Montreal, McCord Museum
of Canadian History, Notman
Photographic Archives

43a. Edward Maxwell
Elevation for the main house ("Bois de la Roche"), Louis-Joseph Forget Estate
Undated
Ink on linen
36.25 x 82
Montreal, McGill University,
Canadian Architecture Collection

43b. William Notman & Son
Main house ("Bois de la Roche"), Louis-Joseph Forget Estate
Undated (printed 1991)
Gelatin silver print
20.3 x 25.4
Montreal, McGill University,
Canadian Architecture Collection

43c. William Notman & Son
Main house ("Bois de la Roche"), Louis-Joseph Forget Estate
Undated (printed 1991)
Gelatin silver print
20.3 x 25.4
Montreal, McGill University,
Canadian Architecture Collection

43d. Edward & W.S. Maxwell
Elevations and sections for the chapel,
Louis-Joseph Forget Estate
Undated
Black ink on linen
53.8 x 39.1
Montreal, McGill University,
Canadian Architecture Collection

43e. William Notman & Son
Louis-Joseph Forget
1887 (printed 1991)
Gelatin silver print
12.7 x 17.8
Montreal, McCord Museum
of Canadian History, Notman
Photographic Archives

43f. William Notman & Son
Mrs. Louis-Joseph Forget
1887 (printed 1991)
Gelatin silver print
12.7 x 17.8
Montreal, McCord Museum
of Canadian History, Notman
Photographic Archives

44a. W.W. Scott & Co., Montreal
Dining room chair for the Louis-Joseph
Forget House (Sherbrooke Street,
Montreal)
1902
Oak (reupholstered)
118 x 69 x 54
Sculptor: George William Hill
Montreal, private collection

44b. Edward & W.S. Maxwell
Elevations for a dining room chair for
the Louis-Joseph Forget House
(Sherbrooke Street, Montreal)
Undated
Ink and watercolour on paper
18.1 x 19
Montreal, McGill University,
Canadian Architecture Collection

44c. Edward & W.S. Maxwell
Elevations for a dining room chair for
the Louis-Joseph Forget House
(Sherbrooke Street, Montreal)
Undated
Ink and watercolour on paper
18.1 x 16.2
Montreal, McGill University,
Canadian Architecture Collection

44d. W.W. Scott & Co., Montreal, and
Steinway & Sons, New York
Piano from the Louis-Joseph Forget
House (Sherbrooke Street, Montreal)
1902
Wood and brass
143 x 163 x 75
Sculptor: George William Hill
Elgin, Quebec, private collection

44e. Edward & W.S. Maxwell
Elevations for a piano case for the
Louis-Joseph Forget House (Sherbrooke
Street, Montreal)
Undated
Ink on linen
32.8 x 53.8
Montreal, McGill University,
Canadian Architecture Collection

44f. Castle & Son, Montreal
Stained glass window from the Louis-
Joseph Forget House (Sherbrooke Street,
Montreal)
1905-1906
Glass and lead
101.5 x 110.5; 101.5 x 111
Montreal Museum of Decorative
Arts, Château Dufresne

45a. Edward & W.S. Maxwell
Perspective for the main house ("Pine
Bluff"), Richard B. Angus Estate
Undated
Watercolour and graphite on
vellum paper
44.4 x 72.6
Montreal, McGill University,
Canadian Architecture Collection

45b. Edward & W.S. Maxwell
Elevation for the main house ("Pine
Bluff"), Richard B. Angus Estate
Undated
Black ink on linen
45.5 x 114.8
Montreal, McGill University,
Canadian Architecture Collection

45c. Brigitte Ostiguy
Peach house, Richard B. Angus Estate
1982
Gelatin silver print
17.1 x 25.4
Quebec City, France Gagnon
Pratte collection

46a. Edward & W.S. Maxwell
Elevation for the Frederick W.
Thompson House ("Meadow Lodge")
1909
Black, red and blue ink and
graphite on linen
58.8 x 80
Dated upper centre: *Oct 1909*
Montreal, McGill University,
Canadian Architecture Collection

46b. Brigitte Ostiguy
Frederick W. Thompson House
("Meadow Lodge")
1982
Gelatin silver print
22.2 x 35.6
Quebec City, France Gagnon
Pratte collection

46c. Edward & W.S. Maxwell
Sketch for dining room chair for the
Frederick W. Thompson House
("Meadow Lodge")
Undated
Graphite on tracing paper
52.4 x 48.6
Montreal, McGill University,
Canadian Architecture Collection

46d. Castle & Son, Montreal
Wheat motif dining room chair,
Frederick W. Thompson House
("Meadow Lodge")
1910
Mahogany
104 x 58.5 x 55
Dr. and Mrs. John A. Findlay

INSTITUTIONAL AND
CULTURAL BUILDINGS

At a time when governments were only minimally involved in public welfare and Catholic institutions looked after the needs of the French-speaking community, Montreal's business leaders assumed the responsibility and cost of providing educational, medical and cultural institutions for the city's English-speaking population. In addition to founding and funding these institutions and organizations, they controlled them as members of the boards of directors. Many of these leading businessmen were Maxwell clients. Significant Maxwell commissions in this realm include a nurses' residence for the Royal Victoria Hospital, the Alexandra Hospital, the Montreal Museum of Fine Arts (originally the Art Association of Montreal) and the High School of Montreal, as well as the Arts Club, of which William Maxwell was an energetic member.

Cat. 47c. *The Montreal Museum of Fine Arts (formerly the Art Association of Montreal)*

47
Edward & W.S. Maxwell
The Montreal Museum of Fine Arts

1379 Sherbrooke Street West
Montreal, Que.
1911-1912

The building designed by the Maxwells for the Montreal Museum of Fine Arts (formerly the Art Association of Montreal) is one of the outstanding examples of Beaux-Arts design in Canada (cat. 47c).[1] It reflected the brothers' awareness of the American trend towards Beaux-Arts inspired public buildings at the end of the nineteenth century. This commission offered the Maxwells an opportunity to draw on William's French training in Beaux-Arts planning and to demonstrate the firm's ability to provide excellent workmanship and fine materials in the construction of the building.

The Art Association's first gallery was built on the east side of Phillips Square in 1879.[2] In 1910, after some discussion over the possibility of renovating the Phillips Square building, the Association's Council decided to build a new gallery in the "Square Mile", on Sherbrooke Street at what is now Avenue du Musée. Among the councillors were some of the wealthiest and most influential businessmen in Montreal: Sir William Van Horne, James Ross, Richard B. Angus and Sir Edward Clouston. Most lived in the Square Mile, and in their eyes the new site was a most desirable location for the Association's new quarters – within strolling distance of their homes, away from the hubbub of the commercial area and close to McGill University, with which the Association had strong ties.

In February 1910, a Building Committee was appointed from the Council, and the land was purchased the next month. The committee included James Ross, David Morrice, Louis-Joseph Forget, R. B. Angus, AAM president Dr. Francis Shepherd and vice-president H. Vincent Meredith.[3] To help choose a suitable architect for the gallery and to bring prestige and experience to the project, the committee hired a Bostonian, Edmund M. Wheelwright, as consulting architect. Wheelwright had acted as a consultant for the design of the Boston Museum of Fine Arts and had visited museums all over Europe and the United States.[4]

The committee decided to hold a limited competition for the new gallery. The three entrants, Brown & Vallance, Edward & W.S. Maxwell and Percy Nobbs, were all based in Montreal and had some recent connection with members of the AAM Council.[5] Members of the Province of Quebec Association of Architects protested the holding of such a limited competition, but the executive decided not to challenge the Art Association because it was a private institution.[6]

Wheelwright served as the assessor and selected the Maxwells as the winners. Their presentation drawings are beautifully rendered plans, elevations and sections for a grand Beaux-Arts design, which includes ornamental details delicately penned in black ink. Neither drawings nor photographs remain of the entries by Nobbs and Brown & Vallance, although a comment in a 1915 article on the gallery refers to the "purely British spirit of the other designs" in the competition.[7] Since Wheelwright had attended the École des Beaux-Arts in Paris, it is not surprising that he favoured the Maxwells' design, which reflected the French school.

Once the Maxwells were named the winners, they were asked to revise their plans because the competition programme had called for a much bigger and grander building than Wheelwright and the Building Committee had ever intended to build. The committee minutes record that Wheelwright "suggested that Messrs. Maxwell should visit Boston and New York and confer with engineers who had had experience in museum problems, and inspect the Boston and Metropolitan Museums".[8]

The Maxwells therefore drew up final plans for a museum on a more modest scale to meet the immediate needs of the Association. The committee, however, did not intend to scrimp when it came to materials and chose white marble from Manchester, Vermont, for the exterior. After some discussion on the possibility of using artificial marble in parts of the interior to cut costs, it was recorded: "It was the opinion of the meeting that this opportunity of erecting a building in itself to be a work of art should not be allowed to pass." No expense was to be spared.[9]

The new gallery was formally opened on December 9, 1912, with a loan exhibition of paintings from private collections in Montreal. The adjectives "dignified" and "monumental" were used over and over again in enthusiastic reviews of the new building. This must have pleased the Art Association Council, who intended their museum to be a stately monument to the arts.

Specific features of the museum's façade contribute to its monumentality and reflect its Beaux-Arts design. The symmetrical composition, the grand staircase leading up to the imposing stone columns (each carved from a single block), the large entrance doors and the use of white marble were all typical of Beaux-Arts work. The Maxwells' historical references, in particular to the Italian Renaissance, were also within the Beaux-Arts tradition. The architectural sculpture clearly refers to the purpose of the building, for example, the bas-reliefs of the façade, which were intended "to represent the traditions of Greek and Roman art being explained to groups of sculptors, artists, painters".[10] The bronze grilles over the entrance doors are each decorated with a cherub posed beside the accoutrements of the various arts.

The monumental grandeur of the building is carried through to the interior of the gallery in the entrance hall, which has a marble floor and Botticino marble walls (cat. 47d). One of the most impressive elements is the marble staircase with a handsome bronze balustrade that leads the visitor to the principal exhibition galleries above. The ceremonial progression towards the main rooms of a building was a key element of Beaux-Arts design, as was a well-defined and clearly thought-out plan. The one criticism of the new gallery after it opened was that having reached the top of the grand staircase, the visitor was confronted with a wall. However, the Maxwells had intended in their future plans to open this wall into a court for cast plaster sculptures, which would have created the missing dramatic effect. Instead the visitor was directed left and right to the galleries or to the areas of passage beside the imposing bronze-capped marble columns around the stairwell. The interior, like the exterior, is restrained in its decoration, except in specific details such as the laurel leaf motifs on the oak door surrounds, which were hand carved by members of the Bromsgrove Guild of Canada. The Guild also executed the furniture designed by the Maxwell firm for the galleries and offices.

Cat. 47d. *Entrance hall, the Montreal Museum of Fine Arts (formerly the Art Association of Montreal)*

It is not surprising that the Maxwells, with their American experience, decided that a Beaux-Arts design was most appropriate for Montreal's new gallery. This type of design had become the fashion for public buildings in the United States at the end of the nineteenth century. By 1910, the outdated buildings of many major American museums had been replaced or expanded: for example, the Art Institute of Chicago (1892-1893) by Edward Maxwell's former employer Shepley, Rutan & Coolidge, the Fifth Avenue entrance façade of New York's Metropolitan Museum of Art, (1895-1902), designed by Richard Morris Hunt, two wings of the Brooklyn Institute of Arts and Sciences (1895-1897 and 1906) by McKim, Mead & White, and the Museum of Fine Arts (1909) in Boston by Guy Lowell.[11] These Beaux-Arts museums symbolized the economic prosperity and national confidence of large American cities at the turn of the century.

One feature that detracted from the monumental character of the museum was its restricted corner site on one of Montreal's main east/west arteries. The architects did not have room to surround the building with landscaped grounds or terraces in appropriate Beaux-Arts fashion, as they no doubt would have wished. Subsequent additions to the museum have also had to contend with the awkward site.

ROSALIND M. PEPALL

1   The name of the Art Association of Montreal, founded in 1860, was formally changed to the Montreal Museum of Fine Arts in 1949. In 1969 its official title became Musée des beaux-arts de Montréal/The Montreal Museum of Fine Arts.

2   A description of the first AAM gallery is given in Rosalind M. Pepall, exhib. cat., *Construction d'un musée Beaux-Arts/Building a Beaux-Arts Museum* (Montreal: Montreal Museum of Fine Arts, 1986), chapter 1.

3   AAM Minutes, February 17, 1910, p. 152, MMFA Archives.

4   Wheelwright (1854-1912) had co-authored a report of his research on museums for the Boston museum: R. Clipston Sturgis and Edmund Wheelwright, "The Museum Commission in Europe", *Communications to the Trustees III* (Boston: Museum of Fine Arts, 1905).

5   Nobbs was the son-in-law of the president of the AAM, Dr. F. Shepherd. Brown & Vallance had just completed the building for the McGill Faculty of Medicine, of which Dr. Shepherd was the dean. Edward Maxwell had been a member of the AAM Council and had built houses for a number of councillors.

6   For a more detailed account of the protest, see Pepall, 1986, pp. 36-37.

7   Thomas Ludlow, "The Montreal Art Gallery: E. and W. S. Maxwell, Architects", *Architectural Record*, vol. 37 (February 1915), p. 133.

8   AAM Minutes of Standing Committees, 1901-1919, Building Committee, June 24, 1910, p. 154, MMFA Archives.

9   *Ibid.*, Building Committee, December 2, 1910, p. 160.

10 "The New Art Gallery, Montreal", *Construction*, vol. 7 (January 1914), p. 8.

11 A more complete discussion on American models for the AAM gallery appears in Pepall, 1986, chapter 4, "Beaux-Arts Design in North America".

Cat. 48. *Clubroom, Arts Club*

48
Edward & W.S. Maxwell
Arts Club (alterations)
2027 Victoria Street
Montreal, Que.
1912-1913 (demolished about 1965)

The Arts Club played a role in bringing together Montreal architects, artists, craftsmen and their patrons for social activities, lectures and exhibitions. The first general meeting of the club took place in the studio of painter Maurice Cullen on May 16, 1912, and soon afterwards the members bought a small, two-storey building on Victoria Street (near the present McCord Museum).[1] William Maxwell carried out the extensive alterations to transform the interior into a club.

The first members of the Arts Club represented a cross section of French- and English-speaking artists and architects working in Montreal and included such names as A. Y. Jackson, M.-A. Suzor-Coté, William Brymner, Percy Nobbs, J. O. Marchand, Charles Saxe and John Archibald, in addition to the Maxwells' friends Cullen, George Hill and Clarence Gagnon. Several people who were simply interested in art as collectors or amateur painters also became members, such as F. Cleveland Morgan, Guy Drummond and H. Mortimer Lamb.[2]

The club building was officially opened on March 1, 1913, with an exhibition of Canadian art from members' collections.[3] According to the president's report of March 12, the club already boasted one hundred and twenty-nine members. The ground floor of the building, which had large display windows, was rented to provide a source of revenue.[4] The upstairs contained a billiard room, a long corridor for displays and the main clubroom. A 1913 photograph of this room shows it to have been a comfortable, spacious lounge and exhibition gallery, lit by a skylight and a large north window (cat. 48). A major focus of the room was the massive chimney and carved mantelpiece designed by William Maxwell, who also designed the cupboards and window seat, and supervised the furnishings of the room. Other members of the club contributed to the room's decoration: Maurice Cullen and Clarence Gagnon painted mural panels, George Hill modelled the plaster designs on the ceiling beams, Paul Beau supplied the wrought iron fireplace accessories, and the Bromsgrove Guild executed the furniture.[5] The exhibition of Japanese prints on view in the early photograph was organized by William Maxwell, who was an avid collector of these prints.[6]

William Maxwell was a driving force behind the formation and operation of the Arts Club in its first years. He acted as its first president, oversaw the renovations to the club's building and served on various committees. Musician Herbert T. Shaw recalled William's active participation in the club: "W. S. Maxwell always took a great interest in club matters, always unruffled and courteous. He took delight in arranging suppers, such as a Chinese supper all done in proper atmosphere. His printed notices of exhibitions were works of art. He was versatile, enjoying his billiards, poker and even learned to play chess. He was always one of our most enthusiastic and valued members from the inception of the Club."[7] The Arts Club was central to William Maxwell's social life, and his daughter confirms that he spent most Friday evenings with his colleagues on Victoria Street.[8]

ROSALIND M. PEPALL

1 "The Arts Club Minute Book 1913-1921", p. 31, Arts Club Archive, MMFA. The Arts Club still exists; a short history of the association by Leo Cox, *Portrait of a Club* (Montreal: Arts Club, 1962), commemorates its fiftieth anniversary.

2 Edward Maxwell gave money for the purchase of the club but does not appear to have been an active member.

3 *Inaugural Loan Exhibition of the Arts Club, Montreal*, March 1, 1913 (Arts Club Archive, MMFA).

4 The lower floor was rented for a short while to the Duncan Fraser decorating firm and subsequently served as a Bromsgrove Guild showroom. E. L. Wren, the manager of the guild, was a member of the Arts Club.

5 For a description of the club when it opened, see "The Arts Club", *Construction*, vol. 6 (June 1913), pp. 223-225.

6 The exhibition was held from March 20 until April 12, 1913 ("Arts Club Minute Book 1913-1921", p. 72).

7 Letter to H. A. Valentine, president of the Arts Club, from Herbert T. Shaw, March 19, 1960 (Arts Club Archive, MMFA).

8 Mary Maxwell Rabbani, interviewed by France Gagnon Pratte and the author, Haifa, April 1, 1989.

Cat. 49a. *High School of Montreal*

49
Edward & W.S. Maxwell
High School of Montreal

3449 University Street
Montreal, Que.
1912-1914

The Maxwells' building for the High School of Montreal is a severely uncompromising design in the Beaux-Arts classical tradition (cat. 49a). When it opened in September 1914, it accommodated two already-existing schools: the High School of Montreal, founded in 1843 to educate boys, and the High School for Girls, established independently in 1875. Both schools, which were important "feeders" for McGill, had been housed since 1892 in a building on Peel Street erected by the Protestant Board of School Commissioners of Montreal.[1] This building, which also contained the board's offices, soon became overcrowded, and it was decided in 1912 to build the present high school on University Street, the first in the Montreal board's system.[2]

The strict axial plan consists of a four-storey central block and two three-storey projecting wings facing a courtyard. The central block contained offices for the male and female principals, common rooms and cloakrooms for teachers, an assembly hall, a museum, and a library. The north wing (on the left) contained classrooms and other facilities for boys; the south wing served the girls. The main entrance, in the central block, faces University Street; the boys' and girls' entrances lie opposite each other across the courtyard.

Faced with yellow Roman brick, the building is sparingly enriched with terra-cotta ornament. The centre of the main block is treated as a three-bay projecting pavilion, with four columns *in antis* linking the first and second floors visually, and topped by an attic and a pediment. Paired columns occur in the University Street ends of the wings as well. The design makes no further acknowledgement of its surroundings: its massing, materials and style are quite unrelated to those of its immediate neighbours. These included a brick neo-Gothic Anglican theological college and the grey stone academic and residential buildings belonging to McGill University.

SUSAN WAGG

---

[1] Elson I. Rexford, I. Gammell and A. R. McBain, *The History of the High School of Montreal*, n.d., n.p., and John Irwin Cooper, "When the High School of Montreal and McGill Were One", *McGill News* (Autumn 1943), pp. 9-14, 55.

[2] According to L. M. Hendrie, "The High School for Girls, Montreal 1875-1930" (typescript, 1930, 15 pp.), MUA (MG 1060, Box 2, item 11), the building, although in use from 1914, was not finished until the mid-twenties. A photograph in the NPA dating from about 1921-1924, shows the completed exterior, with lateral wings of three storeys crowned by a balustrade and a central block one storey higher. Hendrie, 1930, indicates that the swimming pool in the basement was not functional until 1925, at which time the Assembly Hall, at the rear of the central block on the ground floor, was also completed. Until then, the girls' gymnasium in the south wing basement had doubled as an assembly hall.

47a. Edward & W.S. Maxwell
Competition longitudinal section for the Montreal Museum of Fine Arts (formerly the Art Association of Montreal)
Undated [1910]
Ink and grey wash on paper
62 x 93.9
Montreal, McGill University,
Canadian Architecture Collection

47b. Edward & W.S. Maxwell
Staircase detail for the Montreal Museum of Fine Arts (formerly the Art Association of Montreal)
1911
Black and red ink and graphite on linen
54.5 x 87.5
Dated lower right: *May 4th 1911*
Montreal, McGill University,
Canadian Architecture Collection

47c. William Notman & Son
The Montreal Museum of Fine Arts (formerly the Art Association of Montreal)
1913 (printed 1991)
Gelatin silver print
101.6 x 127
Montreal, McCord Museum
of Canadian History, Notman
Photographic Archives

47d. William Notman & Son
Entrance hall, the Montreal Museum of Fine Arts (formerly the Art Association of Montreal)
1913 (printed 1991)
Gelatin silver print
101.6 x 127
Montreal, McCord Museum
of Canadian History, Notman
Photographic Archives

47e. William Notman & Son
Main exhibition gallery, the Montreal Museum of Fine Arts (formerly the Art Association of Montreal)
1913 (printed 1991)
Gelatin silver print
101.6 x 127
Montreal, McCord Museum
of Canadian History, Notman
Photographic Archives

47f. William Notman & Son
Staircase, the Montreal Museum of Fine Arts (formerly the Art Association of Montreal)
1913 (printed 1991)
Gelatin silver print
101.6 x 127
Montreal, McCord Museum
of Canadian History, Notman
Photographic Archives

47g. William Notman & Son
Upper stairhall, the Montreal Museum of Fine Arts (formerly the Art Association of Montreal)
1913 (printed 1991)
Gelatin silver print
101.6 x 127
Montreal, McCord Museum
of Canadian History, Notman
Photographic Archives

47h. William Notman & Son
Lamp standards, the Montreal Museum of Fine Arts (formerly the Art Association of Montreal)
1913 (printed 1991)
Gelatin silver print
101.6 x 127
Montreal, McCord Museum
of Canadian History, Notman
Photographic Archives

47i. William Notman & Son
Detail of entrance, the Montreal Museum of Fine Arts (formerly the Art Association of Montreal)
1913 (printed 1991)
Gelatin silver print
101.6 x 127
Montreal, McCord Museum
of Canadian History, Notman
Photographic Archives

47j. William Notman & Son
Entrance colonnade, the Montreal Museum of Fine Arts (formerly the Art Association of Montreal)
1913 (printed 1991)
Gelatin silver print
101.6 x 127
Montreal, McCord Museum
of Canadian History, Notman
Photographic Archives

47k. Edward & W.S. Maxwell
Façade detail for the Montreal Museum of Fine Arts (formerly the Art Association of Montreal)
Undated
Black ink and graphite on paper
95.6 x 64.2
Montreal, McGill University,
Canadian Architecture Collection

47l. Edward & W.S. Maxwell
Longitudinal section study for the Montreal Museum of Fine Arts (formerly the Art Association of Montreal)
Undated
Graphite on tracing paper
22.9 x 48.2
Montreal, McGill University,
Canadian Architecture Collection

47m. Edward & W.S. Maxwell
Front elevation study for the Montreal Museum of Fine Arts (formerly the Art Association of Montreal)
Undated
Graphite on tracing paper
30.2 x 47.5
Montreal, McGill University,
Canadian Architecture Collection

47n. William Notman & Son
The Montreal Museum of Fine Arts (formerly the Art Association of Montreal)
1913
Gelatin silver print
18.1 x 23.2
The Montreal Museum
of Fine Arts

47o. William Notman & Son
Council room, the Montreal Museum of Fine Arts (formerly the Art Association of Montreal)
1913
Matt gelatin silver print
19 x 24.5
The Montreal Museum
of Fine Arts

47p. William Notman & Son
*Library, the Montreal Museum of
Fine Arts (formerly the Art Association
of Montreal)*
1913 (printed 1991)
Gelatin silver print
19 x 24.1
The Montreal Museum
of Fine Arts

47q. Bromsgrove Guild (Canada) Ltd.
(designed by Edward & W.S.
Maxwell)
Writing table
1912
Oak
75.5 x 128.2 x 75
The Montreal Museum
of Fine Arts

48. William Notman & Son
Clubroom, Arts Club
1913 (printed 1991)
Gelatin silver print
20.3 x 25.4
Montreal, McCord Museum
of Canadian History, Notman
Photographic Archives

49a. Brian Merrett
High School of Montreal
1991
Gelatin silver print
35.6 x 35.6
The Montreal Museum
of Fine Arts

49b. Photographer unknown
*Model for a caryatid ("Research")
from the Atlantic Terra Cotta Co.
for the High School of Montreal*
Undated
Gelatin silver print
(verso exhibited)
29.9 x 8.1
Enlargement of recto (printed
1991), 50.9 x 16.5
Montreal, McGill University,
Canadian Architecture Collection

49c. Photographer unknown
*Model for a caryatid ("Truth")
from the Atlantic Terra Cotta Co.
for the High School of Montreal*
Undated
Gelatin silver print
(verso exhibited)
30.9 x 8.1
Enlargement of recto (printed
1991), 50.9 x 16.5
Montreal, McGill University,
Canadian Architecture Collection

49d. Photographer unknown
*Model for a caryatid ("Greek")
from the Atlantic Terra Cotta Co.
for the High School of Montreal*
Undated
Gelatin silver print
(verso exhibited)
30.5 x 11.5
Enlargement of recto (printed
1991), 50.9 x 16.5
Montreal, McGill University,
Canadian Architecture Collection

49e. Photographer unknown
*Model for a caryatid ("Roman")
from the Atlantic Terra Cotta Co.
for the High School of Montreal*
Undated
Gelatin silver print
(verso exhibited)
29.8 x 12.3
Enlargement of recto (printed
1991), 50.9 x 16.5
Montreal, McGill University,
Canadian Architecture Collection

50. Edward & W.S. Maxwell
*Perspective for the Royal Victoria
Hospital Nurses' Home*
1905
Watercolour, gouache and
graphite on vellum paper
62.4 x 90.9
Delineator: W. S. Maxwell
Signed and dated lower right:
W.S. Maxwell/ July 14. 1905.
Montreal, McGill University,
Canadian Architecture Collection

Although Maxwell-designed government buildings – both executed and un-executed – were not numerous, they enhanced the firm's national reputation. The brothers entered four competitions for important government buildings in Canada: a Justice and Departmental Buildings complex in Ottawa (1907 and 1913), the Saskatchewan Legislative Building (1907) and the Manitoba Legislative Building (1912). They won the two 1907 competitions, although only the Saskatchewan Legislative Building was built. Their success in these and other competitions for important Montreal buildings, including the Montreal Museum of Fine Arts, was undoubtedly in large part due to the Beaux-Arts skills that William had acquired in Boston and Paris.

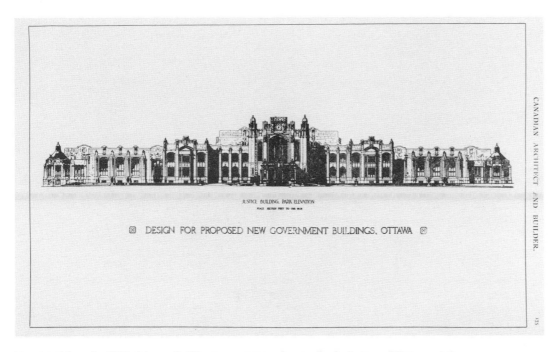

Fig. 43. Edward & W.S. Maxwell, *Winning competition elevation for the Justice and Departmental Buildings at Ottawa*, 1907. Reproduced from *The Canadian Architect and Builder* (1907).

51
Edward & W.S. Maxwell
Competition Designs for the Justice and Departmental Buildings
Ottawa, Ont.
1907, 1913

The first competition the Maxwell firm won outside their native province was for the Justice and Departmental Buildings in Ottawa, held in 1907. Although their winning scheme (fig. 43) was never built and they did not place in a subsequent competition, held in 1913, this project was significant. Not only did it enhance the firm's reputation, but it marked the first time since the completion of the Parliament Buildings that the federal government had dispensed with the services of the Department of Public Works in favour of a competition open to all the architects in the country.

The Canadian Architect and Builder for September 1907 contains an account of the competition, to which twenty-nine schemes were submitted.[1] The judges were David Ewart, chief architect of the DPW; Edmund Burke, president of the Ontario Association of Architects; and Alcide Chaussé, president of the Province of Quebec Association of Architects. Second place was awarded to Darling & Pearson, third to Saxe & Archibald and fourth to Brown & Vallance.

The government did not specify a style for the complex, which comprised a federal courthouse and a departmental office building at the eastern edge of Majors Hill Park, but suggested that some phase of Gothic would best harmonize with the Parliament Buildings, which lay directly west across the Rideau Canal.[2] The Maxwells complied with this suggestion, although their Gothic-inspired forms are composed in a rigidly symmetrical design, evidently showing they believed Beaux-Arts planning principles to be compatible with Gothic work. Their comments were recorded in *CAB*:

> ... varied only as the Gothic style can be varied, but without restlessness, rich without ostentation or undue ornamentation, with simple masses, logical composition, and the purpose of the plan unmistakable.[3]

Like the Church of the Messiah, this was an early essay in a new phase of the Gothic Revival that would become known as Modern Gothic.

The only original document the Maxwell Archive possesses regarding the proposed justice building is an

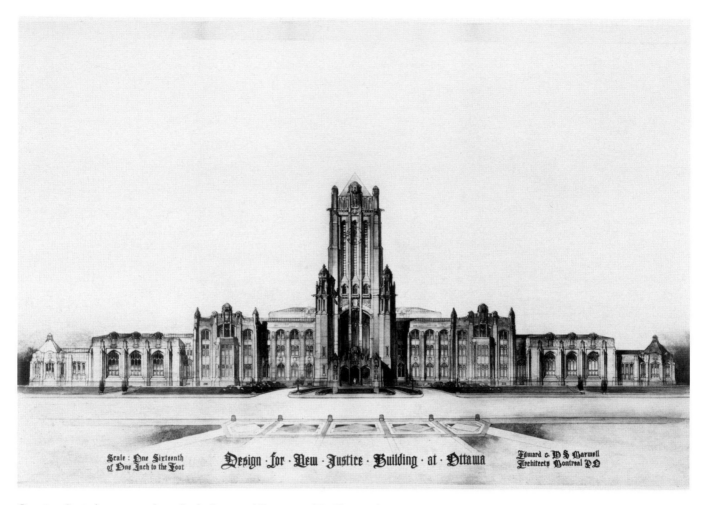

Cat. 51a. *Revised competition design for the Justice and Departmental Buildings at Ottawa*

elevation drawing (cat. 51a), which appears to be a revision of an elevation submitted to the 1907 competition and now known through an illustration in *CAB*. The presumed revision has an additional floor and a central tower. In October 1907 *CAB* recorded that the government found all of the schemes deficient, and the Maxwells may have prepared this revision to meet the criticism of their design.[4] The DPW records reveal that all of the competition drawings were lost in a fire while on public display in Toronto.[5] A note indicates that the Maxwells submitted a photograph of one of their drawings with a letter, presumably intended to keep the matter alive. This could be the 1907 Notman photograph of a perspective drawing, *Design of New Justice Building Ottawa*, a copy of which is in the Maxwell Archive, since it corresponds to the elevation drawing in the present exhibition.[6]

Much to the disgust of the Canadian architectural profession, this 1907 competition turned out to be merely exploratory. In May 1910 it was learned that the government had decided not to build the Maxwells' winning design, but to proceed with a cheaper scheme for a Departmental Building by the DPW's Ewart, who had judged the competition.[7] Known as the Connaught Building, it retains many features of the Maxwells' design.

In 1912 an extensive area west of the Parliament Buildings, between Wellington Street and the Ottawa River, was expropriated to be the site of the Supreme Court and future Departmental Buildings. Landscape architects Frederick Todd of Montreal and Edward White of London were retained to provide separate comprehensive reports and plans for the development of the area. The proposal by White, who was assisted by Sir Aston Webb, was accepted.[8]

In April 1913 it was decided to conduct a two-stage architectural competition open to all British architects – Canadians were considered to be British – for buildings to conform with White's layout. The judges were Thomas E. Collcutt, representing the Royal Institute of

Cat. 51b. *Aerial perspective, design for a Justice and Departmental Building, Ottawa*

British Architects; J.H.R. Russell, representing the Royal Architectural Institute of Canada; and J. O. Marchand, who was appointed by the Canadian government. Of the sixty-two schemes submitted, six were selected for further development. However, this second stage, at first deferred by the war in Europe,[9] was abandoned altogether in 1923, and none of the schemes were developed.

The rejected schemes from stage one, including that of the Maxwells, were presumably returned to their owners; the Maxwell Archive contains the complete set submitted by the Maxwells except for a perspective (cat. 51b), which may be the work William Maxwell gave to the Royal Canadian Academy as his diploma piece. Entitled *Design for a Justice and Departmental Building, Ottawa*, it was shown at the Royal Canadian Academy exhibition of 1914.[10] In it, three detached buildings are grouped around a court, and the recessed centre block has a tall tower – a scheme no doubt inspired by the Parliament Buildings. The detail-

ing is classical, although the central spire has a Gothic quality, akin to the Imperial Baroque manner of Collcutt.

JOHN BLAND

1 *CAB*, vol. 20 (September 1907), p. 184.

2 Kelly Crossman, *Architecture in Transition: From Art to Practice, 1885-1906* (Kingston and Montreal: McGill-Queen's University Press, 1987), p. 138.

3 *CAB*, vol. 20 (September 1907), p. 183.

4 *CAB*, vol. 20 (October 1907), p. 201.

5 National Archives of Canada, Federal Archives Division, RG 11, vol. 4239.

6 Notman 166,968-II, MA, Box 9.

7 *Construction*, vol. 3 (May 1910), p. 72, and Crossman, 1987, p. 142.

8 *Construction*, vol. 6 (May 1913), p. 178.

9 The schemes chosen were by MacFarlane & Raine, Montreal; Robb & Mitchell, Montreal; W. E. Noffke, Ottawa; Moodie, London, England; Hutchison, Wood & Miller, Montreal; and Saxe & Archibald, Montreal (RG 11, vol. 295, 5370-1C, National Archives of Canada).

10 R. H. Hubbard, *The National Gallery of Canada Catalogue of Paintings and Sculpture: Vol. 3, Canadian School* (Toronto, 1960), p. 402.

Cat. 52a. *Perspective for the Legislative and Executive Building, Regina, Saskatchewan*

52
Edward & W.S. Maxwell
Saskatchewan Legislative Building
Regina, Sask.
1908-1912

Soon after their hollow victory in the first Ottawa competition, the Maxwells won a second competition (cat. 52a) that firmly established the classical vocabulary and Beaux-Arts planning principles for major public buildings, particularly in the West, and demonstrated that Canadian architects could hold their own in international competitions. The commission did not come easily, and its complicated history involved many of Canada's leading architects.

When Saskatchewan attained provincehood in 1905, the legislature sat in the unimposing Territorial Legislative Building in downtown Regina. Almost immediately the confident, farsighted premier, Walter Scott, began planning for a new structure. A one-hundred-and-sixty-eight-acre (68 ha) site a kilometre

or two south of the business centre was acquired, and Montreal landscape architect Frederick G. Todd was commissioned to lay out the grounds. Although Todd's plan, submitted in January 1907, would be largely abandoned, his recommendation for the location of the legislative building – facing north and overlooking an artificial lake – was incorporated into the conditions of the competition. It has been suggested that Premier Scott initially approached the Beaux-Arts architect John Lyle, who had recently returned to Toronto from New York to start up a practice, inviting him to come west as the province's chief architect, but Lyle refused.[1] Scott then conferred with the architect Francis Rattenbury, whose British Columbia Parliament Buildings had been completed in 1897. Rattenbury

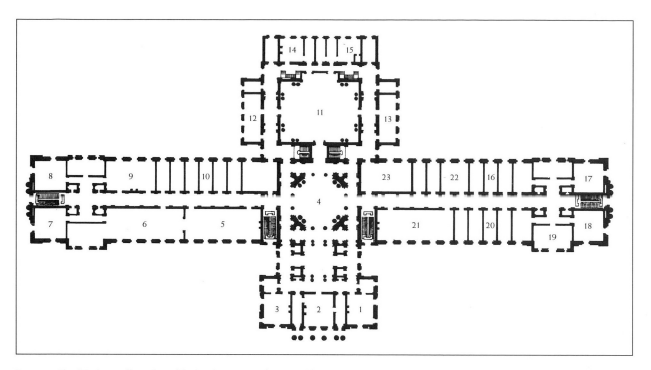

Fig. 44. *Simplified main floor plan of Saskatchewan Legislative Building*. 1. Provincial Governor's room 2. Executive Council Chamber 3. Premier's room 4. Rotunda 5. Reading room 6. Stack room 7.-10. Committee rooms 11. Legislative Chamber 12-13. Smoking rooms 14. Speaker's room 15-20. Offices 21-22. Writing rooms 23.Members' lockers

advised the premier against holding a competition and eagerly offered his own services.[2] However, to avoid political controversy, Scott decided in favour of a competition, asking Percy Nobbs, the director of McGill's Department of Architecture, to take charge. Nobbs later wrote that when he came to Canada from Britain in 1903, "laymen did the selecting [as Scott had initially attempted to do] and sometimes took advice from an architect in the management of the competition only."[3] Nobbs accepted on the condition that the competition follow the guidelines laid down by the Royal Institute of British Architects. It was decided to limit the competition to seven selected architectural firms: one each from the United States, Great Britain and Saskatchewan, and four from elsewhere in Canada. The American was Cass Gilbert, architect of the recently completed Minnesota State Capitol, which Scott greatly admired. After conferring with Sir Aston Webb, a highly successful architect of large public buildings in England, Nobbs chose Mitchell & Raine of London; and Nobbs and Scott together selected the Canadian competitors: Storey & Van Egmond from Regina; Rattenbury; Darling & Pearson; Marchand & Haskell; and the Maxwells. Nobbs, Scott and the New York architect Bertram Goodhue, whose work Nobbs admired, served as assessors. The premier, however, had to withdraw due to ill health, and on the suggestion of Cass Gilbert, his place was taken by Frank Miles Day, presi-

dent of the American Institute of Architects. Nobbs relates what a time he had convincing the premier and his attorney general "that they had the power to delegate the responsibility of the decision on an important competition to three architects; and how grateful was that Premier afterwards when he had to deal with the disappointed".[4]

While the competition programme prepared by Nobbs adhered to Royal Institute of British Architects guidelines, Kelly Crossman has called attention to the strong presence of Nobbs's own ideas regarding appropriate architecture for Canada in his recommendations to the competitors.[5] As a devotee of the Arts and Crafts movement, Nobbs was particularly concerned that local climate, labour skills and materials be taken into account in the design. He went so far as to suggest that the materials be red brick with buff stone dressings, a favourite combination of his.[6] Because the site was at a distance from the city, he suggested that there be "some dominating feature such as a dome or tower" to act as a landmark. No directions were given regarding style, except for the suggestion that the province was politically within the British Empire "and that fact should be expressed in the public buildings".[7]

The competition closed on November 30, 1907; three weeks later it was announced that Edward & W.S. Maxwell had won. The brothers described the style of their monumental domed exterior as "a free adaptation

Cat. 52e. *Anteroom (rotunda),*
Saskatchewan Legislative Building

of English Renaissance work ... a logical, sensible and architecturally interesting solution of the problem that marks it unmistakably as representative of the British sovereignty under which the Province is governed". Following Nobbs's suggestion, the proposed materials were red brick and pale buff stone. The exterior walls were ultimately faced entirely with cream-coloured Tyndall limestone from Manitoba, since the premier felt the appearance of the building would be cheapened if brick was the primary material.[8]

The significance of this competition was considerable. In an era when the most prestigious commissions in the Dominion went to non-Canadians, mostly Americans, the Maxwells' victory "seemed a sign that the Canadian profession had come of age".[9]

The programme for this provincial seat of government had "called for accommodations for the legislative branch of the government, such as a legislative chamber to seat 125 members, with speakers, press and public galleries; and conveniently adjacent, members' retiring room and smoking rooms, a speaker's room, committee rooms, library, executive council chamber, premier's and governor's rooms. The executive group comprised accommodation for the various departments, such as Treasury, Agriculture, Public Works, Education, Railways, etc."[10]

The Maxwells' solution created a simple cruciform plan, with the major axis running north and south, and the longer minor axis running east and west (fig. 44). Marking the intersection is a rotunda, surmounted and lit by an octagonal dome, which rises 183' 8" (56 m), above the ground. The north/south block contains the principal ceremonial elements. The porticoed main entrance, which fronts the north wing, is reached by a broad flight of granite steps and opens onto a vestibule that precedes the main entrance hall, where a great marble staircase ascends. At the top of this staircase is the lofty colonnaded rotunda (cat. 52e), serving as the anteroom of the Legislative Chamber, located just behind it in the south wing. As the Maxwells wrote: "It will be noted that from the point at which one enters the building by the main entrance vestibule, hall, staircase of honor and anteroom, a succession of monumental apartments are traversed, all leading to the Legislative Chamber, the room above all others for which this building will be erected."[11] The entirety of this, the main floor, is devoted to legislative purposes; it is hierarchically arranged, with the Executive Council Chamber (cat. 52f) and the governor's and premier's rooms at the front over the entrance hall, and reading, writing and committee rooms and members' offices along the east/west wings, accessed by a central corridor. With the exception of the main floor and part of the basement that contains dining facilities, the remainder of the three-storey building is given over to offices for the various governmental departments.

A heating plant is located some distance behind the building, its tunnel positioned so as to serve future extensions that might be built at each end.

Final detailed plans were ready for tenders in May 1908. Disregarding the risk of local criticism, the contractor selected was Peter Lyall & Sons of Montreal, the architects' choice, and as Premier Scott put it, "a contracting firm whose experience and equipment leave no room for doubt as to their ability to give us a building up to specifications".[12] By August excavations were well under way, and the sinking of the concrete piles was proceeding by September. Erection of the reinforced concrete framework was begun in the spring of 1909.

The structure of the building was advanced for the time, although it did not involve true skeleton construction, since the massive outer walls helped to carry floor loads. Steel construction fireproofed with concrete was used for the Legislative Chamber and south wing generally, and the remaining framework was reinforced concrete following the new Kahn system, supplied by the Kahn-owned Trussed Concrete Steel Company of Youngstown, Ohio. This system of reinforcing concrete with trussed steel bars had been developed by Albert and Julius Kahn in Detroit and was first used by the Kahn architectural firm at the Packard Motor Car Company plant in 1905. When completed, the Legislative Building was the largest reinforced concrete building in the Canadian West. The framework as far as the drum base of the dome was completed by October 4, 1909, the day the governor-general laid the cornerstone. The setting of the Tyndall stone facing had begun in August. The governmental offices were able to move in by the end of 1910, when the bulk of the interior was completed; the Legislative Assembly first met in their new chamber on January 25, 1912. The following June a cyclone devastated Regina but caused only minor damage to the Legislative Building. Repairs were completed in time for the official opening on October 12. The pediment sculpture over the main entrance, designed by the English Bromsgrove Guild of Applied Arts and representing Canada as a mother protecting the American Indian and the pioneer, was executed during the latter part of 1914.[13]

The previous year, the provincial government had commissioned Thomas Mawson & Sons of Lancaster, England, and Vancouver to prepare a revised plan for the treeless site. Mawson's recommendations for driveways, terraces, paths and gardens on the grounds of the Legislative Building were carried out promptly, but with the war and a slackening of immigration, his general plans for Wascana Park and for the city of Regina were never carried out.[14]

This new building (cat. 52b) was immediately and widely praised. Although the extraordinarily long corridors — five hundred and thirty-five feet (163 m) —

Cat. 52f. *Cabinet meeting room, Saskatchewan Legislative Building*

of the east/west block were criticized, the imposing exterior and the grandly conceived, superbly fitted ceremonial rooms were a source of pride to all Canadians. The Edwardian Free Classic manner allowed the Maxwells to work within the French Beaux-Arts tradition that was William's forte, and they exploited Beaux-Arts strengths in the design: clear, efficient, large-scale planning and fine sequences of majestic public spaces. Although the architects described their treatment as a free adaptation of English Renaissance, the predominant feeling is French. While the heavy Palladianism of the main entrance and end pavilions terminating the east and west wings does provide a British flavour, Le Vau and Hardouin-Mansart's garden front at Versailles rather than the work of an English architect appears to have inspired the long east and west wings. The classical domed and porticoed capitol building had, of course, an American ancestry — reaching back to Bulfinch's Massachusetts State House (1795-1797) and the national Capitol in Washington (1793-1865) — different from the Victorian Gothic parliament buildings in Westminster and Ottawa. It is the dome shape, reminiscent of Wren at Greenwich, that has to carry the bulk of the imperial symbolism.

Cat. 52b. *Saskatchewan Legislative Building*

The striking central feature of the rotunda – a marble well, similar to the Tomb of Napoleon in Les Invalides in Paris – also evokes France. The magnificence of this chamber and of the approach to the Legislative Chamber was intensified during the final design process, huge solid green marble columns brought from Cyprus being substituted for the plain white columns that were originally intended. The marble for the floors of the rotunda came from Vermont, that of the walls from Italy. All of the fittings and furnishings of the principal apartments and spaces were of the best quality. They were provided by the Bromsgrove Guild and Waring & Gillow of England, and Castle & Son of Montreal.

Although Regina never grew into the great prairie city that Premier Scott envisioned, his insistence on excellence left Canada with one of its finest buildings, and one designed by Canadian architects besides. The premier expressed his motivation in Ruskin's words: "Therefore when we build, let us think that we build forever. Let it not be for present delight, nor for present use alone; let it be such work as our descendants will thank us for, and let us think, as we lay stone upon stone, that a time is to come when those stones will be held sacred because our hands have touched them, and that men will say as they look upon the labor and wrought substance of them 'See, this our fathers did for us.'"[15]

SUSAN WAGG

[1] Kelly Crossman, *Architecture in Transition: From Art to Practice, 1885-1906* (Kingston and Montreal: McGill-Queen's University Press, 1987), p. 143.

[2] Anthony A. Barett and Rhodri Windsor Liscombe, *Francis Rattenbury and British Columbia: Architecture and Challenge in the Imperial Age* (Vancouver: University of British Columbia Press, 1983), p. 181.

[3] Percy Nobbs, "Competition Reform", *JRAIC*, vol. 12 (September 1935), p. 150.

[4] *Ibid.*

[5] Crossman, 1987, p. 148.

[6] See Susan Wagg, *Percy Erskine Nobbs: Architect, Artist, Craftsman* (Kingston and Montreal: McGill-Queen's University Press, 1982), p. 14.

[7] Lewis H. Thomas, "The Saskatchewan Legislative Building and Its Predecessors", *JRAIC*, vol. 32 (July 1955), p. 251.

[8] Crossman, 1987, p. 175, note 47.

[9] *Ibid.*, p. 148.

[10] "Saskatchewan Legislative Buildings, Regina", *JRAIC*, vol. 2 (April-June 1924), p. 41.

[11] "Legislative Buildings, Regina, Sask., E. & W.S. Maxwell, Architects, Montreal", *CAB*, vol. 22 (February 1908), p. 11.

[12] Thomas, 1955, p. 251. Messrs. Ballantyne of Montreal were responsible for the plumbing and heating; Hastings & Willoughby of Regina carried out the roofing, tin and copper work; the plastering was done by C.W. Sharpe & Company of Winnipeg; the painting and glazing by W. Talbot of Winnipeg (J. H. Puntin, "The New Legislative Building at Regina", *Contract Record*, vol. 27 [January 8, 1913], p. 42).

[13] Construction information can be found in Diana Lynn Bodner, "The Prairie Legislative Buildings of Canada" (Master's thesis, University of British Columbia, 1979), pp. 83-84.

[14] Also never carried out, perhaps because of the war, was a design by the Maxwell firm for a Lieutenant-Governor's Residence overlooking the lake (linen drawings dated 1913, Project 168.0, MA).

[15] Thomas, 1955, p. 252.

- FRONT - ELEVATION -
- SCALE: SIXTEEN-FEET-TO-ONE-INCH -

- PROPOSED -LEGISLATIVE - AND - EXECVTIVE - BVILDING - WINNIPFG - CANADA -

Cat. 53. *Competition elevation for the Manitoba Legislative Building*

53
Edward & W.S. Maxwell
Competition Design for the Manitoba Legislative Building
Winnipeg, Man.
1912

The Maxwells' unsuccessful design for the Manitoba Legislative Building developed some of the themes stated at Regina. A two-stage competition for a new legislative and executive building for the Province of Manitoba was announced in November 1911. Restricted to British architects (including Canadians), the conditions, which were published in December, were prepared by the province's deputy minister of Public Works and the chief architect.[1] Preliminary schemes were received by February 15, 1912, and final proposals prepared, judged and reported by November.

The design (cat. 53) submitted by Edward & W.S. Maxwell was one of five accepted to be further developed for the final competition. Both stages were judged by the English architect Leonard Stokes, a former president of the Royal Institute of British Architects. In the final stage Stokes chose the proposal of Frank Worthington Simon (1862-1933), an architect from Liverpool.[2] Like W. S. Maxwell, Simon had been a pupil of Jean-Louis Pascal in Paris, which may partially explain the similarity in their submissions.

The site of the Winnipeg building invited a composition with four important façades, unlike the site of the Maxwells' Saskatchewan Legislative Building, which clearly invited only one. To both Frank Simon and the Maxwells, this evidently suggested a compact composition with shorter lateral wings than those in Regina, whose long corridors had been criticized. The Maxwells' elevations were more French than British, and the scale was smaller. A two-storey Corinthian order stood upon a strongly defined rusticated base, whereas Simon employed a colossal Ionic order that encompassed a less defined base and the two upper floors. The central feature of the Maxwell proposal was a tall dome, whereas the Simon scheme was a four-sided tower with a domical roof over the rotunda of the legislative chamber. Two unusual aspects of this competition were the speed with which it was carried out and the fact that the building was erected without any evident change from the competition design.[3]

JOHN BLAND

---

[1] *The Builder*, vol. 101 (September 24, 1911), p. 604.

[2] "New Legislative and Executive Building Winnipeg", *Construction*, vol. 5 (November 1912), p. 69.

[3] Marilyn Baker, *Manitoba's Third Legislative Building* (Winnipeg: Hyperion, 1986), and Diana Lynn Bodnar, "The Prairie Legislative Buildings of Canada" (Master's thesis, University of British Columbia, 1979).

51a. Edward & W.S. Maxwell
Revised competition design for the Justice and Departmental Buildings at Ottawa
Undated, probably 1907
Black-and-white reproduction of a drawing
49.4 x 76.2
Montreal, McGill University, Canadian Architecture Collection

51b. Edward & W.S. Maxwell
Aerial perspective, design for a Justice and Departmental Building, Ottawa
1914
Pen and ink and wash on paper
58.4 x 85.1
Delineator: W. S. Maxwell
(Royal Canadian Academy of Arts diploma work, deposited by the artist, Montreal, 1915)
Signed and dated lower right:
W.S. Maxwell/1914 Del.
Ottawa, National Gallery of Canada

52a. Edward & W.S. Maxwell
Perspective for the Legislative and Executive Building, Regina, Saskatchewan
1909
Watercolour and pen and ink on paper
53.5 x 78.8
Delineator: Edward Maxwell
(Royal Canadian Academy of Arts diploma work, deposited by the artist, Montreal, 1911)
Signed and dated lower right:
Edward Maxwell/ Del. 1909./ Montreal
Ottawa, National Gallery of Canada

52b. Photographer unknown
Saskatchewan Legislative Building
Undated (printed 1991)
Gelatin silver print
50.5 x 60.8
Montreal, McCord Museum of Canadian History, Notman Photographic Archives

52c. Photographer unknown
Entrance hall, Saskatchewan Legislative Building
Undated
Gelatin silver print
20.3 x 25.4
Montreal, McGill University, Canadian Architecture Collection

52d. Photographer unknown
Staircase hall, Saskatchewan Legislative Building
1924
Gelatin silver print
20.3 x 25.4
Montreal, McGill University, Canadian Architecture Collection

52e. Photographer unknown
Anteroom (rotunda), Saskatchewan Legislative Building
Undated
Gelatin silver print
20.3 x 25.4
Montreal, McGill University, Canadian Architecture Collection

52f. Photographer unknown
Cabinet meeting room, Saskatchewan Legislative Building
1924
Gelatin silver print
22.2 x 19.1
Montreal, McGill University, Canadian Architecture Collection

52g. Photographer unknown
Premier's office, Saskatchewan Legislative Building, Regina
Undated (printed 1991)
Gelatin silver print
20.3 x 25.4
Regina, Saskatchewan Archives Board

52h. GLAF Maquettes, Gerald Laforest with François Leblanc
Model of the Saskatchewan Legislative Building
1991
Lindenwood
120.3 x 191.1 x 48.8
The Montreal Museum of Fine Arts

52i. Photographer unknown
Legislative Chamber, Saskatchewan Legislative Building
1924
Gelatin silver print
19.1 x 24.5
Montreal, McGill University, Canadian Architecture Collection

52j. William Notman & Son
Construction photograph showing west and south wings, Saskatchewan Legislative Building
April 20, 1910
Gelatin silver print
19.2 x 24.6
Montreal, McGill University, Canadian Architecture Collection

52k. William Notman & Son
Construction photograph showing dome, Saskatchewan Legislative Building
July 23, 1910
Gelatin silver print
19.8 x 19
Montreal, McGill University, Canadian Architecture Collection

52l. William Notman & Son
Construction photograph showing north and east wings, Saskatchewan Legislative Building
August 1, 1910
Gelatin silver print
16.2 x 21.7
Montreal, McGill University, Canadian Architecture Collection

52m. William Notman & Son
Construction photograph showing north wing and dome, Saskatchewan Legislative Building
December 20, 1910
Gelatin silver print
24.6 x 19.2
Montreal, McGill University, Canadian Architecture Collection

53. William Notman & Son
Competition elevation for the Manitoba Legislative Building
1912
Photographic print of a drawing by Edward & W.S. Maxwell
25.5 x 30.5
Montreal, McGill University, Canadian Architecture Collection

Religious buildings form a comparatively small proportion of the Maxwell brothers' oeuvre. Their major church commissions were all in Montreal: Edward's Knox Presbyterian Church (1893, demolished), Melville Presbyterian Church (1900-1902), the Unitarian Church of the Messiah (1906-1908, destroyed) and Saint Giles Presbyterian Church (1911-1913). The first three exhibit little stylistic correlation. The Knox Church, with its arched openings and broad surfaces of rusticated limestone had affinities with Shepley, Rutan & Coolidge's Richardsonian Shadyside Presbyterian Church in Pittsburgh, which was under construction during Edward's Boston sojourn. The brick Melville Church in Westmount, with its self-contained compound comprising church and rectory, is reminiscent of English Victorian urban churches of the latter half of the nineteenth century. However, the simplified "Modern Gothic" of the Church of the Messiah was later used for Saint Giles, although brick was substituted for the more costly Indiana limestone in which the Church of the Messiah was faced.

Between 1948 and his death in 1952, William was engaged in designing a magnificent superstructure for the shrine on the slopes of Mount Carmel in Haifa, Israel, which houses the remains of the Báb, one of the two prophet-founders of the Bahá'í Faith. It was a fitting last work for an architect who, as a young Canadian, had gone to Boston and then to Paris to gain the training needed to create splendid architecture of this magnitude, and who subsequently became the first Canadian to embrace the Bahá'í Faith.

Cat. 54b. *Church of the Messiah*

54
Edward & W.S. Maxwell
Church of the Messiah

3415 Simpson Street (at Sherbrooke Street)
Montreal, Que.
1906-1908 (destroyed by fire May 26, 1987)

The Church of the Messiah (Unitarian Church of Montreal) was designed for a prominent site on Sherbrooke Street (cat. 54b). Its urbane exterior and the fine craftsmanship of its unified programme of Arts and Crafts decoration make it perhaps the Maxwells' most successful church building in Montreal.

At the turn of the century, the Church of the Messiah's congregation was dwindling. The building at Beaver Hall Hill and de La Gauchetière Street was in poor repair and no longer near its membership. A change of location was proposed, and in 1904 a build-

ing committee was formed. By July 1905 a convenient parcel of land on the northeast corner of Sherbrooke and Simpson Streets, in the heart of the residential district, had been purchased from the McDougall estate.

On February 13, 1906, the building committee unanimously recommended the plans of Edward & W.S. Maxwell over all others submitted,[1] and two weeks later William attended a meeting to answer questions. The Maxwells' design called for a church with a Sunday school on the floor above; instead, the committee suggested building a church hall and Sunday school

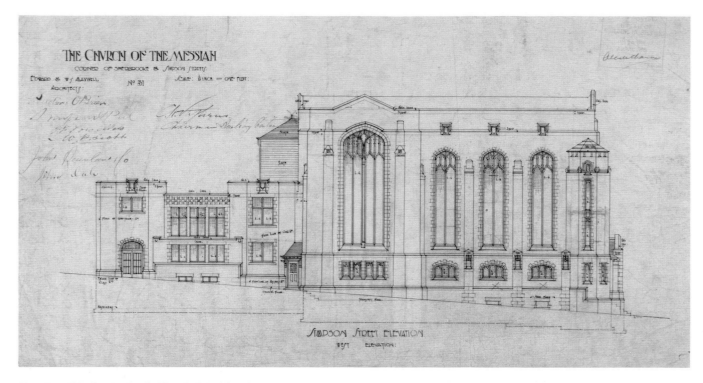

Cat. 54c. *Side elevation for the Church of the Messiah*

on the ground level at the rear of the church, in order to reduce the $75,000 cost by almost $25,000.[2] Although the committee had "considerable difficulty" in securing these changes from the architects, by June 1906 they were able to approve the new plans and let contracts. The building permit was issued in November,[3] and the church was dedicated on January 5, 1908.[4]

Constructed on a rusticated grey limestone foundation, the church was faced in buff Indiana limestone with sandstone trim crandalled and chiselled to give textural and tonal variety. The masonry concealed brick walls and steel supports and roof trusses; these modern building methods resulted in thin exterior walls. Bands of cut stone marked the horizontal divisions of the elevations.

The restrained detail was Tudor Gothic in inspiration. Crenellated octagonal turrets supporting sculpted angels rose at either corner of the main elevation on Sherbrooke Street, stopping short of the parapet. The gabled entrance porch, finished in chequered stonework, incorporated small panels of sculpted decoration, as did the midpoint of the gable above the large Perpendicular-type window. The secondary elevation, on Simpson Street, had three shallow bays divided by

buttresses that disguised exhaust vents (cat. 54c).[5] These bays were almost entirely filled by tall Gothicizing windows, below which projected a low side aisle whose corresponding bays contained a series of three small windows set in a compressed Gothic arch. The shallow north transept was dominated by a large window, with four smaller windows beneath. Extending beyond the transept, and not as high, the Sunday school façade was distinguished from the main body of the church by its blunted volumes and squared windows. It contained the minister's office in addition to the Sunday school, which also served as the church hall. While this elevation repeated to some extent the Sherbrooke Street façade, the formula was inverted by means of corner turrets that rose above the wall. The effect, however, was cramped and somewhat awkward, suggesting a certain difficulty in modifying the plan in response to the building committee's request. Because the east elevation was blocked from view, for economy's sake it was left undecorated; likewise, the rear wall of the Sunday school wing was faced only in brick.

The simplicity of the exterior treatment and the omission of the traditional tower, spire and pinnacles represent an early exercise – perhaps Montreal's first – in Modern Gothic, the twentieth-century revision of

Cat. 54d. *Maxwell memorial window, Church of the Messiah*

the Gothic Revival, which featured simpler forms and modern building methods.[6] Modern Gothic was also the Maxwell's choice in their 1907 competition design for the Justice and Departmental Buildings in Ottawa (see cat. entry 51). An important source of this style was the widely published winning competition design for Liverpool Cathedral (1901-1902) by Giles Gilbert Scott. Scott freely manipulated Gothicizing elements into a well-modulated and tightly knit plan notable for its bold and sober massing. The influence of this design on the Church of the Messiah is seen in the restrained treatment of the façade, whose shape, corner modulations and narrow Gothic window recall Liverpool Cathedral's transepts and west end. Other sources for the Church of the Messiah can be found in the work of the American firm Cram, Goodhue & Ferguson, whose intriguing designs for Modern Gothic churches were appearing in American and Canadian architectural journals at the time.[7]

The interior arrangement of the Church of the Messiah was essentially cruciform. A wide nave was flanked by narrow side aisles that ended where the transepts opened. A celestial organ (later dismantled)

hung in the larger south transept, while a gallery over the inner vestibule housed the organ's console and main case. A hammer-beamed ceiling, carried over in the chancel, accentuated the white plaster walls. The scooped-out volumes of the narrow chancel, transepts and side aisles added architectonic richness to the large open space of the nave.

The church's minister, William Sullivan Barnes, conceived of an extensive programme of memorial gifts, which was carried out in the Arts and Crafts manner.[8] These included the elaborately carved woodwork of the reredos, screen and oak furniture of the chancel, and handcrafted metalwork fixtures, such as lanterns, tablets, vases and candlesticks.[9] However, it was the impressive and carefully co-ordinated series of stained glass windows designed in England by the Bromsgrove Guild of Applied Arts that formed the key element in the church's decorative programme. Edward and William Maxwell themselves donated the middle window of the north aisle, representing David's instructions to Solomon for the building of the Temple of Jerusalem (cat. 54d). The inscription read, "And the house that is builded for the Lord must be exceedingly magnifical."[10]

It suggests the brothers felt considerable pride in their achievement.

The main body of the church and most of its contents were destroyed by fire on May 26, 1987.[11] The church hall and offices survive.

SANDRA COLEY BYRON

1   [Montreal Unitarian Society Minute Book E], entry for February 13, 1906, Concordia University Archives. The architects who submitted the other plans were not identified. However, the Maxwells may have already submitted a proposal, including an oil sketch by William (now in the CAC), in June 1905. See [Minute Book E], entry for June 7, 1905.

2   Notes from the Annual Meeting, transcribed in [Minute Book E], entry for January 14, 1907.

3   The *Canadian Contract Record* of July 4, 1906 (vol. 17, p. 4), reported that plans for the church had been accepted. In September 1906, *CAB* (vol. 19, p. 136), announced under "Montreal Notes" that the church was to be built, and in November (vol. 19, p. 171) that the building permit had been issued, that John Quinlan & Company had been named as contractors, and that on October 22 the foundation stone had been laid.

4   A year after the church's completion, *The Builder* (London) published a photograph of it, together with McKim, Mead & White's Mount Royal Club and Bank of Montreal Extension, as examples of recent architecture in Montreal, noting that only the church was designed by Canadian architects (July 10, 1909, p. 47). I am indebted to Robert Lemire for this reference.

5   See Project no. 215.0, MA (drawings 30, 42, 45). *The Gazette* (Montreal) noted that "The most scientific principles of heating and ventilation are to be utilized, on the model of the [Maxwells'] Alexandra Hospital" (October 22, 1906, p. 5).

6   See R. H. Hubbard, "Modern Gothic in Canada", *Bulletin, the National Gallery of Canada*, vol. 25 (1975), pp. 3-18.

7   Perspectives of Emmanuel Church in Cleveland suggest the stonework, fenestration, entrance porch and peaked façade of the Unitarian Church (*American Architect and Building News* [June 11, 1904]). A perspective drawing for the Cathedral of All Saints, Halifax, indicates a similar treatment of the façade and transept (*CAB*, vol. 22 [January 1908], pp. 11-13).

8   British Unitarians were great patrons of the Arts and Crafts movement and often commissioned the Bromsgrove Guild, the Birmingham Guild and related craftsmen for their church decoration. See Alan Crawford, *By Hammer and Hand: The Arts & Crafts Movement in Birmingham* (Birmingham: Birmingham Museums and Art Gallery, 1984), pp. 32, 34-36, 38, 70-73, 76.

9   Most of the wood carving was done by Félix Routhier, and Paul Beau made the metalwork fixtures ([Work Costs Book M, 1904-1914], pp. 261, 263, MA, Series C). For further information, see the essay "Craftsmen and Decorative Artists" in the present catalogue.

10 Dr. Nevil Norton Evans, *Memorials and Other Gifts in the Church of the Messiah, Montreal* (Montreal, 1943), p. 8.

11 "Church Organist Held after Collapse of Wall Kills Two Firefighters on Ladder", *The Gazette* (Montreal), May 26, 1987, p. A-1.

DESIGN FOR THE MASHRAK-EL-AZKAR TO BE ERECTED IN CHICAGO

Cat. 55. *Competition elevation for Bahá'í House of Worship (Mashriqu'l-Adhkár)*

55
William Maxwell
Competition Design for Bahá'í House of Worship (Mashriqu'l-Adhkár)
Wilmette, Ill.
1919

Although William Maxwell did not win the competition held in 1919 for the first Bahá'í house of worship in the Western world, to be located in Wilmette, Illinois (cat. 55), it provided him with an opportunity to design such a building prior to his appointment some three decades later as architect for the Shrine of the Báb in Haifa, Israel. The Bahá'í Faith imposes only two constraints on the design of a house of worship, or temple: that it be nine-sided, with a central hall, and that it admit natural light. The architect is encouraged to strive for the highest quality and for innovative design. The Wilmette competition was won by a Canadian, Louis J. Bourgeois.
HUGH LOCKE

Fig. 45. *Original structure of the Shrine of the Báb*, undated. Haifa, Bahá'í International Community Photographic Archives.

56
William Maxwell
Superstructure of the Shrine of the Báb
Bahá'í World Centre
Haifa, Israel
1948-1953

The superstructure of the Shrine of the Báb was William Maxwell's last major commission, and the elegant and highly original design is a consummate testament to his architectural talents.

As with Judaism, Christianity and Islám, historical circumstance binds the Bahá'í Faith, youngest of the world's independent religions, to the Holy Land. The houses and other places in Haifa and nearby Acre associated with the exile of Bahá'u'lláh, Founder of the Bahá'í Faith, are visited every year by thousands of Bahá'í pilgrims from around the world. Among the most important of these sites is the gold-domed Shrine of the

Báb on the slopes of Haifa's Mount Carmel, built to entomb the remains of the forerunner to Bahá'u'lláh.

William and his wife May were prominent members of the Bahá'í Faith.[1] In 1941, the year following his wife's death, William went to live in Haifa with his daughter, Mary Maxwell Rabbani, and her husband, Shoghi Effendi Rabbani, great-grandson of Bahá'u'lláh and Guardian of the Bahá'í Faith.[2] It was Shoghi Effendi who, shortly after Maxwell's arrival, appointed him architect for the Shrine of the Báb.

The original structure of the Shrine was a simple six-room, one-storey building of local stone (fig. 45),

Cat. 56a. *Shrine of the Báb*

built between 1900 and 1908[3] under the supervision of 'Abdu'l-Bahá, eldest son of Bahá'u'lláh. 'Abdu'l-Bahá himself interred the remains of the Báb there in 1909. In 1929 Shoghi Effendi added three rooms along the south side, changing the oblong structure to a perfect square.[4]

Maxwell worked closely with Shoghi Effendi to design a superstructure that envelops the original building with an arcade, from the roof of which rises an octagon, a drum and a dome. The resulting building, in both conception and detail, combines Eastern and Western design elements into an original yet recognizably classical style (cat. 56a).

The arcade is repeated on four sides and in each case is defined by a colonnade of six columns and two pilasters, all of Rose Baveno granite. The colonnades are joined at each corner by four large curved recesses, which in turn support a beautifully carved setting for an oval panel of green marble into which is set a Bahá'í symbol in fire-gilt bronze. The arches, capitals, corners and balustrade are of a light straw-coloured Chiampo marble.[5] The balustrade's panels are carved in low relief against a background of blue-green glass mosaic inlaid with scarlet blossoms. In describing the arcade, Bahá'í author Ugo Giachery wrote: "As the columns of Rose Baveno granite proclaim the glory of classic Roman architecture, the majestic ogee arches, seven on each side, bring the flavour of the Orient ... This harmony of epochs and styles, perpetuating the artistic aspects of two spiritual forces that have been at variance through the centuries, is one of the inspired creations of the architect, who enhanced the uniqueness of his design by placing a composite Corinthian capital between each shaft and the base of the arch."[6]

The marble and granite for the Shrine were quarried and carved in Italy and then shipped to Haifa by sea. Since building materials were scarce in the newly formed state of Israel, most of the remaining construction material – cement, structural steel, lumber for scaffolding and shuttering, even nails – was also imported from Italy.[7]

An octagon rises above the arcade from a platform that begins approximately thirty centimetres above the roof of the original building. Supported by reinforced concrete piers that pass unobtrusively through the edifice, this platform was built to ensure that the original Sepulchre would not have to carry the more than nine hundred tonnes of the combined weights of the octagon, drum and dome.[8] Each side of the octagon, also faced with Chiampo marble, is punctuated by three stained glass windows whose shape echoes the ogee profile of the arches of the colonnade below. Rising from the cornice and running between eight pinnacles is a wrought iron balustrade, much of which is gilt.

The circular drum that emerges from the roof of the octagon consists of eighteen marble panels that alternate with a like number of vertical stained glass windows incorporating floral motifs. Around the base of the dome is a wide brim of marble that casts a strong shadow, even when the sky is overcast. Atop this brim is a carved "garland" that alternates two sizes of foliate uprights. The dome was made by spraying concrete onto wooden shuttering, to which reinforcing rods were affixed. Its exterior is particularly striking, being covered between its eighteen marble ribs with twelve thousand overlapping terra-cotta tiles, each of which has been covered by a chemical reduction process with a thin layer of pure gold.[9] A marble floral ornament appears between each set of ribs near the base, and the overall effect is completed by a cupola with five Rose Baveno granite columns and a Chiampo marble "bell" and finial.

William Maxwell died in the year before the Shrine of the Báb was completed. It is his last, and in many ways his definitive work; bold in concept, it unites Western and Eastern styles, with details that are unparalleled within the legacy of one who was a master of ornamental and symbolic design.

In announcing the completion of the Shrine of the Báb to the Bahá'í world in October 1953, Shoghi Effendi wrote, "... Queen of Carmel enthroned on God's Mountain, crowned in glowing gold, robed in shimmering white, girdled in emerald green, enchanting every eye from air, sea, plain and hill".[10]

HUGH LOCKE

1 American-born May Maxwell introduced the Bahá'í Faith to Canada, and William Maxwell was the first Canadian Bahá'í. He was given the special appointment of "Hand of the Cause" by Shoghi Effendi, Guardian of the Bahá'í Faith, in 1951.
2 The Bahá'í World, A Biennial International Record: Vol. 12, 1950-1954 (Wilmette, Illinois: Bahá'í Publishing Trust, 1956), p. 661.
3 Shoghi Effendi, God Passes By (Wilmette, Illinois: Bahá'í Publishing Trust, 1944), pp. 275-276.
4 Ugo Giachery, Shoghi Effendi: Reflections (Oxford: George Ronald, 1973), p. 83.
5 Ibid., p. 73.
6 Ibid., p. 84. In 1948 Shoghi Effendi appointed Ugo Giachery as his personal representative for all the work in Italy associated with the erection of the superstructure of the Shrine of the Báb.
7 Ibid., p. 78.
8 Ugo Giachery, "An Account of the Preparatory Work in Italy", in The Bahá'í World..., 1956, p. 244.
9 Giachery, 1973, p. 106.
10 Shoghi Effendi, "Construction of the Superstructure of the Shrine of the Báb", in The Bahá'í World..., 1956, p. 239.

54a. Edward & W.S. Maxwell
*Front elevation and transverse section
for the Church of the Messiah*
Undated
Black ink on linen
34.3 x 67
Montreal, McGill University,
Canadian Architecture Collection

54b. Barnes (Montreal)
Church of the Messiah
Undated (printed 1991)
Gelatin silver print
20.3 x 25.4
Montreal, McCord Museum
of Canadian History, Notman
Photographic Archives

54c. Edward & W.S. Maxwell
*Side elevation for the Church of the
Messiah*
Undated
Black, brown and red ink on
linen
34 x 66.6
Montreal, McGill University,
Canadian Architecture Collection

54d. Helen P. Mackey
*Maxwell memorial window, Church of
the Messiah (made by the Bromsgrove
Guild of Applied Arts, Worcestershire,
England, 1908)*
1962
Chromogenic colour print
27.9 x 35.6
Montreal, Helen P. Mackey
collection

54e. Bromsgrove Guild of Applied
Arts, Worcestershire, England
*Stained glass window from the Church
of the Messiah*
1908
Glass and lead
75 x 51 x 2
Montreal, Church of the Messiah

55. William Sutherland Maxwell
*Competition elevation for Bahá'í House
of Worship (Mashriqu'l-Adhkár)*
1919
Chromogenic colour print
12.7 x 17.7
Delineator: W. S. Maxwell
Haifa, Bahá'í Archives

56a. Photographer unknown
Shrine of the Báb
Undated
Chromogenic colour print
43.6 x 36.7
Montreal, McGill University,
Canadian Architecture Collection

56b. John Tusa Design Inc., New York
Model of the Shrine of the Báb
1991
Acrylic, polystyrene, etched
metal, paint, gilt
78.7 x 78.7 x 78.7
Courtesy of the National
Spiritual Assembly of the Bahá'ís
of Canada, Thornhill, Ontario

CITY PLANNING AND LANDSCAPE DESIGN

The Maxwells, responding to principles of Beaux-Arts teaching and of the Arts and Crafts movement, looked upon buildings as total works. Thus, not only did they encourage a number of Canada's leading artists and craftsmen by collaborating with them on the exterior and interior decoration of their buildings, but also they concerned themselves with settings and the beautification of their native city of Montreal. To this end, they worked with such eminent landscape architects as Frederick Todd, Rickson Outhet and the Olmsted firm, and with various local civic improvement and planning committees. Among their better-known public works are the "Lookout" on the top of Mont Royal and the base of the Sir George-Étienne Cartier monument, which overlooks Park Avenue. On the first project, they collaborated with Todd and the architectural firm of Marchand & Haskell. On the latter, they worked with the sculptor George Hill and – in the planning of the boulevard and park – Rickson Outhet.

57a. Brian Merrett
Monument to Sir George-Étienne Cartier
1990
Chromogenic colour print
35.6 x 35.6
The Montreal Museum
of Fine Arts

57b. Edward & W.S. Maxwell
*Preliminary sketch for location of the Sir
George-Étienne Cartier monument on
Park Avenue, Montreal*
1913
Graphite on paper
27.4 x 21.4
Dated lower centre: *1913*
Montreal, McGill University,
Canadian Architecture Collection

57c. William Sutherland Maxwell
*View of the Sir George-Étienne Cartier
Monument*
1917
Watercolour
27.8 x 21.8
Signed and dated lower right:
W.S. Maxwell/ 18.VIII.17
Thornhill, Ontario, National
Spiritual Assembly of the Bahá'ís
of Canada

57d. Photographer unknown
*Model for the Sir George-Étienne Cartier
Monument*
1914 (printed 1991)
Gelatin silver print
35.6 x 27.8
Montreal, McGill University,
Canadian Architecture Collection

57e. Brian Merrett
*Detail of the Sir George-Étienne Cartier
Monument*
1991
Gelatin silver print
20.3 x 20.3
The Montreal Museum
of Fine Arts

57f. Brian Merrett
*Detail of the Sir George-Étienne Cartier
Monument*
1991
Gelatin silver print
20.3 x 20.3
The Montreal Museum
of Fine Arts

58a. Edward & W.S. Maxwell and
Marchand & Haskell
*Elevation for the pavilion, Mount Royal
Park*
Undated
Black and blue ink on linen
38.2 x 78.3
Montreal, McGill University,
Canadian Architecture Collection

58b. Edward & W.S. Maxwell and
Marchand & Haskell
*Site plan for the "Lookout", Mount
Royal Park*
Undated
Black ink and graphite on linen
51 x 54.2
Montreal, McGill University,
Canadian Architecture Collection

58c. Photographer unknown
*Pavilion and "Lookout", Mount Royal
Park*
Undated (printed 1991)
Gelatin silver print of half-tone
reproduction
20.3 x 25.4
Montreal, McGill University,
Canadian Architecture Collection

As most of the Maxwell firm's drawings are undated, the following is based on the research done by the contributors to the present catalogue and on citations from *Canadian Contract Record*, 1890-1922, provided by Robert G. Hill. The works mentioned constitute a small but significant part of the Maxwell oeuvre. Buildings are in Montreal unless otherwise stated.

1867
Edward Maxwell born December 31 in Montreal to Edward John, founder of E.J. Maxwell & Co., lumber merchants, and Johan MacBean.

1874
William Sutherland Maxwell born November 14 in Montreal.

1888
Edward listed as draftsman in Shepley, Rutan & Coolidge office, Boston.

1891
Edward returns to Montreal to supervise construction of Montreal Board of Trade Building.

1892
(January) H.V. Meredith House is in planning stage. When Board of Trade Building Committee objects to outside work, Edward sends resignation to Shepley, Rutan & Coolidge. (February) William begins working as a draftsman in Edward's office. New Board of Trade Building Committee allows Edward to carry on private work in hand while supervising completion of Board of Trade. Begins designing McIntyre-Angus Houses. (April) Receives commission for Henry Birks & Company (later Henry Birks & Sons) Building. Designs pair of houses for business partners James Crathern and J. B. Learmont.

1893
Designs E.S. Clouston House. Construction begins on Henry Birks & Sons Building. Edward becomes member of the AAM; visits World's Columbian Exposition, Chicago.

1894
Contracts awarded for H.A. Allan House, H.V. Meredith House and R.A.E. Greenshields House. Designs Merchants Bank of Halifax Building and Bell Telephone Company of Canada Building.

1895
William goes to Boston to work for Winslow & Wetherell. Contracts awarded for Bell Telephone Company of Canada Building. Edward travels to Venice and Ravenna. Probable construction of Edward Maxwell House, Côte-Saint-Antoine Road.

1896
Designs T. Hodgson Cottage, Sainte-Agathe, Que. Edward visits Milan; marries Elizabeth Ellen Aitchison.

1897
Revises design of Edward Colonna's CPR Station and Offices, Vancouver.

1898
(May) William returns to Montreal from Boston and resumes work as draftsman in Edward's office. Firm designs J. Ross House additions and London & Lancashire Life Assurance Company Building. Contracts awarded for J.H. Birks House. Begins extension and remodelling of "Pine Bluff" for R.B. Angus Estate, Senneville, Que.

1899
Designs Windsor Station extension, CPR Hotel and Station, Winnipeg, and farm buildings for W.C. Van Horne Estate, Minister's Island, N.B. Receives commission to design "Le Bois de la Roche" for L.-J. Forget Estate, Senneville, Que. (August) Edward forms partnership with George Cutler Shattuck (1864-1923). (September) William is in Paris as special student at the École des Beaux-Arts, in the Atelier Pascal.

1900
(March) Studies accepted for C.R. Hosmer House. (July-September) William travels to Normandy, Brittany, Venice, Padua, Milan, Florence and Rome. (December) William resumes working as a draftsman in Edward's office.

1901
Building permit granted for Hosmer House. Studies ordered for new "Pine Bluff" house for R.B. Angus Estate, Senneville, Que. Edward travels to New York, Paris and London.

1902
Partnership of Edward & W.S. Maxwell formed. William marries May Ellis Bolles; travels to Europe.

1903
Building permit granted for Edward Maxwell House, Peel Street, and Montreal Stock Exchange Building (designed by George B. Post, New York; supervised by Edward & W.S. Maxwell). Prepare plans for CPR Hotel and Station, Winnipeg, and Royal Bank of Canada Westmount Branch. Edward elected Associate, R.C.A.

1904
Bank of Montreal Westmount Branch and Royal Bank of Canada Westmount Branch completed.

1905
Contracts awarded for Alexandra Hospital. Building permit granted for Nurses' Home, Royal Victoria Hospital.

1906
Plans accepted for Church of the Messiah.

1907
Win competition for Saskatchewan Legislative Building, Regina. Construction begins on R.R. Mitchell House. Win first competition for Justice and Departmental Buildings, Ottawa (project abandoned).

1908
Prepare final plans for Saskatchewan Legislative Building, Regina; excavation begun. Construction begins on J.K.L. Ross House. Edward elected Academician, R.C.A. William becomes Councillor, PQAA.

1909
Design F.W. Thompson House, Saint Andrews, N.B. W.S. Maxwell and E.M. Renouf Houses under construction. Contracts awarded for J.T. Davis House. William elected Associate, R.C.A.; travels to Europe.

1910
Design Dominion Express Building. Win competition for Art Association of Montreal (later the Montreal Museum of Fine Arts).

1911
Design Palliser Hotel, Calgary.

1912
Design High School of Montreal. Enter competition for Legislative and Executive Building for the Province of Manitoba, Winnipeg. Alterations for Arts Club of Montreal.

1913
William elected President, Arts Club of Montreal. Enter second competition for Justice and Departmental Buildings, Ottawa (project never realized).

1914
William elected Academician, R.C.A.; becomes President, PQAA.

1919
Design central tower and additional wings for Château Frontenac Hotel, Quebec City. William enters competition for Bahá'í House of Worship (Mashriqu'l-Adhkár), Wilmette, Illinois.

1920
Construction begins on additions to Château Frontenac Hotel, Quebec City.

1923
Death of Edward Maxwell. William forms partnership with Gordon McLeod Pitts (1886-1954).

1925
William travels to Europe.

1928
William elected Fellow, RIBA.

1935
William becomes President, RAIC; travels to Germany, Belgium, France and England.

1938
William becomes Vice-president, R.C.A.

1948
William begins work on superstructure of the Shrine of the Báb, Haifa.

1952
Death of William Maxwell.